souplemoncaesarsalad**grilledcheesepanin**

stonewall kitchen **favorites**

stonewall
kitchen
favorites

Delicious Recipes to Share with Family and Friends Every Day

jonathan king, jim stott,
and kathy gunst

foreword by ina garten

photographs by jim stott

Clarkson Potter/Publishers
New York

Also by Jonathan King, Jim Stott, and Kathy Gunst
Stonewall Kitchen Harvest

Photograph on page 282 by Dan Gair/Blind Dog Photo.
Photograph on page 283 by Lynn Garlin.

Published in the United States by Clarkson Potter/Publishers, an imprint of
the Crown Publishing Group, a division of Random House, Inc., New York.
www.crownpublishing.com
www.clarksonpotter.com

Clarkson N. Potter is a trademark and Potter and colophon are registered trademarks
of Random House, Inc.

Library of Congress Cataloging-in-Publication Data
King, Jonathan.
Stonewall kitchen favorites : delicious recipes to share with family and friends every day /
by Jonathan King, Jim Stott, and Kathy Gunst ; foreword by Ina Garten.—1st ed.
    1. Cookery, American.   I. Stott, Jim.   II. Gunst, Kathy.   III. Title.
TX715.K525   2006
641.5973—dc22   2005027750

ISBN-13: 978-0-307-33681-1
ISBN-10: 0-307-33681-6

Printed in Japan

Design by Jane Treuhaft

10   9   8   7   6   5   4   3

First Edition

to our families,
where all our favorites began.

contents

foreword

This is the true American success story. We all dream of pursuing our passion and then building a company doing what we love. Jonathan King and Jim Stott have done just that. Fifteen years ago, they cooked up some fresh blueberry jam on their kitchen stove in Maine and took it to a nearby farmer's market to see if it would sell. On that very day, the owner of Tuttle's, the oldest operating family farm in America, happened to be walking by, tasted the jam, and asked if she could order hundreds of jars for their gourmet section. Most of us would have panicked, but not Jonathan and Jim! They asked, "When would you like it delivered?" They cooked all day and all night for weeks, poured each jar by hand, wrote each label, and filled their first order on time. And so, Stonewall Kitchen, a great American food company, was born.

In 2005, my business partner Frank Newbold and I were looking for a company to manufacture and distribute a line of Barefoot Contessa pantry products and our first thought was to talk to Stonewall Kitchen. I had owned a specialty food store in East Hampton, New York, where I sold Stonewall Kitchen's products, and I always believed they made the best quality specialty foods on the market. Jonathan and Jim had never had a partnership with another company, but fortunately they agreed to work with us. We love working with them not only because we adore them personally—they live life with both feet on the accelerator!—but also because we admire their insistence on the best quality possible.

This wonderful book comes from Jonathan, Jim, and Kathy's love of cooking and good food. They have an uncanny sense of exactly what you want to eat and the recipes are really easy. Everything I've made is absolutely delicious and I can't wait to work my way through the rest of the book.

—ina garten, author of the Barefoot Contessa cookbooks

introduction

Where were you when you tasted your first real Caesar salad—with crunchy Romaine and croutons, and salty Parmesan cheese and anchovy fillets, tossed with a creamy egg-based dressing? Or your first coq au vin, that fabulous French stew, redolent of smoky bacon, sweet onions, and hearty red wine, with meat so tender it nearly falls off the bone? Do you remember when you tasted your first brownie? Rich, creamy chocolate, dense and chewy, full of unforgettable sweetness, butter, and nuts. Was it at your grandmother's kitchen table? A favorite childhood restaurant?

akes**macaroniandchees**

Like certain scents or songs, favorite foods evoke lasting memories. They have the power to make us smile (or cry), as we remember the people, the places, and the great meals of our past.

Many of the dishes in this book are based on childhood memories. These are the foods we begged for on birthdays and looked forward to every holiday. As we sat around the kitchen table, noting our list of favorites for this book, the stories began to spill out. "My mother made an amazing meat loaf," one of us began. And then the other two would chime in, "Did she use bacon?" "Did she smother it in ketchup?" Kathy recalled her mother's deviled eggs and the buttery walnut cookies her grandmother Lulu made every December. For Jim it was the stellar roast beef his dad made once a month, always on a Sunday. And Jonathan rhapsodized about his mom's fantastic spaghetti and meatballs with garlic bread. These memory sessions made us nostalgic. But mostly they made us hungry. Very, very hungry.

And while we yearn for many of the flavors and scents of our childhoods, we also acknowledge that our tastes have grown up and become more sophisticated over the years. So this book is not simply a look back. It's a collection of recipes for our time— old favorites with a new spin.

What does it mean to remake a classic? In many cases we lightened the original— got rid of excessive amounts of butter or cream. In our New Eggs Benedict, for example, we layer baby spinach and smoked salmon and top it with a poached egg. We did away with the heavy hollandaise sauce and replaced it with a simple chive-lemon butter. In other cases, we gave traditional dishes interesting new ingredients such as lemon zest, fresh ginger, fresh herbs, or miso paste. We took these old standards and found their essence, the elements that make them so attractive to begin with, and then brightened them and gave them a new take that complements the way we eat now.

Your mother or grandmother may have taught you to make chocolate cake, but chances are they never baked one like ours—made in individual ramekins with 65 percent cacao bittersweet chocolate and a layer of ripe, fat raspberries. When you cut open our cake and take a bite, a virtual volcano of chocolate and fresh fruit erupts in your mouth.

Another good example of a classic that never fades is onion soup. Ours is a tribute to that thick, hearty broth topped with a blanket of cheese and bread that you tasted on your first trip to Paris. However, this version is sweetened with five types of onion

deviledeggs**cornchowder**

(Vidalia, red onions, leeks, shallots, and garlic) in a simple beef broth enriched with hard New England–made apple cider instead of the traditional red wine and Cognac. To top it off, a single oversize crouton, modestly topped with sharp cheddar cheese.

And then there's our take on a BLT sandwich. We got rid of the bread and piled thick bacon, juicy sweet tomatoes, and buttery lettuce into a refreshing salad. Our spaghetti carbonara is still comfort food—creamy, rich, smoky, and peppery with pancetta instead of bacon—but it has a new wake-up flavor: a swirl of basil puree that adds a taste of the garden. Cardamom in a pineapple upside-down cake? Why not? Coconut milk and mango in an icy cold frozen milkshake? Sure!

We like to think about the favorites offered in this book as being kin to the little black dress (hereafter referred to as t.l.b.d.), a fashion classic, a woman's perennial answer to the dilemma "What should I wear tonight?" It is an article of clothing every woman intrinsically understands is almost always a good choice. In the world of food, t.l.b.d. could be considered a rack of lamb, tomato soup, Cobb salad, or cheesecake. These foods are standards, the solutions to that other age-old question: "What should I serve tonight for dinner?"

Although t.l.b.d is a classic, it does, in fact, change from season to season—it may be ultrashort one year, below the knee the next, or have a plunging neckline and off-the-shoulder look for summer. Like t.l.b.d, the favorite dishes presented in this book are classics, but they all offer some sort of flair, fit for this season—and many seasons to come. Each of these recipes is filled with vibrant flavors that let you know, yes, this is a familiar favorite, but it's also kept up with the times.

esemeatloafroastchicken

Chapter after chapter we took a new, fresh look at our most cherished dishes—soups, sandwiches, salads, roasts, desserts, even breakfast and drinks. And at the bottom of nearly every recipe you'll find something called Favorite Variations. These are ideas for further tweaking our recipes—ways to make our favorites your favorites, ways to account for everyone's ever-changing tastes.

When we first started working on this book, we were pretty sure we knew what we defined as our "favorites." But cooking and reworking these recipes we discovered a new collection of dishes that we find ourselves making night after night. As you cook from this book, we hope you will find some new favorites, too.

—Jonathan King, Jim Stott, and Kathy Gunst

oatmealfig**cookies**

breakfast

1

trio of **fruit salads** with flavored sugar syrups

These three fruit salads are bursting with freshness thanks to a simple herb- or citrus-flavored syrup that infuses each one. You can prepare one salad to serve four, or make all three varieties to serve twelve. You can make these up to a few hours in advance; cover and refrigerate until ready to serve.

■ **berry salad** with mint syrup

SERVES 4

1 cup raspberries
1 cup blackberries
1 cup quartered ripe strawberries

½ cup blueberries
1 to 2 tablespoons Mint Syrup (page 20)
Fresh mint leaves for garnish

In a medium bowl, gently mix all four types of berries. Taste the berries. If they are very sweet you will need only 1 tablespoon of syrup; add enough syrup—up to 2 tablespoons—to flavor the berries without oversweetening. Serve cold, garnished with mint leaves.

■ **melon salad** with lime syrup

SERVES 4

4 cups honeydew melon balls (see Note)
2 cups cantaloupe melon balls (see Note)
2 cups seedless watermelon balls (see Note)

1 to 3 tablespoons Lime Syrup (page 20), Lemongrass Syrup (page 20), or Mint Syrup (page 20)
Paper-thin slices of lime

In a medium bowl, gently toss the three types of melon. Taste the melons. If they are very sweet and juicy, you will need only about 1 to 2 tablespoons of syrup; add enough syrup—up to 3 tablespoons—to flavor the melon without oversweetening. Serve cold, garnished with the lime slices.

NOTE: To make melon balls, cut a small ripe melon in half and remove the seeds. Using a melon scooper or baller, scoop out balls from the melon flesh. If you don't have a scooper or baller, use a small spoon.

RECIPE CONTINUES ▶

■ **tropical fruit** salad

SERVES 6

2 cups cubed mango
2 cups cubed pineapple
1 cup cubed papaya
1 cup thinly sliced kiwi

1 banana, cut into thin slices
1 to 3 tablespoons Lime Syrup (page 20) or
    Lemongrass Syrup (page 20)
Paper-thin slices of lime

In a medium bowl, gently toss the mango, pineapple, papaya, kiwi, and banana slices. Taste the fruit. If it is very sweet, you will need only 1 tablespoon of syrup; add enough syrup—up to 3 tablespoons—to flavor the fruit without oversweetening. Serve cold, garnished with the lime slices.

how sweet it is

making simple sugar syrups

Sugar syrups can add a subtle sweetness to fruit salads (page 00), drinks, dessert sauces, and coffee and tea, and are lovely drizzled over pound or angel food cake. Here is the master recipe; see below for some flavor combination ideas to get you started:

In a small saucepan mix ½ cup sugar and 1 cup water. Bring to a boil over high heat, stirring frequently to make sure all the sugar is dissolved. Reduce the heat to low, add the herbs or flavoring, and simmer for 10 minutes. Strain the syrup into a small glass jar or bowl and let cool. Cover and refrigerate until ready to use, or for up to 3 to 5 days.

MAKES ABOUT ½ CUP SYRUP.

favoritevariations
- **Mint Syrup:** Add ¼ cup coarsely chopped fresh mint leaves. Use with fruit salads (page 00), in mojitos, and ice tea.
- **Ginger Syrup:** Add 2 tablespoons chopped fresh ginger.
- **Lemongrass Syrup:** Add 2 tablespoons chopped fresh lemongrass. If you can't find fresh lemongrass, add 1 tablespoon grated lemon zest and 2 tablespoons lemon juice.
- **Lime Syrup:** Add 1 teaspoon grated lime zest and 2 tablespoons fresh lime juice,
- **Basil Syrup:** Add 2 tablespoons coarsely chopped fresh basil leaves.
- **Lavender Syrup:** Add 2 tablespoons organic lavender leaves.

raspberry muffins with crumb topping

MAKES 18 MUFFINS

Kathy's friend Neil Kleinberg is the owner of the Clinton Street Baking Company, a fabulous bakery/restaurant in lower Manhattan that is famous for its muffins and scones. We've tasted (and tested) an awful lot of muffins over the years, and when we say this is one of the best we've ever tried, we really mean it. Best of all, you can make these muffins year-round—with fresh berries in summer, or any time of year using good-quality frozen raspberries. See photograph on page 5.

for the topping
½ cup all-purpose flour
½ cup sugar
¼ cup (½ stick) unsalted butter, cut into small pieces, at room temperature

for the muffins
Vegetable oil spray, for the pans
2¾ cups all-purpose flour
3 teaspoons baking powder

1¼ teaspoons baking soda
½ teaspoon salt
½ cup (1 stick) unsalted butter, room temperature
1½ cups sugar
4 large eggs
½ teaspoon vanilla extract
1½ cups sour cream
2½ cups raspberries, fresh or frozen

Place a rack in the middle of the oven and preheat the oven to 375°F.

To make the topping: Mix the flour and the sugar together in a medium bowl until blended. Add the butter, and using your hands or a fork, mix the ingredients until homogenous and crumbly. Set the topping aside.

To make the muffins: Spray 18 regular muffin tins with the vegetable oil. Whisk the flour, baking powder, baking soda, and salt together in a medium bowl until blended, and set aside.

Beat the butter and sugar together on medium speed with a handheld or stand mixer fitted with the paddle attachment until light and fluffy, about 3 minutes. Add the eggs, one at a time, mixing the batter on low speed until smooth after each addition and scraping down the sides and bottom of the bowl if necessary. Add the vanilla, and mix to combine.

Add about one-third of the dry ingredients to the batter, and mix on low until blended. Add half of the sour cream, mix, and repeat with another third of the dry ingredients, the rest of the sour cream, and the remaining dry ingredients, mixing between each addition. Use a wooden spatula to stir in the raspberries by hand.

Fill the prepared muffin tins until almost full, and sprinkle 1 tablespoon of the topping onto each muffin (don't worry if it looks like a lot of topping).

Bake the muffins for 25 to 30 minutes, or until a toothpick inserted into the center of a muffin comes out clean. Cool the muffins in the pan for 5 minutes. Using a kitchen knife, gently lift the muffins out of their tins and transfer to a cooling rack.

blueberry-buttermilk muffins

What is better than warm, fluffy muffins bursting with tart summer berries? Serve these straight from the oven with butter, blueberry jam, and hot or iced coffee or tea. A bowl of mixed berries topped with crème fraîche or one (or all) of our Trio of Fruit Salads (page 18) would also make an ideal accompaniment.

If you have any of these left over the next day, cut the muffins in half and broil them, or place cut side down in a hot skillet with a touch of butter until just brown.

The muffins are best made with fresh berries, but if using frozen berries be sure to carefully separate them so they don't clump together; you may need to add a bit of flour to your hands to separate them easily.

Vegetable oil spray for the pans
1¾ cups all-purpose flour
1 tablespoon baking powder
1 teaspoon baking soda
¼ teaspoon salt
½ cup (1 stick) plus 2 teaspoons unsalted butter, at room temperature
¾ cup granulated sugar

2 large eggs
¼ teaspoon vanilla extract
1 cup buttermilk
1 teaspoon grated lemon zest
2 cups fresh blueberries, or 1½ cups frozen blueberries
¼ cup packed light brown sugar

Place a rack in the middle of the oven and preheat oven to 375°F.

Spray 18 regular muffin tins (including the flat surface of the muffin pan) with the vegetable oil spray. Whisk together the flour, baking powder, baking soda, and salt until blended; set aside.

Beat 1 stick of the butter and the granulated sugar together in a stand mixer or using a hand-held mixer fitted with the paddle attachment on medium speed until light and fluffy, about 4 minutes. Add the eggs, one at a time, mixing well after each addition and scraping down the sides of the bowl as needed. Add the vanilla and mix to combine.

Add half of the dry ingredients and mix to combine. Add the buttermilk and mix until smooth. Add the remaining dry ingredients and mix until just blended. Remove the paddle, and using a spatula, gently fold in the lemon zest and blueberries by hand. Fill the prepared tins about three-quarters full. Bake for 17 minutes.

While the muffins are baking, in a small bowl mix the brown sugar with the remaining 2 teaspoons butter until crumbly. After the muffins have baked for 17 minutes, sprinkle a scant teaspoon of the mixture over the top of each muffin. Bake for another 2 to 3 minutes, or until a toothpick inserted in the center comes out clean. Remove from the oven and let cool for a few minutes before carefully inverting the tins and tapping out the muffins. Serve warm.

favoritevariations

- Substitute fresh raspberries or blackberries for the blueberries.
- Add 1 teaspoon ground ginger to the flour mixture.
- Use 1 cup berries and 1 cup cubed ripe peaches or nectarines.
- Omit the brown sugar topping and sprinkle with sanding (or coarse) sugar—available in specialty food shops.
- If you don't have buttermilk, substitute 1 cup warm milk plus 1 tablespoon lemon juice.

fruit and nut **maple granola**

We've never been able to understand why so many cooks think making granola at home is difficult. It's as easy as mixing a few ingredients together on a cookie sheet and baking them; the whole process takes under an hour. The only hard part is choosing the ingredients. Here is our basic recipe, one of the most popular dishes served at the Stonewall Kitchen Café. Think of this as a master recipe that you can add or subtract from; see Favorite Variations below for more ideas. Place the granola in a small clear bag, tie with a ribbon, and bring as a hostess gift.

3 cups rolled old-fashioned oats
1 cup unsweetened shredded coconut
¾ cup unsalted raw sunflower seeds
¾ cup slivered almonds
¼ cup packed light brown sugar
2 teaspoons ground cinnamon
1 to 2 teaspoons ground ginger

¾ cup pure maple syrup
⅓ cup canola oil
1 teaspoon vanilla extract
¾ cup raisins, golden raisins, or dried
  cranberries
½ cup dried chopped apricots

Position a rack in the middle of the oven. Preheat the oven to 300°F.

On a large cookie sheet or two smaller ones, combine the oats, coconut, sunflower seeds, almonds, brown sugar, cinnamon, and ginger. Drizzle the maple syrup, canola oil, and vanilla over the oat and nut mixture and stir well to coat the entire mixture. Add the raisins and apricots and stir well to incorporate.

Bake for 30 to 40 minutes, stirring the granola about every 10 minutes so it doesn't clump up and rotating the cookie sheet once or twice so the granola bakes evenly. The granola is ready when it just begins to turn a light golden color.

Remove from the oven and stir well. Let cool, stirring once or twice to avoid clumping. Store the granola in a sealed container at room temperature for up to 6 weeks.

favorite variations

- Substitute dried blueberries, dried cherries, dried cranberries, or dried strawberries for the raisins, or use a combination.
- Substitute pecans, walnuts, macadamia nuts, pine nuts, or cashews for the almonds, or add a combination of several nuts.
- Substitute ¼ cup honey for the brown sugar.
- Add ½ cup wheat germ to the granola.
- Add ½ cup sesame seeds or flax seeds to the granola.
- Add ¼ cup bran flakes to the granola.
- Increase the amount of ginger to 2 teaspoons.
- Add 1 teaspoon allspice to the mixture.

bacon and chive **biscuits**

MAKES 12 BISCUITS

Light, fluffy, and full of flavor, these biscuits are addictive. Serve them warm, straight from the oven, with omelets, fried eggs, or a fruit salad (see page 18). Use them instead of bread for a BLT or a tomato and avocado sandwich. Serve the biscuits as a side dish to the Summer Tomato and Basil Soup (page 51), or to accompany any soup or stew. For real bacon lovers, these make a great side dish to our BLT Salad on page 71, and our Dry Rubbed Paper Bag Pork Ribs on page 202. (Conversely, you can easily omit the bacon and make this a buttery chive biscuit.)

The basis for this recipe is the much-loved biscuits from Lundy's in Brooklyn, New York, as they appeared in Kathy's book, *Lundy's—Reminiscences and Recipes*.

$1/2$ pound bacon (about 8 slices)
$1^1/2$ cups plus 3 tablespoons all-purpose flour
1 tablespoon baking powder
1 tablespoon sugar
$1/4$ teaspoon salt

$1/4$ cup ($1/2$ stick) unsalted butter, chilled
$1/4$ cup shortening, chilled
$1/2$ cup minced fresh chives
$1/2$ cup milk

Place a rack in the center of the oven and preheat the oven to 375°F.

In a large skillet, cook the bacon over medium heat until crisp on both sides, about 10 minutes. Drain on paper towels. Finely chop and set aside.

Sift the flour, baking powder, sugar, and salt together into a large bowl. Stir well. Cut the butter and shortening into small pieces and add to the flour mixture. Using a pastry cutter, your hands, or two kitchen knives, crumble the fats into the flour mixture until the butter and shortening are pea-sized and the mixture resembles coarse cornmeal. Add the bacon and chives. Add the milk and mix the dough until it just comes together, making sure not to overmix.

Knead the dough gently on a lightly floured work surface. Roll out the dough to a half-inch thickness. Be sure the dough is $1/2$ inch thick; if it's too thin the biscuits will be dry. And if it's rolled too thick, the biscuits won't cook properly. Using a 2-inch glass or biscuit cutter, cut out the biscuits and place on an ungreased cookie sheet. Roll the scraps together and cut out additional biscuits. (The biscuits can be made several hours ahead of time; cover and refrigerate.)

Bake for 14 to 15 minutes, or until the biscuits begin to turn a pale shade of golden brown. (If the biscuits have come straight out of the refrigerator they will need to bake for closer to 19 or 20 minutes.) Serve hot or at room temperature.

favoritevariations

- Substitute a few tablespoons chopped fresh herbs for the chives.
- Add 1 to 2 tablespoons chopped sun-dried tomatoes.
- Add $1/4$ cup grated cheddar, Asiago, Parmesan, or your favorite cheese to the biscuit mixture.

walnut pancakes with caramelized bananas

We are huge fans of these light, nutty, crunchy cakes. Served with a caramelized banana topping, and drizzled with warm maple syrup, these are a real Sunday morning favorite. Best of all, the batter can be made up to 2 hours ahead of time, covered and refrigerated, and the pancakes and topping can be cooked at the last minute. Be sure to let the batter return to room temperature before cooking the pancakes.

for the pancakes
1½ cups all-purpose flour
2 teaspoons baking powder
1 teaspoon salt
2 tablespoons sugar
2 large eggs
1½ cups buttermilk
¼ cup (½ stick) unsalted butter, melted, plus more for the pan

½ cup finely chopped walnuts, or toasted walnuts (see page 260)
½ teaspoon vanilla extract

for the banana topping
2 tablespoons unsalted butter
¼ cup packed light brown sugar
4 small bananas, sliced into ½-inch rounds
1 cup pure maple syrup

To make the pancakes: Whisk the flour, baking powder, salt, and sugar together in a medium bowl and set aside. In a large bowl, whisk the eggs and the buttermilk together until blended. Add the melted butter, and whisk again to combine. Add the dry ingredients, and stir with a wooden spoon until just combined. Fold in the walnuts and vanilla, and let the batter sit for about 10 minutes.

While the batter sits, prepare the banana topping: Melt the butter in a large skillet over medium heat. Add the brown sugar and stir until the sugar has melted and the mixture begins to simmer. Cook over low heat for 1 minute, stirring continuously. Add the banana slices to the pan in a single layer and cook for about 2 minutes, or until soft and lightly browned. Using a small spatula, carefully flip the bananas over. Remove the pan from the heat immediately and set aside until the pancakes are done.

Preheat the oven to 250°F.

Heat a large skillet or griddle over medium heat. When the pan is hot, add about a teaspoon of butter. Ladle ⅓ cup of the pancake batter into the pan, allowing the pancake to spread on its own; it should be about 4 inches wide. Repeat, making sure not to crowd the skillet. Cook the pancakes for 1 to 2 minutes per side, or until golden brown and puffy.

Repeat with remaining pancake batter, stacking the finished pancakes on an ovenproof platter and keeping them warm in the oven. Place the maple syrup in a small saucepan and warm over low heat, about 3 to 4 minutes. Before serving, heat the bananas over medium-high heat for a minute or two, until the bananas begin to caramelize and the brown sugar sauce is bubbling. Pour the bananas over the hot pancakes and serve the warm maple syrup on the side.

favoritevariations

- Substitute $\frac{1}{2}$ cup whole-wheat flour for $\frac{1}{2}$ cup of the all-purpose flour, and add another tablespoon of buttermilk.
- Substitute chopped pecans, almonds, or pistachios for the walnuts, or use a combination.
- Add $\frac{1}{8}$ teaspoon ground cinnamon, nutmeg, or allspice to the pancake batter with the flour.
- Use thinly sliced apples or pears instead of bananas for the topping, cooking until the fruit becomes just soft.
- Add a dollop of crème fraîche, plain or vanilla-flavored yogurt, or sour cream as a topping for the pancakes.

almond-crusted challah french toast
with spiced maple syrup

MAKES 6 SLICES; SERVES 3 TO 6

French toast made with sweet challah bread (or brioche or any type of egg-based bread) is dipped into a nutmeg–cinnamon–maple syrup–egg mixture and then one side of the bread is coated in sliced almonds. The coating gives the French toast a fabulous crunchy texture and a delicious nutty flavor.

This dish reheats beautifully, so you can prepare it when you wake up and reheat it for breakfast or brunch when everyone's ready to eat. Surround the French toast with a big bowl of seasonal fruit; a collection of summer berries is a particularly good match.

for the french toast
4 large eggs
¼ cup half-and-half or whole milk
2 tablespoons pure maple syrup
¼ teaspoon salt
⅛ teaspoon ground nutmeg
⅛ teaspoon ground cinnamon
¼ teaspoon almond extract (optional)
1 cup thinly sliced almonds

6 pieces challah, brioche, or other sweet egg bread, sliced ¾ inch thick
2 to 4 teaspoons unsalted butter

for the spiced maple syrup
1½ cups maple syrup
¼ teaspoon ground nutmeg
¼ teaspoon ground cinnamon

Preheat the oven to 350°F.

To make the French toast: Whisk the eggs, half-and-half, maple syrup, salt, nutmeg, cinnamon, and almond extract together in a wide, shallow bowl until well blended. Place the almond slices on a large plate. Dip a piece of bread in the egg mixture, being sure to coat each side thoroughly. Then place the bread on the almond plate, pressing down lightly to get a solid layer of almond slices on one side of the bread. Set the bread aside, almond side-up, on a platter or cookie sheet and repeat with the remaining bread slices.

Heat a large nonstick pan or griddle over medium heat. When hot, melt 2 teaspoons of the butter in the pan. Add a few pieces of bread almond side down (taking care not to overcrowd the pan) and cook for 3 to 4 minutes, or until the almonds are golden brown (you may need to rotate the pieces halfway through cooking to toast the almonds evenly). Carefully flip the bread over and cook the other side, another 2 to 3 minutes, until golden. Serve immediately and repeat with the remaining bread and butter.

The finished toasts can be made several hours ahead of time; transfer to a cookie sheet, cover, and refrigerate until ready to serve. To rewarm, place in a preheated 350°F oven for 5 to 10 minutes.

To make the spiced syrup: Place the maple syrup, nutmeg, and cinnamon in a small saucepan. Warm over low heat until the syrup just begins to simmer. Serve hot with the French toast.

- **Jam-Stuffed French Toast:** Before dipping the challah in the batter, make a cut that almost separates the bread slice into two thinner pieces of bread, stopping so that one side of the bread remains intact. Spread about 1 to 1½ tablespoons of good berry jam on the inside of the bread, close again, and continue as directed.

- **Orange-Almond French Toast:** Add 1 tablespoon freshly grated orange zest and substitute orange juice for the maple syrup in the batter.

spinach, prosciutto, sun-dried tomato, and cheese **frittata**

SERVES 4 TO 6

You're in the mood for eggs, but you want something a bit more special than fried or scrambled. This frittata, made in minutes with prosciutto, spinach, fresh eggs, and grated cheese, bakes in the oven until it puffs up like a soufflé. Serve with toast, muffins (pages 21 and 22), a collection of jams and jellies, fruit salad (page 18), some good, strong coffee, and you've got the makings of a memorable brunch. The frittata is also a great choice for lunch or a light dinner.

1 tablespoon olive oil
$\frac{1}{3}$ cup chopped prosciutto, cooked ham, or cooked bacon
12 ounces baby spinach
Salt and freshly ground black pepper
4 drained and chopped sun-dried tomatoes (the kind packed in olive oil), or $\frac{1}{4}$ cup chopped fresh tomatoes

6 large eggs
2 tablespoons whole milk or heavy cream
$\frac{1}{3}$ cup fresh grated cheese (Parmesan, cheddar, Manchego, goat, Fontina, or your favorite cheese)

Place rack in the middle of the oven and preheat the oven to 400°F.

Heat the oil in a large, heavy, ovenproof skillet (we use a 10-inch cast-iron pan). Add the prosciutto and cook about 1 minute. Add the spinach in batches, stirring frequently, until soft, about 6 minutes. Pour any excess liquid out of the pan, or blot the spinach dry with paper towels. Season with salt and pepper, add the sun-dried tomatoes, and cook for 1 minute.

In a small bowl, whisk the eggs; season with salt, pepper, and add the milk. Add the eggs to the skillet, tilting the pan so the eggs distribute evenly over the spinach mixture. Cook for 2 minutes. Remove from the heat and sprinkle with the cheese. Place in the oven and bake for 10 to 14 minutes, or until puffed and just set in the center; you don't want the eggs to be dried out.

Cut the frittata into wedges and serve hot or at room temperature.

favoritevariations

- Add $\frac{1}{4}$ cup chopped Kalamata olives.
- Whisk 1 tablespoon black or green tapenade into the eggs.
- Add 1 tablespoon chopped fresh chives to the eggs.
- Sauté 1 thinly sliced sweet red bell pepper with the prosciutto and spinach until soft.
- Add 1 cup sliced mushrooms (wild or cultivated varieties) to the spinach as it cooks.

bacon, cheese, leek, and mushroom quiche

MAKES 2 QUICHES; SERVES 8 TO 12

Yes, we know. Quiche is so seventies. But there was a reason quiche was so hot: it's fast to make (particularly if you use a premade crust), satisfying, and the combinations are endless. This recipe makes enough for two quiches. You can freeze the second one uncooked, covered tightly with plastic wrap, for several months, thaw and bake, or cover and refrigerate the baked quiche for 1 day before serving.

½ pound bacon (about 8 slices) or thinly sliced pancetta
2 tablespoons olive oil
3 small leeks (white and light green parts only), sliced lengthwise and then into 1-inch pieces, or 1 medium onion, very thinly sliced
Salt and freshly ground black pepper
⅛ cup chopped fresh thyme leaves

¾ pound crimini or portabella mushrooms, sliced (about 2½ cups)
Two 8-inch premade (uncooked) pie crusts
1½ cups freshly grated Parmesan cheese
4 large eggs
2 cups sour cream
½ cup heavy cream
¼ cup minced fresh parsley leaves

Cook the bacon or pancetta in a large skillet over medium heat until crisp on both sides, 8 to 10 minutes. Drain on paper towels. Remove all but 1 teaspoon of the fat from the skillet.

Heat the bacon fat over low heat and add the olive oil. Add the leeks and cook for 5 minutes, stirring occasionally. Season with salt, pepper, and half of the thyme. Add the mushrooms and cook, stirring, for another 5 minutes. The vegetables should be tender and slightly golden brown. Remove from the heat and let cool.

Place a rack in the middle of the oven and preheat the oven to 425°F.

Sprinkle 1 tablespoon of the thyme into the bottom of each pie shell, spreading it out evenly along the bottom. Add 2 tablespoons of the cheese to each crust, spreading it out on top of the thyme.

In a large bowl, whisk the eggs. Add the sour cream and heavy cream and whisk until smooth. Add the remaining cheese, the parsley, and the remaining thyme, and season with salt and pepper. Crumble the bacon or pancetta and add to the mixture.

Divide the vegetables between the bottoms of both crusts, spreading them out evenly. Pour the egg mixture over the vegetables, dividing it evenly between both crusts.

Place the quiches on a cookie or baking sheet and bake for 10 minutes. Reduce the temperature to 350°F and bake for another 45 to 50 minutes, or until the quiche is slightly puffed up and a toothpick inserted in the center comes out clean. Serve hot or at room temperature. Once cool, the quiche can be tightly wrapped and refrigerated for 1 day, or frozen for up to a month, thawed and reheated in a 300°F oven until warm.

favoritevariations

- To make a meat-free quiche, omit the bacon completely and sauté the vegetables in 2 table-spoons olive oil.
- Omit the mushrooms and add 1 small thinly sliced zucchini.
- Substitute basil for the thyme.
- Use grated cheddar, Swiss, or any other hard cheese instead of, or in addition to, the Parmesan.
- Use a soft goat cheese for half of the Parmesan.
- Sauté the leeks and add ¾ pound lump crabmeat or lobster and 2 tablespoons chopped fresh chives instead of the mushrooms and cook for only 2 minutes.
- Use ½ pound smoked ham, turkey, or chicken, cut into cubes or thin slices, instead of the bacon or pancetta.
- Line the bottom of the crusts with 1 small thinly sliced ripe tomato and add 1 cup chopped black olives to the egg mixture.
- Substitute 1 cup fresh or frozen corn kernels for the mushrooms.
- Substitute ½ pound Italian sausage taken out of the casing for the bacon. Add 1 red or green sweet pepper instead of the mushrooms.
- Add 8 ounces baby spinach or regular spinach, stemmed and chopped, instead of the mushrooms.

huevos rancheros

Huevos rancheros (which translates roughly to "ranch-style eggs") have traveled a long way from Mexico, where this tortilla, fried egg, black bean, and salsa breakfast treat first gained popularity. Making them at home is much easier than you might guess; the beans and salsa can be made ahead of time and the eggs cooked at the last minute. You can make our fabulous Mango Salsa (page 236), Fresh Tomato Salsa (page 237), and Chunky Guacamole (page 234), or opt for good quality store-bought versions to save time.

3 tablespoons olive oil
1 small red onion, chopped
1 small yellow onion, chopped
Salt and freshly ground black pepper
Two 15-ounce cans black beans, rinsed and
    drained
1/2 teaspoon ground cumin
2 tablespoons chopped fresh cilantro leaves
Dash of hot pepper sauce

Four 6-inch corn tortillas
4 large eggs
1 1/2 cups shredded Monterey Jack cheese
1/2 cup sour cream
1 cup Chunky Guacamole (page 234), or
    store-bought
Mango Salsa (page 236), Fresh Tomato Salsa
    (page 237), or about 2 cups store-bought
    salsa

Preheat the oven to 300°F.

Heat a large skillet over medium heat. Add 1 tablespoon of the olive oil. When hot, add the red and yellow onions and season with salt and pepper. Cook, stirring, until the onions are soft, about 5 minutes. Add the beans and cumin, and cook over low heat for 5 minutes, stirring occasionally. Stir in 1 tablespoon of the cilantro and a dash or two of hot sauce, season again with salt and pepper to taste, and set aside. (The beans can be made a day ahead of time; cover and refrigerate. Place over low heat to rewarm. If they seem dry, add 1 to 2 tablespoons water.)

Wrap the corn tortillas in a clean, damp kitchen towel. Place in the oven and heat the tortillas for 5 minutes.

Meanwhile, heat 1 tablespoon of the remaining olive oil in a large skillet over medium heat. When hot, crack 2 eggs (or more if they fit without overlapping) into the pan and fry for 1 to 2 minutes on each side, or until the egg whites solidify, depending on how soft you like your eggs. Transfer to a warm plate and repeat with the remaining oil and eggs.

Place 1 warm tortilla on each of four plates. Divide the beans among the 4 tortillas. Sprinkle the cheese over the beans and top with a fried egg. Garnish with sour cream, guacamole, and the remaining cilantro. Surround the tortillas with a small dollop of each of the salsas. Serve hot pepper sauce on the side.

the good egg?

Our heads spin trying to keep up with what's healthy and what's not. We know that eggs—one of our all-time breakfast favorites—are good for you, but we also know they are high in cholesterol. So what's an egg lover to do? Much like the question Dorothy asked Glinda, the Good Witch of the North in *The Wizard of Oz*, we want to ask eggs: Are you a good food or a bad food?

Like so many things, it turns out that, in moderation, eggs *are* very good for you. One large egg provides more than 12 percent of the daily recommended intake of protein with only 74 calories and 1.5 grams of saturated fat. It's the yolks—the center of the egg and of all its rich, delicious flavor—that contain the fat but they're also where you'll find good amounts of vitamins A, D, and B_{12}, as well as iron and folate. And about that cholesterol? Well, the American Heart Association currently suggests that we eat no more than 300 milligrams of cholesterol a day. If you're watching your cholesterol (and who isn't?), keep in mind that one egg provides 212 milligrams of that daily limit. So about that three-egg omelet . . .

The egg world is filled with all kinds of facts and trivia. Here are some of our favorite egg tidbits:

- Eggs come in many colors and sizes, but what's most important to know is that brown or white, pink or beige, there is no nutritional difference in the color of an egg. The color of the shell is determined by the breed of the chicken. For instance, brown eggs come from hens with reddish brown feathers, while white-shelled eggs come from breeds with white feathers.
- The color of the yolk—which can vary from a sunshiny yellow to gold to lemon or pale yellow—is determined by the hen's diet. Many commercial egg farmers feed their hens marigold petals to darken and richen the color of the yolks. The reason for this deception: Many of us are under the mistaken belief that a dark yellow yolk indicates a superior egg. But unless that rich deep color comes from a good, healthy, nonmedicated diet, the color of the yolk is not your best indicator of flavor.
- Eggs come in many sizes. Jumbos are the granddaddies of the egg world, followed by extra-large, large, medium, small, and pee-wee. Most recipes (and the ones used in this book) are based on large eggs.
- What's a free-range egg? These are eggs produced by hens that have been raised outdoors or with access to the outdoors. Because these hens are allowed to roam and search for tidbits their diets tend to be more varied, which is why these eggs tend to have deep yellow yolks and a more distinct eggy flavor.
- What about organic eggs? Organic eggs are produced by hens that are fed a diet free of pesticides, fungicides, and herbicides. No hormones go into their food. They cost more than regular eggs but have the same nutrients as regular eggs. But there's no denying that a fresh, organically fed egg has superior flavor. If you've ever tasted an egg freshly laid from a chicken on the farm, where the animals are allowed to roam and eat all manner of organic scraps, you know what a truly delicious egg tastes like. The hen's diet is the largest contributor to an egg's flavor. There is also the issue of safety. Because they are raised in much healthier conditions, organically raised eggs have less risk than regular eggs for salmonella.
- Salmonella is a bacteria that causes food poisoning and is sometimes found in commercially raised eggs. Many believe the cause for this problem is the overcrowded and often unsanitary conditions found in huge egg production centers. For those with compromised immune systems (as well as babies, young children, and the elderly), eggs should be cooked to an internal temperature of 160°F., which is when salmonella is killed and the

yolk is cooked all the way through and hard. We use fresh organic eggs when soft boiling eggs and when using raw eggs in dressings and meringue.

- Nutrient-enhanced eggs have recently appeared on supermarket shelves. This describes eggs that come from hens that are fed nutrient-rich diets. These eggs are being touted as having lower saturated fat, while others claim they have higher omega-3 fatty acid content.

- Freshness is key to a good egg. Many eggs have a date listed on the carton and the fresher the egg, the better the flavor. Keeping eggs refrigerated and out of humidity is also important. A one-week-old egg kept in ideal conditions can be fresher than a one-day-old egg left at room temperature.

- Despite the plastic egg containers that come in virtually every new refrigerator, the best way to store eggs and keep them fresh is to store them in the carton they arrived in, protecting them from odors.

- As eggs age their whites become thinner and their yolks become flatter. Really fresh eggs hold their shape rather than spread out in the pan or bowl. On the other hand, eggs that are a week old and then hard boiled are easier to peel than hard-boiled fresh ones. This is because the pocket of air at one end grows as the egg ages.

- Some egg math: 5 large eggs = 1 cup. 6 small eggs = 1 cup. 7 large whites = 1 cup. 8 medium whites = 1 cup.

- When you crack an egg and a small bit of the shell accidentally falls into the bowl or pan, the best way to scoop it up is to use another piece of shell. Take half an egg shell (after you've cracked the egg) and use it as a scoop to gather the broken bit of shell. It seems that shell is attracted to shell and cuts through the whites, which makes getting rid of those little pieces that invariably fall into our batters, sauces, and omelets a whole lot easier to get rid of.

- For more on eggs, see pages 40 and 85.

new **eggs benedict**

SERVES 2 TO 4

There's only one thing that used to keep us from making regular eggs benedict at home: the fussy hollandaise sauce. We decided to lighten things up by opting for smoked salmon over the traditional Canadian bacon, layering it with sautéed spinach between the poached egg and English muffin, and doing away with the hollandaise entirely. Instead we top the eggs with a lemon and chive butter sauce for a light, colorful New Eggs Benedict. Without the heavy sauce, the entire breakfast can be made quickly, and the flavor of each ingredient comes through.

1 tablespoon olive oil
12 ounces washed baby spinach
Salt and freshly ground black pepper
¼ cup (½ stick) unsalted butter
2 teaspoons grated lemon zest
2 tablespoons fresh lemon juice

2 tablespoons chopped fresh chives, plus
  more for garnish
2 whole English muffins
4 large eggs
¼ pound sliced smoked salmon

Heat a large skillet over medium-high heat. When hot, add the olive oil, then add the spinach in batches. Season with salt and pepper. Cook the spinach, stirring with tongs, until it has completely wilted, about 5 minutes. Remove from the heat and set aside.

Make the sauce: Melt the butter in a small saucepan over low heat. Remove from the heat, stir in the lemon zest, juice, and chives, and season with salt and pepper. Set aside.

Separate and toast the English muffins.

Poach the eggs: See below. Lift the eggs from the water with the slotted spoon, and place on a paper towel–lined plate.

While the eggs are cooking, place a quarter of the spinach on half of each muffin, and place the salmon over the spinach. Top each portion with a poached egg, and garnish with extra chives. Drizzle the warm sauce over each egg and serve immediately.

favoritevariations

- Substitute smoked trout or finnan haddie for the salmon.
- Substitute cooked crab or coarsely chopped lobster for the salmon.
- Replace the salmon with cooked bacon, pancetta slices, prosciutto, or slices of smoked, cooked ham or traditional Canadian bacon.
- Make the sauce with fresh chopped dill or fennel fronds instead of chives.

coaching on poaching

Poaching eggs instills fear in otherwise confident breakfast chefs. Why does dropping an egg into simmering water seem so . . . scary? We have absolutely no idea, because poaching is an easy, simple, healthful way to cook eggs.

The basic method is as follows: Fill a large skillet or saucepan (with sides at least 2 inches high) about three-quarters of the way with water. Bring the water to a simmer and season with salt. Crack one egg at a time into a small bowl.

Using a slotted spoon, stir the water in a circular motion to create a little whirlpool in the pan—this will help keep the egg white near the yolk when cooking. Slip the egg into the center of the swirling water. Repeat with one or two other eggs, being sure not to crowd the skillet. Cook the eggs for 2 to 3 minutes, or until the whites have set (yolks should remain a bit runny). Use a slotted spoon to lift the eggs from water; drain off any water and serve.

bacon, egg, spinach, and
blue cheese breakfast sandwiches

We are huge fans of breakfast sandwiches but tire of the same old egg, bacon, and cheese combo. We thought we'd play with the classic a bit and found that the addition of blue cheese and spinach adds just the right touch. (The recipe can be easily doubled or tripled.) Serve this sandwich for breakfast, brunch, lunch, or cut into quarters as an hors d'oeuvre at a cocktail party. You can use either a panini press or a regular skillet; see page 99 for directions on creating a makeshift panini press using kitchen skillets.

¼ pound bacon (about 4 slices)
2 large eggs
Salt and freshly ground black pepper
1 tablespoon soft unsalted butter, divided
    into 4 pieces

4 slices good crusty bread
2 tablespoons crumbled blue cheese, at
    room temperature
½ cup baby spinach

Heat a large skillet over medium heat. Add the bacon and cook until crispy on both sides, flipping occasionally, about 10 minutes. Drain the bacon on paper towels and set aside. Discard most of the bacon fat, leaving a thin film on the bottom of the pan.

Increase the heat to medium high. When the pan is hot, crack the eggs into the pan and season with salt and pepper. Cook for 1 to 2 minutes, or until the egg whites solidify. Carefully flip the eggs and cook for another 1 to 2 minutes on the other side (the yolk should still be soft). Remove to a plate.

Preheat a panini press, large skillet, or grill pan over medium-high heat.

Spread the bread with the butter. Place 2 slices buttered side down on a plate and spread each with 1 tablespoon blue cheese. Arrange an equal amount of spinach on each slice, add a fried egg, yolk side up, and 2 slices of cooked bacon to each, and gently top with the remaining bread slices, buttered side up.

Cook the sandwiches in a hot panini press for 2 to 3 minutes, or until the bread is golden on both sides. If using kitchen skillets, cook the sandwiches until golden on the bottom, 3 to 4 minutes, then flip and repeat on the other side.

favoritevariations

- Substitute grated Parmesan, cheddar, Manchego, or crumbled goat cheese for the blue cheese.
- Substitute arugula or watercress for the spinach.
- Use cooked pancetta or deli ham in place of the bacon, or omit the meat.
- Add a few slices of fresh tomato to each sandwich.

roast beef **hash**

This hash, a quick easy blend of sautéed onions, buttery potatoes, and roast beef, is what hash is all about—hearty and just begging to be topped with a poached egg. While we love corned beef hash, we've found that making hash with roast beef elevates the status of this breakfast classic. Use leftover beef (see page 195) or a good-quality roast beef from your deli sliced just a bit thicker than usual—about ¹⁄₈ inch thick. Serve with home fries, toast or crusty bread, and a good hot pepper sauce.

The hash can be made several hours ahead of time and reheated in the skillet just before serving.

1½ pounds potatoes (about 2 medium),
   peeled and cut into ½-inch cubes
3 tablespoons olive oil
2 medium onions, chopped
Salt and freshly ground black pepper

1 tablespoon chopped fresh thyme leaves,
   or ½ teaspoon dried
¾ pound roast beef, preferably rare, sliced
   about ⅛ inch thick, cut into ½-inch
   squares
¼ cup minced fresh parsley leaves

Bring a large pot of water to a boil. Add the potatoes and simmer over medium heat for about 10 minutes, or until almost tender. Drain well.

While the potatoes are cooking, in a large, heavy skillet (cast iron is ideal), heat 2 tablespoons of the oil over medium-low heat. Add the onions and cook, stirring frequently, for 10 minutes. Season with salt and pepper.

Add the potatoes to the skillet with the onions and raise the heat to medium high. Add the thyme and cook for 5 minutes, stirring occasionally. Add the beef and drizzle the remaining tablespoon of oil over the mixture. Press down on the potato mixture with the back of a spatula. Cook undisturbed for about 5 minutes and then very carefully, using the spatula to help, flip the hash over as if it were a large pancake. (It may be easier to flip it in three or four large sections.) Cook for another 5 to 7 minutes. The idea is to create a golden brown "crust" on the hash. Sprinkle with the parsley. Taste for seasoning and serve hot and crispy.

favoritevariations

■ For Red Flannel Hash, add 1 cooked cubed red beet when you add the beef.
■ Substitute cooked corned beef, chicken, or turkey for the roast beef.
■ Add additional chopped fresh herbs such as rosemary, chives, basil, or tarragon when you add the thyme.

trio of **flavored cream cheeses**

We love those fancy flavored cream cheeses you find in gourmet food stores. But it seems a little crazy to spend so much money for cream cheese mixed with one or two ingredients when it's so easy to whip up these flavored cream cheeses at home. Not only will you save money, but you can create just about any flavor you can think of. Here are three of our favorites. We like to present all three at a brunch, accompanied by assorted bagels, scones, muffins, and artisanal breads.

These flavored cream cheeses will keep, covered and refrigerated, for about 5 days.

■ **double olive** cream cheese

MAKES 1¼ CUPS

1 cup (½ pound) whipped cream cheese
2 tablespoons tapenade (olive puree), or
   chopped Kalamata (or black) olives,
   available in specialty food shops

½ cup chopped green olives
Freshly ground black pepper, to taste

Mix all of the ingredients in a small bowl until blended.

■ **roasted sweet red pepper and scallion** cream cheese

MAKES 1¼ CUPS

1 cup (½ pound) whipped cream cheese
¼ cup finely chopped roasted sweet red bell
   peppers or pimientos

2 scallions (white and green parts), finely
   chopped
Salt and freshly ground black pepper to
   taste

Mix all of the ingredients in a small bowl until blended.

■ **spiced maple-walnut** cream cheese

MAKES 1¼ CUPS

½ cup chopped walnuts, or toasted walnuts
   (see page 260)
1 cup (½ pound) whipped cream cheese

2 tablespoons pure maple syrup
⅛ teaspoon ground nutmeg
⅛ teaspoon ground cinnamon

Mix all of the ingredients in a small bowl until blended.

favoritevariations

Mix any of the following ingredients into 1 cup whipped cream cheese and season with salt and freshly ground pepper to taste.

- **Lemon-Pistachio Cream Cheese:** Zest and juice of 1 large lemon and $1/2$ cup chopped toasted pistachio nuts.
- **Sun-Dried Tomato, Olive, and Onion Cream Cheese:** $1/4$ cup chopped sun-dried tomatoes (packed in oil), $1/2$ cup chopped Kalamata olives, and $1/4$ cup finely chopped red onion.
- **The Whole "Schmear" Cream Cheese:** $1/2$ cup chopped smoked salmon or lox, $1/4$ cup drained capers, and $1/4$ cup finely chopped red onion.
- **Lemon-Herb Cream Cheese:** $1/4$ teaspoon grated lemon zest, 1 tablespoon lemon juice, and 2 tablespoons chopped fresh herbs (such as basil, chives, thyme, lemon verbena, rosemary, or lavender).
- **Hot Stuff:** $1/4$ cup chopped pickled jalapeño peppers with 1 teaspoon pickling juice from the jar.
- **Chive-Scallion Cream Cheese:** $1/3$ cup chopped fresh chives and 2 scallions (white and green parts), finely chopped.
- **Garden Vegetable Cream Cheese:** $1/4$ cup diced carrots, $1/4$ cup diced celery, $1/4$ cup diced red onion, and 1 tablespoon diced radish (optional).

2

soups and chowders

chunky gazpacho with piquillo-scallion relish

On a stifling hot summer day there is nothing that refreshes like a good gazpacho. This is the dish to make when it's too hot to cook, when even the thought of turning on the grill leaves you sweating. Once you do a bit of chopping, this gazpacho takes no time to make—just mix the chopped crisp cucumbers, fresh red tomatoes, and a few sweet peppers together and set the mixture aside for an hour, and the vegetable juices appear almost magically. The resulting "soup" is like a summer garden in a bowl, topped with a minty relish of smoky, sweet piquillo peppers and chopped scallions. It's perfect for a picnic.

Look for roasted piquillo peppers packed in oil in a small jar in your grocery store, often near the pickled items or in the ethnic foods section, or in specialty food stores. You can substitute roasted sweet red peppers, finely chopped, with a pinch of smoky paprika.

for the gazpacho
1½ pounds ripe tomatoes (about 3 medium), cut into ¼-inch dice
2 seedless cucumbers (skin left on), cut into ¼-inch dice
1 red bell pepper, cut into ¼-inch dice
1 yellow bell pepper, cut into ¼-inch dice
1 green bell pepper, cut into ¼-inch dice
1 medium red onion, finely chopped
1 garlic clove, minced
¼ cup white wine or Champagne vinegar
2 tablespoons olive oil
Dash of hot pepper sauce
Salt and freshly ground black pepper

for the relish
½ cup drained roasted piquillo peppers, finely chopped
½ cup chopped scallions (white and green parts)
3 tablespoons chopped fresh mint leaves
1 garlic clove, minced
2 tablespoons white wine or Champagne vinegar
1 tablespoon olive oil
Salt and freshly ground black pepper

To make the gazpacho: Gently mix all of the gazpacho ingredients in a large bowl until well combined. Puree about 3 cups of the vegetable mixture in a food processor or blender until almost liquid. Return the pureed mixture to the bowl, mix well, and season again to taste with salt and pepper, if necessary. Let the gazpacho sit at room temperature for about an hour, allowing the natural juices to accumulate at the bottom of the bowl. Cover and chill if not serving right away.

To make the relish: Mix all of the ingredients in a bowl until blended (makes about 1 cup relish).

Stir the gazpacho to distribute the juices, and serve it in small bowls, garnished with a spoonful of relish.

favoritevariations

- Add 2 finely chopped jalapeño peppers.
- Add 2 cups corn kernels (fresh are best).
- Replace some or all of the red tomatoes with yellow or green tomatoes.
- Replace one of the bell peppers with orange or purple bell peppers.
- Spoon a tablespoon or so of the gazpacho onto fresh raw oysters or clams on the half shell.
- Serve the gazpacho with cooked shrimp.

summer **tomato and basil soup**

SERVES 8 TO 10; MAKES 10 CUPS

Use the very freshest, ripest, plumpest, bursting-with-flavor tomatoes you can find—preferably ones from your, your neighbor's, or a local farmer's garden. Fresh basil and slowly cooked onions add extra dimension to this delicious soup. Serve it chilled or hot, with or without the basil cream. The soup can be made a day ahead of time or frozen for several months.

for the soup
4 pounds tomatoes (about 6 medium), cored
2 tablespoons olive oil
1 pound yellow or Vidalia onions (about 3 medium), sliced
Salt and freshly ground black pepper
1/3 cup packed coarsely chopped fresh basil leaves, plus extra whole leaves for garnish

4 cups low-sodium canned chicken or vegetable broth, or homemade chicken broth (see page 63)
A few fresh basil leaves for garnish

for the basil cream
1 cup packed fresh basil leaves
1/2 cup heavy cream
Salt and freshly ground black pepper

To make the soup: Bring a large pot of water to a boil. Fill a large bowl with ice water. Gently drop the tomatoes into the boiling water and cook for about 20 seconds. Remove with a slotted spoon and immediately place in the bowl of ice water. Using your fingers or a small, sharp knife, peel the tomatoes. Coarsely chop the tomatoes and set aside.

In a large pot, heat the oil over low heat. Add the onions, salt and pepper to taste, and cook, stirring occasionally, for 10 minutes. Add the tomatoes and cook for 2 to 3 minutes, stirring well. Add half of the chopped basil and raise the heat to high. Add the broth and bring to a boil. Reduce the heat, cover, and let simmer for 30 minutes. Remove from the heat and set aside for 5 minutes.

To make the basil cream: Place the basil, cream, and salt and pepper in a food processor or blender and whirl until almost fully pureed. The basil cream can be made several hours ahead of time; cover and refrigerate until ready to use. Bring the cream to room temperature before serving.

Add the remaining chopped basil to the soup and, working in batches, puree the soup in a food processor or blender. Taste for seasoning.

If serving hot, return the soup to the pot and bring to a simmer over low heat. Alternatively, the soup can be refrigerated and served chilled. Swirl about a tablespoon of the basil cream into the soup, and garnish with the basil leaves.

favoritevariations
■ Serve with the Parmesan croûtes on page 165.
■ Replace the basil cream with basil whipped cream: Chop the basil finely and gently stir into 1/2 cup (unsweetened) whipped cream; season with salt and pepper.

shellfish chowder

SERVES 8

There are certain dishes that take time and some work, but the pay-off is so huge that you forget all that went into them. This is one such dish, a chowder chock full of plump steamer clams, delicate littlenecks clams, lobster meat, and sea scallops. Much of the chowder can be prepared ahead of time and then put together just before serving. Serve with warm Bacon and Chive biscuits (page 27) and a good green salad.

One 2-pound live lobster
2 pounds steamer clams, scrubbed clean
1½ dozen littleneck clams (about
    1½ pounds), scrubbed clean and soaked
    (see page 54)
4 ounces bacon, preferably thick-sliced
    (3 to 4 slices)
1 tablespoon unsalted butter
2 medium onions, finely chopped
2 pounds white potatoes (about 3 medium),
    peeled and finely chopped

2 stalks celery, finely chopped
2 tablespoons flour
Freshly ground black pepper
1 cup milk
½ cup heavy cream
8 ounces sea scallops, cut in half, tabs
    removed (see Note on page 54)
3 tablespoons chopped fresh chives
Salt
Sweet Hungarian paprika

Fill a large pot with 6 cups of water and bring to a boil over high heat. Add the lobster, shell side down, cover, and steam for 14 minutes. Remove the lobster from the pot and set aside; be sure to save all of the lobster water/broth.

Bring the lobster broth to a boil over moderately high heat and add the steamer and littleneck clams; cover the pot. Cook for about 3 minutes, or until the clams just begin to open their shells. Use a slotted spoon to remove the clams as they start to open a tiny bit; you don't want the shells to open all the way or the clams will be overcooked in the final chowder. Transfer the open clams to a bowl and set aside to cool. Do not discard the cooking broth, but do get rid of any clams that refuse to open.

Remove the clams from their shells; discard the shells. Be sure to pull the skin off the long rubbery-looking neck (also called the siphon) of the steamer clams. Coarsely chop the clams. Remove the lobster meat from the claws. Use a paring knife to cut a slit down the back of the tail and remove the thin black vein. Coarsely chop the lobster meat and set aside.

Pour the broth through a fine sieve into a bowl, making sure to discard any bits of debris that have settled at the bottom of the pot. You should have 5 to 5½ cups of broth. If not, add enough water to make 5 cups broth and set aside. You can cover the shellfish and the broth and refrigerate for up to 24 hours.

RECIPE CONTINUES ▶

Heat a large pot over medium heat. When hot, add the bacon and cook until crisp on both sides, about 10 minutes. Drain on paper towels and then chop coarsely; set aside. Remove all but 1 teaspoon of the grease in the bottom of the pan. Return the pan to the stove, and add the butter and onions and cook over medium-low heat, stirring, for 5 minutes. Add the potatoes and cook for 5 minutes, stirring occasionally. Add the celery and cook for 3 minutes. Sprinkle in the flour and a grinding of pepper and cook, stirring, for 2 minutes more. Slowly add the 5 cups broth and bring the soup to a simmer. Reduce the heat to low, cover, and cook for 15 minutes, or until the potatoes are tender.

Meanwhile, in a small saucepan, heat the milk and cream over low heat until just simmering.

Add the chopped clams, lobster, and scallops to the pot and cook for 3 minutes. Add the hot milk and cream and cook for 3 minutes over very low heat; do not let the chowder boil. Add the chopped bacon and the chives and lightly season with salt, if necessary. Serve piping hot with a dusting of paprika on top of each bowl.

NOTE: Tabs are the small, thick, rectangular pieces of tissue on the side of the scallop that can become tough when cooked. Some fishmongers trim them off; some don't. To remove, simply pull off the tab with your fingers or a small knife.

favoritevariations

- Leave a few clams in the shell to use for garnishing each bowl of chowder.
- Substitute 2 dozen mussels for the littleneck clams.
- Add 1 pound whitefish (such as haddock, cod, or scrod), cut into $1\frac{1}{2}$-inch cubes. Add during the last 5 minutes of cooking.
- Add 1 tablespoon chopped fresh tarragon, rosemary, or basil during the last 5 minutes of cooking.

soaking clams

Soaking clams helps remove sand and other grit from them. Place the clams in a large bowl filled with cold water. Add a teaspoon of cornmeal or oatmeal and let the clams sit for about 15 minutes. (They open their shells to eat the cornmeal and spit out any sand.) Drain the clams, rinse well, and drain again.

classic **oyster stew**

You don't want to mess around with oysters. They have such a clean, briny essence that it's a shame to infuse them with too many flavors. This stew combines lightly sautéed shallots and whole fresh-shucked oysters with hot milk and cream. Believe us when we say that once you've shucked the oysters the stew takes no more than 15 minutes to make. Serve with Bacon and Chive Biscuits (page 27). The recipe can easily be doubled or tripled to serve a crowd.

¾ cup milk
½ cup heavy cream
1 tablespoon unsalted butter
2 shallots, minced

12 oysters, shucked (be sure to keep all the juices)
⅛ teaspoon Worcestershire sauce
Salt and freshly ground black pepper
Sweet Hungarian paprika

In a small saucepan, heat the milk and cream over low heat until hot but not simmering.

In a medium saucepan, melt the butter over low heat. Add the shallots and cook, stirring, for 5 minutes. Add the oysters and cook, stirring gently, for 1 minute. Add the Worcestershire sauce and salt and pepper to taste. Add the liquid from the oysters and cook for 2 minutes. Pour the hot milk mixture on top of the oysters and let warm for about 1 to 2 minutes. Sprinkle each serving with paprika.

favoritevariations

- Use shucked littleneck clams instead of oysters or a combination of the two.
- Sprinkle the stew with 1 tablespoon chopped fresh chives or Italian parsley.
- Add ¼ cup chopped cooked lobster to the stew during the last 2 minutes of cooking.

corn and sweet potato chowder
with saffron cream

This chowder is a sensory explosion. First there's the color: The broth is a gorgeous rich sunflower yellow, thanks to the saffron, sweet potatoes, and golden yellow corn and peppers. Then there's the scent: the earthy aroma of corn and saffron. And, of course, the taste: rich, creamy, summery, and satisfying. Serve with Bacon and Chive Biscuits (see page 27), rolls, crusty bread, or oyster crackers.

2 tablespoons olive oil
1 large onion, chopped
1 large red bell pepper, cut into 1/2-inch squares
1 small yellow bell pepper, cut into 1/2-inch squares
1 large sweet potato, peeled and cut into 1/2-inch squares (about 2 cups)
Salt and freshly ground black pepper
1 tablespoon flour

4 cups low-sodium canned chicken or vegetable broth, or homemade chicken broth (see page 63)
6 large ears fresh corn, or 3 cups frozen corn kernels, thawed
1 cup heavy cream
About 1 teaspoon crumbled saffron
3 scallions (white and green parts), finely chopped

In a large pot, heat the oil over low heat. Add the onion and cook, stirring occasionally, for 10 minutes. Add half of the red pepper and all of the yellow pepper and cook, stirring, for 2 minutes. Add the sweet potato, season with salt and pepper, and cook for 8 minutes, stirring occasionally. Stir in the flour and cook for 2 minutes. Raise the heat to high, stir in the broth, and bring to a boil. Reduce the heat to low, cover, and cook for about 12 minutes until the potatoes are just tender.

Meanwhile, if using fresh corn, shuck it and remove the silks. Using a sharp knife, remove the kernels from the cob by standing each cob on one end on a cutting board and working the knife straight down the cob; you should have about 3 cups of kernels. Remove the corn milk (see page 57) and mix in the kernels; set aside.

In a small saucepan, heat the cream and saffron over low heat for about 5 minutes, until just simmering.

Add the saffron cream to the chowder and stir in the corn. Heat over low heat for 5 minutes. Taste for seasoning. Serve piping hot, topped with the scallions and remaining red pepper.

favoritevariation

- Sauté 3 slices thick-sliced bacon in the pan as the first step. Remove the bacon and keep 1 tablespoon bacon fat in the pan. Sauté the onions in the bacon fat instead of adding olive oil. Crumble the bacon into the soup just before serving.

milking the cob

When you cut the kernels off a fresh cob of corn, don't throw it out. There is a delicious corn "milk" contained just at the edge of the cob that is easily released and adds great flavor to soup, fritters, and salads.

Using the blunt side of a large knife, scrape the cob after the kernels have been removed. The corn "milk" adds great flavor to your cooking. Then you can throw the cobs away.

asian-style **chicken noodle soup**

SERVES 4 GENEROUSLY

It's a freezing cold winter day and the weather isn't supposed to go over 5 degrees all week. You simmer up a pot of chicken broth laced with ginger and scallions, ladle it into oversized bowls with a dab of Chinese chile paste, Asian noodles, slices of cooked chicken, and top it with bean sprouts and a drizzle of sesame oil. Ahhhh, instant warmth.

8 cups low-sodium canned chicken or
    vegetable broth, or homemade chicken
    or turkey broth (page 63)
3 scallions (white and green parts), cut into
    1-inch pieces
3 tablespoons peeled, thinly sliced fresh
    ginger, cut into matchsticks
Freshly ground black pepper

1 to 4 teaspoons Chinese chile paste
4 teaspoons soy sauce
1 cup shredded or cubed cooked chicken
6 ounces Asian wheat or udon noodles
1 small bunch watercress, stems removed
1 cup bean sprouts
1 tablespoon Asian sesame oil

In a large pot bring the broth, scallions, and ginger to a simmer over medium heat. Season with pepper and simmer for about 10 minutes. Meanwhile bring a large pot of water to a boil.

In four oversized soup bowls, add a dab of chile paste. You can make the soup as spicy or mild as you like. Add 1 teaspoon of soy sauce to the bottom of each bowl. Divide the chicken among the four bowls.

Cook the noodles in the boiling water for 4 to 5 minutes, depending on the thickness of the noodles, until tender. Drain.

Divide the hot noodles among the four bowls and ladle on the hot broth. Top with the watercress and bean sprouts and a drizzle of sesame oil.

favoritevariations

- Use cooked duck, turkey, pork, or beef instead of the chicken.
- Add 2 tablespoons chopped fresh cilantro to the top of the soup.
- Add roasted vegetables to the soup (see page 59).
- Roast baby bok choy and add it to the soup: Place whole (ends trimmed) in a small roasting pan, drizzle with olive oil, and roast for about 15 minutes. Slice the bok choy in half lengthwise before adding to the soup bowls.

roasted **winter vegetable soup**

SERVES 6

Cubes of winter vegetables—parsnips, winter squash, celery root, carrots, and celery, along with shallots, leeks, and garlic—are roasted until just tender, golden brown, and caramelized and then tossed with a splash of white wine and some good broth. The soup takes less than an hour from start to finish but the resulting flavor is startlingly complex. See photograph on page 46.
Serve with Winter Parsley Pesto (page 232), and Cheddar Croûtes (page 64).

10 ounces parsnips (about 3 medium), peeled and cut into ½-inch pieces

2 medium carrots, peeled and cut into ½-inch pieces

One 2-pound butternut squash, or any type of winter squash, peeled and cut into ½-inch cubes

3 stalks celery, cut into ½-inch pieces

1 medium celery root (about 1¼ pounds), peeled and cut into ½-inch cubes

3 leeks (whole and light green parts only), halved lengthwise, and cut into ½-inch pieces

2 shallots, quartered

8 garlic cloves, thinly sliced

Salt and freshly ground black pepper

1½ tablespoons chopped fresh thyme leaves, or 2 teaspoons dried

2½ tablespoons olive oil

5 cups low-sodium canned vegetable or chicken broth, or homemade chicken broth (see page 63)

1 bay leaf

¾ cup dry white wine

Winter Parsley Pesto (page 232)

Cheddar Croûtes (page 165)

Place a rack in the center of the oven and preheat the oven to 400°F.

Toss the parsnips, carrots, squash, celery, celery root, leeks, shallots, garlic, salt and pepper, thyme, and olive oil together in a large, very shallow roasting pan. Place in the oven and roast for 20 minutes. Raise the heat to 450°F and roast for another 10 to 20 minutes, or until the vegetables are just tender.

Meanwhile, combine the broth in a large pot with the bay leaf and bring to a boil over high heat.

Remove the vegetables from the oven and deglaze the pan with the wine, using a spatula to loosen any bits clinging to the bottom of the pan. Pour the vegetables and the liquid from the bottom of the pan into the pot with the simmering broth. Reduce the heat to low and simmer for 10 minutes, partially covered. Serve piping hot with the pesto and croûtes.

pasta e fagioli
(italian-style pasta and bean soup)

SERVES 8

Scented with rosemary, our thick, hearty version of Italy's traditional pasta and bean soup is simple and satisfying. We make it a one-bowl meal by adding generous chunks of cubed boneless pork loin roast, or you can substitute bacon or pancetta. Serve with the Parmesan Croûtes (see page 165).

The soup can be stored in airtight containers in the refrigerator for up to 3 days or in the freezer for up to 2 months.

2 tablespoons flour
Salt and freshly ground black pepper
¾ pound boneless pork loin roast, cut into
   ½-inch cubes
3 tablespoons olive oil
1 cup dry white wine
1 large onion, diced
6 garlic cloves, coarsely chopped
1 medium carrot, diced
1 stalk celery, diced
¼ cup packed chopped fresh parsley leaves

2 teaspoons chopped fresh rosemary leaves
6 cups homemade chicken broth (see page
   63), or low-sodium canned
One 28-ounce can crushed or whole peeled
   tomatoes
¾ cup small pasta (conchigliette, ditalini,
   and orzo work well)
Two 15-ounce cans cannellini (white kidney)
   beans, rinsed and drained
Dash of hot pepper sauce (optional)
About 1 cup freshly grated Parmesan cheese

Put the flour in a bowl or plate and season with salt and pepper, and lightly coat all sides of the pork with the flour. Heat a large soup pot over medium-high heat. When the pot is hot but not smoking, add 2 tablespoons of the olive oil. Working in batches, brown the pork, stirring occasionally, about 5 minutes per batch. Transfer the browned pork to a bowl. Add the wine to the pot, raise the heat to high, and simmer for 2 minutes, stirring with a spoon to release any bits clinging to the bottom of the pan. Pour the wine mixture into the bowl with the cooked pork and set aside.

Reduce the heat under the pot to medium, and add the remaining tablespoon olive oil. Add the onion and garlic to the pan, and cook, stirring, until the onion begins to soften, about 3 minutes. Add the carrot, celery, half of the parsley and half of the rosemary, and season with salt and pepper. Cook for another 3 minutes, stirring occasionally. Add the broth and tomatoes (if using whole tomatoes crush them first; see page 61), and bring the mixture to a strong simmer. Stir in the pasta and cook, stirring, for about 5 minutes. Add the beans and the browned pork with all the wine juices, and simmer for another 5 minutes. Taste for seasoning.

Just before serving, stir in the remaining parsley and rosemary, and a dash of hot sauce, if using. Serve the soup piping hot in large bowls, topped with grated Parmesan.

favoritevariations

■ Substitute ½ pound bacon or pancetta for the pork. Be sure to remove all but 1 tablespoon of the bacon fat from the pan before adding the garlic and onions.

■ Substitute boneless, skinless chicken breasts for the pork.

■ Top the hot soup with plenty of chopped fresh basil.

crushing tomatoes

There's an easy way to crush a can of whole, peeled tomatoes by hand. Open the can and remove the lid, making sure there are no jagged edges. Drain the liquid contents of the can into your soup, stew, or sauce, holding back the tomatoes. Then put your whole hand into the can, and squish the tomatoes to break them up, before adding them to the pot. No tomato chopping!

greek-style **turkey-lemon-rice soup**

SERVES 6 TO 8

Whenever we roast a turkey (page 183) we like to use the leftovers to create this soothing, deeply comforting soup. A light turkey broth (made from the carcass; see page 63), or chicken broth is simmered with cooked white rice, chunks of tender turkey, egg yolks, and lots of fresh lemon juice, parsley, and thyme. The rice causes the soup to thicken and the yolks give it a creamy texture.

About 6 cups turkey broth (see page 63), or
    low-sodium canned chicken broth
1/2 cup minced fresh parsley leaves
2 tablespoons minced fresh thyme leaves
2 cups cooked white rice, at room
    temperature

2 cups cubed cooked turkey
2 large egg yolks
Salt and freshly ground black pepper
Juice of 2 lemons (about 1/2 cup)
1 lemon, preferably organic, cut into
    paper-thin slices, seeds removed

Place the turkey broth in a large pot and bring to a simmer over medium-high heat. Add half of the parsley and half of the thyme. Add the rice to the soup, making sure to break up any clumps. Add the turkey and simmer over very low heat.

In a small bowl whisk the egg yolks with salt and pepper. Add about 1/2 cup of the hot broth to the bowl and whisk with the yolks. Pour the yolks back into the pot and whisk until fully incorporated. Add the lemon juice and season to taste. It is important that you don't let the soup boil; if it does the egg yolk will curdle. You can whisk the soup gently to smooth it out if the egg begins to curdle, but past a certain point there's not much you can do. Add the lemon slices and heat very gently for about 5 minutes. The longer the soup sits the thicker it will become; add more broth if necessary.

favoritevariations

- Add 2 tablespoons chopped fresh dill instead of thyme.
- Use Meyer lemons instead of regular lemons.

don't throw away that carcass!

making a simple, rich poultry broth

After you've roasted a turkey or chicken and removed the meat from the bones, *don't throw away the carcass* because there is still a lot of flavor left over: use it to make a richly flavored simple broth. Turkey broth has a more pronounced flavor than most chicken broths and can be used in soups, stews, or virtually any dish calling for chicken broth.

You can make the broth with any size poultry carcass, adding enough water to cover the entire carcass. For a smaller carcass, use the lower measurement when there's a range in the ingredients list, since you'll be starting out with less water to flavor. The broth can be covered and refrigerated for several days or will keep in the freezer for months.

Of course, you can also make an extraordinary broth using a whole *uncooked* chicken. Simply replace one 2- to 3-pound raw chicken for the carcass and follow the recipe.

MAKES ABOUT 5 TO 10 CUPS

1 turkey or chicken carcass
1 to 2 carrots, cut into chunks
1 to 2 stalks celery, cut into chunks
1 to 2 large onions, quartered
1 bay leaf
A few sprigs fresh parsley
3 to 6 peppercorns
Salt

Place the carcass in a large stockpot and add the carrot, celery, onion, bay leaf, parsley, peppercorns, and some salt. Add enough water to cover (about 5 cups for a 3-pound chicken carcass and about 12 cups for a 10- to 12-pound turkey carcass), and bring to a boil over high heat. Reduce the heat to low and simmer, covered, for about 1 hour. Taste for seasoning. The broth should be flavorful; if it still tastes weak, simmer uncovered, for another 30 to 45 minutes.

Strain the broth and refrigerate for about 4 days or freeze up to 3 months.

new england **five-onion soup**
with cheddar croûtes

SERVES 8 TO 10

We've all enjoyed French onion soup—a rich beef broth infused with loads of caramelized onions and then topped with a thick chunk of bread and gobs of melted cheese. While we have always loved this bistro classic, lately we've found it a bit heavy. We decided to take all the best elements of French onion soup and lighten it up a bit, giving it a New England twist. Our first step is to lighten the broth with New England–made sparkling hard cider. We then sauté five different types of onions (red, yellow, shallots, leeks, and garlic) and let them cook long and slow until they caramelize and turn naturally sweet. The final touch: Instead of the heavy layer of cheese that usually tops the soup, we serve it with a simple cheddar croûte (like a large crouton).

The soup can be made a day ahead and reheated before serving. Serve with hard cider.

for the soup
¼ cup olive oil
5 medium yellow onions, halved and cut into ¼-inch-thick slices
5 large red onions, halved and cut into ¼-inch thick slices
3 large shallots, cut into ¼-inch rings
2 medium leeks (white and bright green parts only), halved and cut into ½-inch pieces
10 garlic cloves, peeled and left whole
Salt and freshly ground black pepper

10 cups low-sodium canned beef broth
1½ cups sparkling hard cider, or red wine
3 tablespoons Cognac
1 tablespoon chopped fresh thyme leaves

for the cheddar croûtes
1 baguette, cut into ¾-inch slices (about 16 slices)
2 tablespoons olive oil
2 cups packed grated high-quality sharp cheddar cheese
Freshly ground black pepper

Divide the oil between two large skillets and place them both over low heat. When the oil is hot, add some of the yellow onions, red onions, shallots, leeks, and garlic to each skillet. Cook, stirring frequently, until the onions are soft and golden brown, about 1 hour. (If the onions don't all fit into two skillets at first, add more as the onions cook down. You can also cook the onions in 2 batches.) After an hour, increase the heat to medium low and cook the onions for another 10 to 15 minutes, or until they are well caramelized and begin to stick to the bottom of the pan. Season the onions with salt and pepper.

Bring the beef broth to a simmer in a large soup pot. When the onions are done, carefully transfer them to the simmering broth. Divide the cider and Cognac between the two skillets. Increase the heat to high and bring to a boil, scraping any browned bits clinging to the bottom of the skillets with a spatula, until the alcohol has cooked off, 2 to 3 minutes. Empty the skillets into the soup pot, add the thyme, and stir to combine. Simmer the soup for 5 minutes. Taste the soup for seasoning.

To make the croûtes: Place a rack in the top of the oven and preheat to 400°F.

Arrange the baguette slices on a baking sheet. Lightly brush some of the olive oil over each slice. Bake for 5 to 7 minutes, or until the bread is just beginning to turn golden brown.

Remove the bread from the oven, carefully flip each piece, and top each with a generous tablespoon of cheese. Bake the croûtes again until the cheese has just melted, about 3 minutes. Season the croûtes with pepper. (The croûtes can be made up to 4 hours ahead and reheated for about 3 minutes in a 400°F oven before serving.)

Spoon a good portion of soup into each bowl and top with a cheddar croûte. Serve piping hot.

favoritevariations

- For a more traditional soup, substitute 2 cups dry red wine for the cider.
- For a stronger Cognac flavor, spike each bowl of soup with about a teaspoon of Cognac just before serving.

3

salads

the new **waldorf**

Remember those mayonnaise-filled salads of days past, with apples and nuts and grapes? They had all the right elements but that gloppy mayonnaise was a real turnoff. We thought it would be fun to revisit this classic salad and give it a makeover. In our version, we feature sweet roasted beets layered with crunchy fennel, tart apples, toasted walnuts, and a lemon and ginger vinaigrette. The result is much improved and full of vivid flavors.

If you roast the beets and walnuts ahead of time, the salad can be put together at the last minute.

for the salad

1 pound beets (about 3 medium large), red, golden, or a combination
1 medium bulb fennel, cored, thinly sliced, with some of the fennel fronds reserved as a garnish
1 Granny Smith apple, peeled, cored and sliced into thin rounds
½ cup walnut pieces, toasted (see page 260), and coarsely chopped

for the vinaigrette

1 tablespoon grated, peeled fresh ginger
1 tablespoon grated lemon zest
3 tablespoons fresh lemon juice
¼ cup plus 2 tablespoons olive oil
Sea salt and freshly ground black pepper
About ½ teaspoon sugar

Preheat the oven to 400°F.

Wrap the beets in foil and roast for 1 hour to 1 hour and 15 minutes, or until the beets feel soft when a small, sharp knife is inserted in the center. Remove from the oven, unwrap, and let cool until just warm. Using your hands or a small, sharp knife, peel and then thinly slice the beets. Place in a bowl, cover, and refrigerate until ready to serve.

To make the vinaigrette: In a small bowl, whisk the ginger, lemon zest, lemon juice, and oil. Add salt, pepper, and sugar to taste. Cover and refrigerate until ready to serve. The vinaigrette can be made a day ahead of time up to this point.

To assemble the salad: Place the fennel slices on the bottom of a serving dish. Arrange the beet slices on top, making sure the outside edges of the fennel layer aren't covered. Drizzle with a few teaspoons of the vinaigrette. Place the apples on top of the beets, again making sure to keep some of the outside edges of the beet exposed. Sprinkle the top of the salad with the walnuts and drizzle with the remaining vinaigrette. Garnish with the reserved fennel fronds. Serve within 1 hour.

favoritevariations

- Use pine nuts or cashews, lightly toasted, instead of walnuts.
- Use peeled and thinly sliced pears instead of apples.
- Add a layer of thinly sliced jicama or Napa cabbage.

blt salad

SERVES 4 TO 6

This dynamic trio makes a perfect salad, particularly when it's tossed with an herb-filled, bright green vinaigrette. Serve with the Parmesan croûtes on page 165.

for the salad
1 pound bacon (12 to 14 slices), preferably thick sliced
1 medium head Romaine lettuce, torn into bite-size pieces
¾ pound tomatoes (about 4 medium), cubed

for the vinaigrette
1 teaspoon Dijon-style mustard
Salt and freshly ground black pepper
2 tablespoons chopped fresh parsley leaves
2 scallions (white and green parts), thinly sliced
2½ tablespoons red wine vinegar
¼ cup plus 1 tablespoon olive oil

In a large skillet, cook the bacon over medium heat until crisp on both sides, 8 to 10 minutes, depending on the thickness of the meat. Drain well on paper towels. Crumble the bacon into ½-inch pieces and set aside.

Make the vinaigrette: In a small bowl, combine the mustard, salt and pepper to taste, parsley, and scallions. Add the vinegar and then the oil, whisking to create a smooth dressing. The bacon and the vinaigrette can be made a day ahead of time; cover and refrigerate until ready to assemble the salad.

Arrange the lettuce in the center of a serving plate or salad bowl. Surround the outside of the lettuce with the tomato cubes. Sprinkle the bacon into the center of the salad. Toss with the vinaigrette just before serving.

favoritevariations

- Replace the bacon with pancetta.
- Use a combination of yellow and red tomatoes or cherry tomatoes instead of just regular tomatoes.
- Substitute a variety of greens for the Romaine, but keep in mind that a good crunch is nice in this salad.
- Add 1 tablespoon chopped fresh basil or tarragon leaves to the vinaigrette.
- Sprinkle the top of the salad with thinly shaved slices of Parmesan or crumbled blue or goat cheese.

shaving cheese

Thin slices from a chunk of Parmesan (or any type of hard cheese) makes a great garnish for salads. Simply use a wide vegetable peeler and shave off thin slices of the cheese. Try it with our Ultimate Lemon Caesar Salad (page 72) or on top of mixed greens, Tuscan-Style White Bean Salad (page 75), or with seafood or any composed salads.

ultimate **lemon caesar salad**

SERVES 4 TO 6

We can remember a time when Caesar salad was a real treat, served only at *special* restaurants. But these days it seems the famed salad is on the menu just about everywhere—coffee shops, mediocre dinner spots, even fast-food restaurants. It's become a cliché of modern cuisine.

When you make the real thing using fat fillets of anchovies and pungent garlic crushed together with a raw egg yolk, good olive oil, and a dash of Worcestershire sauce, tossed with crispy romaine leaves and thin shavings of Parmesan cheese, this dish still ranks as one of the great salads of all time.

Note: We always use fresh organic eggs for this salad since the yolk is raw (see page 38). You may simply omit the egg or use a hard-boiled egg yolk instead. See photograph page 10.

4 to 6 anchovy fillets, or to taste
1 garlic clove, peeled
¼ teaspoon salt
Freshly ground black pepper
1 large egg yolk (see Note)
1 teaspoon Worcestershire sauce
2 tablespoons freshly squeezed lemon juice

½ cup extra-virgin olive oil
3 medium to small heads Romaine lettuce, separated into leaves (about 1 pound)
½ cup packed freshly grated Parmesan cheese
½ cup packed thinly shaved Parmesan cheese

To make the dressing: Place the anchovies, garlic, salt, and pepper in the bottom of a large salad bowl. Use the back of a wooden spoon to mash the ingredients together into a paste. Add the yolk, and combine. Whisk in the Worcestershire sauce and lemon juice. Slowly drizzle the olive oil into the bowl with one hand as you whisk with the other, stirring until the olive oil is completely incorporated. Fold in the grated Parmesan cheese.

Just before serving, toss the lettuce with the dressing until all of the leaves are coated. Place a few long leaves on each plate, and top with the Parmesan shavings. Serve with Parmesan croûtes (see page 165) on the side.

favoritevariations

- Add 2 thinly sliced, grilled or broiled boneless, skinless chicken breasts.
- Add 1 pound grilled or cooked shrimp.
- Add 1 pound grilled or sautéed fish fillets.
- Add 1 ripe avocado cut into cubes.
- Add crumbled blue cheese instead of Parmesan.
- For real anchovy lovers, garnish the salad with 4 to 6 anchovy fillets.
- Add 2 tablespoons heavy cream to the dressing for a creamier salad.

tangy **coleslaw**

SERVES 6

What makes this slaw unique is the addition of low-fat yogurt, instead of mayonnaise, to create a tangy, creamy sauce for the shredded red and white cabbage, carrots, and scallions. The slaw can be made several hours ahead of time. It's an ideal side dish to Dry Rubbed Paper Bag Ribs (page 202). See photograph page 66.

1 small red cabbage (about 1 pound), cored and thinly shredded (about 4 cups) (see Note)

1 small cabbage (about 1 pound), cored and thinly shredded (about 4 cups) (see Note)

3 medium carrots, grated

1½ teaspoons Dijon-style mustard

1 cup plain low-fat yogurt

¼ cup minced fresh parsley leaves

4 scallions (white and green parts), finely chopped

2 tablespoons white wine or cider vinegar

Salt and freshly ground black pepper

In a large salad bowl, toss together the two cabbages. Add the carrots and mix well. Add the mustard, yogurt, parsley, and scallions and mix with salad tongs or a wooden spoon. Add the vinegar and salt and pepper to taste and toss. The slaw can be made 2 to 3 hours ahead of time; cover and refrigerate until ready to serve.

NOTE: Shred the cabbage with a long, sharp knife, grate it on the largest hole on a box grater, or use the grater attachment on a food processor.

favoritevariations

- Add 1 cup raisins, golden raisins, sun-dried cranberries, or dried cherries.
- Add 1 cup coarsely chopped toasted walnuts or almonds (see page 260).
- Add ¼ cup minced fresh basil, thyme, or chives.
- Add 3 slices crumbled crisp cooked bacon.
- Add several dashes of hot pepper sauce.
- Add 1 teaspoon grated lemon zest and 2 tablespoons fresh lemon juice.
- Add ¼ cup olive oil for a moister slaw.

tuscan-style **white bean salad**

SERVES 8 TO 10

Find a really good-quality dry white cannellini bean for this luscious salad; it will make all the difference. Sure, you can substitute canned white beans, but believe us when we say it won't even come close to the fresh taste, and the buttery, almost creamy texture of home-cooked beans. Soak the beans overnight and simmer them the next day.

The salad can be made a day ahead of time and served warm, room temperature, or chilled. Serve the beans as part of the Antipasti Platter on page 217. The salad is also a delicious, colorful accompaniment to grilled meats and poultry, seafood, or tacos. There's enough salad here to serve a crowd.

for the beans
- 2 cups dried white cannellini (white kidney) beans
- 1 medium yellow onion, peeled and cut into quarters
- 2 garlic cloves, peeled
- 1 bay leaf
- 1 tablespoon chopped fresh thyme leaves, or 1 teaspoon dried
- 6 peppercorns
- ⅛ teaspoon salt

for the salad
- ⅓ cup red or white wine vinegar
- 2 tablespoons fresh lemon juice
- 2 tablespoons chopped fresh thyme leaves
- 2 tablespoons chopped fresh rosemary leaves
- ½ cup plus 2 tablespoons olive oil
- Salt and freshly ground black pepper
- 2 ripe medium tomatoes, cubed (about 2 cups)
- 1 small red onion, finely chopped
- ¼ cup thinly sliced fresh basil leaves

Place the beans in a large bowl and cover with 6 to 8 cups cold water. Let soak for at least 2 hours or, preferably, overnight.

To cook the beans: Drain the beans and rinse under cold running water. Place the beans in a large pot and add the onion, garlic, bay leaf, thyme, peppercorns, and salt. Cover with cold water and bring to a simmer over medium-high heat. Reduce the heat to low and let simmer for 30 to 50 minutes, depending on the beans (see page 74). Drain the beans, discarding the onion, garlic, bay leaf and peppercorns. (You can save bean cooking liquid and use it as a soup base.)

To make the salad: In a large bowl, whisk together the vinegar, lemon juice, thyme, rosemary, oil, and salt and pepper to taste. Gently stir in the warm beans, the tomatoes, onion, and basil.

favoritevariations
- ▪ Add 1 cup coarsely chopped black olives.
- ▪ Add ½ cup chopped sun-dried tomatoes.
- ▪ Add 6 to 8 cloves coarsely chopped roasted garlic (see page 161).

black bean salad

We like to serve this cumin-spiked salad at our Burrito Party (page 187), but it's also delicious with Dry Rubbed Paper Bag Pork Ribs (page 202), grilled or roasted chicken (page 173) or grilled fish, as a dip with corn chips, or piled into buttery lettuce leaves. Serve with ice cold Mexican beer.

Two 15-ounce cans black beans, rinsed and drained
1 large ripe red or yellow tomato, chopped
½ small red onion, finely chopped
2 tablespoons chopped fresh cilantro leaves

2 tablespoons olive oil
2 tablespoons fresh lime juice
¼ teaspoon cumin
Salt and freshly ground black pepper

Mix the beans, tomato, onion, cilantro, olive oil, lime juice, and cumin together in a medium bowl. Season to taste with salt and pepper.

favoritevariations

- Add 1 finely chopped sweet red, green, or yellow pepper
- Add 1 tablespoon finely chopped chile pepper or some hot pepper sauce to taste.

beans that will blow you away

What's the best method for telling when dried beans are cooked and tender as opposed to overcooked and mushy or undercooked and crunchy? There's a thin line between perfectly cooked, buttery beans and those that cook just a little too long. Here's a little trick: After you have simmered dry beans for about 15 minutes (always simmer; never boil!), scoop a few beans up onto a large fork. Blow on the beans and when the skin begins to peel back it means the beans are almost cooked. Cooking times vary considerably with dried beans (depending on how old they are and what variety you are using); it's always best to test the beans early, before they become overcooked. After the skin peels back you want to taste a bean. It should still have a slight bite (the equivalent to al dente pasta), but the inside of the bean should also have a somewhat soft, creamy consistency. Immediately drain the beans before they become overcooked, soft, and mushy.

asian **pulled chicken salad**

SERVES 4

This is an elegant chicken salad—we shred the chicken and lightly dress it with ginger, scallions, red pepper, and crunchy, salty peanuts, making this a truly Asian-style salad. Serve the salad on a bed of mixed greens, roll it up burrito-style in a large leaf of buttery lettuce, or serve it traditionally on your favorite sandwich bread. The leftover poaching liquid is very flavorful, so be sure to save it for a soup or sauce.

4 cups homemade chicken broth (see page 63), or low-sodium canned
1 bay leaf
5 black peppercorns
1 pound boneless, skinless chicken breast halves (about 2 large), cut in half
One 1-inch piece fresh, peeled ginger, cut into thin matchsticks
8 scallions (white and green parts), cut into 1½-inch pieces, then cut into thin matchsticks

1 red bell pepper, cut into thin matchsticks
½ cup peanuts, coarsely chopped
1 tablespoon olive oil
¼ cup fresh lime juice
1 tablespoon Asian sesame oil
2 tablespoons chopped fresh cilantro leaves (optional)
Salt and freshly ground black pepper

Bring the chicken broth, bay leaf, and peppercorns to a simmer over high heat in a large skillet or a wide saucepan. Place the chicken in the simmering liquid and reduce the heat to medium. Cook for 7 minutes at a bare simmer, carefully flip the chicken, and cook for another 5 to 7 minutes, or until the chicken is cooked through. Transfer the chicken to a plate to cool, and reserve the broth for another use. (The broth can be frozen for several months.)

Use your hands to shred the chicken into thin 1- to 2-inch-long strands, as if you were peeling string cheese. Put the chicken in a medium bowl and add the ginger, scallions, red pepper, and peanuts, and toss. Add the olive oil, lime juice, sesame oil, cilantro, and salt and pepper to taste. Toss the salad gently to combine. Serve cold or at room temperature.

favoritevariations

■ Add 1 cup thinly sliced jicama to the salad.
■ Substitute cashews for the peanuts.
■ Sprinkle the salad with 2 to 3 tablespoons sesame seeds.
■ Add about 1 cup thinly sliced, peeled fresh water chestnuts, or drained canned water chestnuts.
■ Serve with rice crackers.

fresh **asian tuna salad**

SERVES 4

It may be a stretch to say that this salad has anything to do with the mayonnaise-drenched tuna fish salad we all grew up with. We've taken a classic tuna fish salad and given it a great new spin for the twenty-first century.

We coat a fresh tuna steak in coarsely ground peppercorns, sear it over high heat, and then finish it off in a hot oven until medium rare. The tuna is thinly sliced, dotted with wasabi, and served alongside an Asian-flavored celery-radish salad. The red radishes are a nice mirror of the rare pink color inside the seared tuna.

for the salad

8 stalks celery, thinly sliced on the diagonal
    (about 3 cups)
8 medium radishes, thinly sliced
2 scallions (white and green parts), thinly
    sliced
¼ cup rice vinegar or white wine vinegar
2 tablespoons Asian sesame oil
1 tablespoon soy sauce
Freshly ground black pepper

for the tuna

1 pound fresh tuna steak, about 1½ inches
    thick
Coarsely ground pepper
Coarse sea salt
1½ tablespoons vegetable oil
3 tablespoons soy sauce
Juice of 1 large lemon (about ⅓ cup)
1 tablespoon prepared wasabi (optional)

Place a rack in the middle of the oven and preheat the oven to 400°F.

To make the salad: In a bowl, mix the celery, radishes, scallions, vinegar, sesame oil, soy sauce, and a good grinding of pepper. Set it aside. The salad can be made several hours ahead of time; cover and refrigerate until ready to serve.

Place the tuna on a plate and coat it lightly with the pepper and sea salt on both sides.

In a heavy, medium, ovenproof skillet, heat the oil over high heat. When the oil is hot, add the tuna and cook for 1½ minutes until lightly browned. Gently flip the tuna over and cook another 1½ minutes. Transfer to the oven for 7 to 9 minutes, depending on how rare or well done you like your tuna. Remove the tuna to a plate and let it sit for about 2 minutes.

Meanwhile, place the hot skillet over medium heat and add the soy sauce and lemon juice and cook for about 2 minutes, scraping up any juices from the bottom of the pan.

Thinly slice the tuna on the diagonal. Place the celery salad in the middle of a large serving plate. Arrange the tuna slices around the outside of the salad. Spoon the soy sauce from the skillet on top of the tuna slices (there will only be enough to very lightly dab each piece.) Place a tiny dollop of the wasabi on every other piece of the tuna. Serve warm or at room temperature.

favoritevariations

- Add 1 cup thinly sliced water chestnuts or jicama to the salad.
- Place 1 cup arugula or watercress under the salad.
- Add a bit of wasabi to the skillet when you add the soy sauce.
- Add ½ teaspoon chopped lemongrass or grated lemon zest to the skillet when you add the soy sauce.
- Add ¼ cup coarsely chopped salted peanuts or cashews on top of the finished dish.

arugula, prosciutto, and grilled asparagus salad with lemon-chive dressing

SERVES 2 AS A MAIN COURSE OR 4 AS AN APPETIZER

Fresh, light, and satisfying is how we'd describe this salad. The combination of tart, crunchy arugula, buttery, meaty prosciutto, and smoky grilled asparagus is a winning one, particularly when it's tossed with this light lemon-chive dressing. Serve with warm bread or Bacon-Chive Biscuits (page 27) or the Olive and Anchovy Toasts (page 166).

for the salad
1 pound medium asparagus, ends trimmed
1 tablespoon olive oil
Salt and freshly ground black pepper
3 ounces baby arugula, or stemmed regular
   arugula or watercress (2 packed cups)
¼ pound (about 8 thin slices) prosciutto

for the dressing
Juice of 1 large lemon (about ⅓ cup)
Salt and freshly ground black pepper
⅓ cup olive oil
2 tablespoons minced chives

Place the rack in the middle of the oven and preheat the broiler.

Place the asparagus in a small, shallow roasting pan, ovenproof skillet, or on a large sheet of aluminum foil. Pour the oil, salt, and pepper on top and toss to coat the asparagus. Broil for 4 to 5 minutes; then turn over the asparagus. Broil for another 4 to 5 minutes, depending on the thickness and freshness of the asparagus, or until golden brown and almost tender. The asparagus will keep cooking when they are removed from the broiler; be sure not to overcook them or they will be soft and limp.

Meanwhile, arrange the arugula on a serving platter. Roll the slices of prosciutto into cigar shapes and arrange (or simply drape them) along the outside of the plate.

To make the dressing: In a small bowl, whisk together the lemon juice, salt and pepper to taste, olive oil, and chives.

Place the hot asparagus in the middle of the plate on a diagonal and pour the dressing on top. Serve hot or at room temperature.

favoritevariations

- Substitute fresh basil for the chives.
- Serve with Italian-style breadsticks.
- Sprinkle the top of the salad with oil-cured black olives.

trio of **deviled eggs**

We used to think deviled eggs were fussy old lady food, but there are few dishes that take such little effort and give back such a huge payoff. Our deviled eggs each have a little makeover. We stuff the bottom of the cooked whites with a few surprises—sun-dried tomatoes, Kalamata olive tapenade, and a chive-scallion combination, and then top the fillings with a creamy egg mixture, so that each bite reveals a burst of flavor inside. Place the eggs on top of a bed of baby watercress and serve as a salad or first course.

Once you get the hang of these deviled egg surprises, you can create your own flavors; see below for some ideas to get you started.

12 hard-boiled eggs (see page 85), peeled
¼ cup mayonnaise
1 teaspoon Dijon-style mustard
Salt and freshly ground black pepper
2 tablespoons chopped sun-dried tomatoes (packed in oil) plus extra for garnish
2 tablespoons black or green tapenade plus extra for garnish

1 tablespoon minced fresh chives plus extra for garnish
1 tablespoon finely chopped scallions (white and green parts), plus extra for garnish
Sweet Hungarian paprika
3 cups baby watercress, or stemmed regular watercress

Using a small, sharp knife, cut each egg in half lengthwise. Carefully remove the yolks and place in a small bowl. Mash the yolks with a fork, and add the mayonnaise, mustard, and salt and pepper to taste.

Divide the sun-dried tomatoes among 8 of the egg white halves. Divide the tapenade among 8 other halves. Mix together the chives and scallions and divide among the remaining 8 halves. Sprinkle the eggs lightly with paprika.

Fill each egg half with a spoonful of the yolk mixture, and then top with its respective garnish. Place the watercress on a serving plate and arrange all three types of eggs on top.

favoritevariations
Substitute 3 tablespoons of any of the following for any of the fillings above:

- Chopped roasted red peppers
- Basil Swirl (page 233)
- Winter Parsley Pesto (page 232)
- Crumbled blue cheese or goat cheese

egg tips

hard-boiled and cracking secrets

The trick to making perfect hard-boiled eggs is all in the timing. There are a few no-fail methods for hard boiling an egg, each resulting in a firm, clear white with a yolk that's bright yellow all the way to the edges. Here's our favorite method:

Place the eggs in a single layer in a large saucepan. Add cold water to cover the eggs by about an inch, and bring the water to a boil over high heat. When the water boils, cover the pan tightly, and move the pan off the heat. Let the eggs sit in the hot water for 14 minutes.

Drain the water you cooked the eggs in out of the saucepan, keeping the eggs in the pan. Shake the pan back and forth and up and down a few times, so that the egg shells crack *just a little*. Then fill the pan with cold water; the water will seep into the cracks in the shells and separate the eggs from the shells, making them easier to peel once they've cooled.

cobb and blossom salad

SERVES 4 TO 6

What we like best about Cobb Salad is that it combines so many of our favorite ingredients in one deeply satisfying salad. There's grilled chicken, ripe tomatoes, pungent blue cheese, crunchy red onions, hard-boiled eggs, buttery avocados, and smoky bacon on top of crunchy Romaine and buttery frisée lettuce. What makes this salad unusual (and gorgeous) is the topping of edible blossoms—chive flowers, nasturtiums, marigold petals, or any edible flower you can find.

Best of all, the whole salad can be made ahead of time, making it an ideal dish for entertaining. Prepare the chicken, eggs, and bacon, and chop the vegetables and clean the lettuce a day before serving and you can put together the salad at the last minute. Slice the avocado and dress the salad just before serving.

The recipe for Blue Cheese–Scallion Vinaigrette (page 90) will make just enough to dress the salad; if you want any extra to pass at the table you should double the recipe.

1 tablespoon olive oil
1 pound boneless, skinless chicken breast
   halves (about 2 large)
Salt and freshly ground black pepper
1 head frisee lettuce, torn into bite-size
   pieces, or 1 cup watercress, stemmed
2 small heads Romaine lettuce, chopped
4 large hard-boiled eggs (page 85),
   quartered lengthwise
8 ounces bacon (about 8 slices), cooked and
   crumbled (see page 27)

1½ pounds ripe tomatoes (about 3 medium),
   chopped
½ small red onion, chopped
4 ounces Roquefort or other blue cheese,
   crumbled (about 1 cup)
2 ripe avocados
Blue Cheese–Scallion Vinaigrette (page 90)
1 cup edible organic flowers or herb
   blossoms (such as chive blossoms,
   nasturtiums, or marigold petals)

Heat a large skillet over medium heat. When hot, add the olive oil. Season the chicken breasts on both sides with salt and pepper. Cook the chicken for 4 to 5 minutes per side, or until the chicken is browned and cooked through. Transfer the chicken to a plate to cool, and refrigerate until ready to assemble the salad.

To assemble the salad: Toss the lettuces and place on a serving platter. Place the eggs, bacon, tomatoes, onion, and cheese in individual piles on top of the lettuce. Cut the chicken into thin slices on the bias or chop into 1-inch cubes and place on the salad. Just before serving, peel and chop the avocados (they should be the same size as the tomatoes), and add to the salad. Drizzle the salad with the vinaigrette and top with the flowers.

favoritevariations

- Use yellow and red cherry tomatoes or pear or grape tomatoes instead of regular tomatoes.
- Use cooked pancetta or raw prosciutto instead of bacon.
- Substitute turkey breast for the chicken.

chopped greek salad with
lemon-caper dressing

SERVES 6 TO 8

Serve this salad any time of year and you will feel rays of bright summer sunshine beaming down on you. Seriously, the colors, textures, and flavors of this chopped salad bring light to the darkest of days. A light lemon-caper dressing and the Olive and Anchovy Toasts (page 166) bring all the Mediterranean flavors of the salad together.

The salad can be prepared, covered, and refrigerated several hours ahead of time, but it shouldn't be dressed until just before serving. This salad is satisfying enough to be a main course, or it can be served as an accompaniment to grilled or roasted lamb (page 200), chicken, or seafood.

for the salad
- 2 medium cucumbers, peeled and cut into ½-inch cubes (about 3 cups)
- 2 large green bell peppers, cut into ½-inch squares
- 1 large red onion, chopped (about 1 cup)
- 2 cups crumbled feta cheese, sheep's or goat's milk
- 1 cup pitted black Kalamata olives
- 2 ripe medium-large tomatoes, cut into ½-inch cubes

for the dressing
- Juice of 1 large lemon (about ⅓ cup)
- ½ cup olive oil, preferably a rich Greek variety
- Freshly ground black pepper
- ¼ cup minced fresh parsley leaves
- 2 tablespoons drained capers

- 8 Olive and Anchovy Toasts (page 166)

To make the salad: On a large serving plate, make a small pile with half of the cucumbers. Place a pile of half of the peppers next to it, and then half of the red onions, half of the feta, and half of the olives working around half the platter. Repeat with the remaining cheese and vegetables working your way around the entire plate. Place the tomatoes in the center. The idea is to intersperse all the colors and shapes in an attractive pattern around the plate.

To make the dressing: In a small bowl, whisk together all the ingredients. The salad and the dressing can be made several hours ahead of time; cover and refrigerate them separately.

Spoon the dressing over the salad and serve with the Olive and Anchovy Toasts.

blue cheese–scallion **vinaigrette**

MAKES ABOUT 1½ CUPS

A basic vinaigrette with the addition of salty crumbled blue cheese and chopped scallions is the perfect dressing for the Cobb and Blossom Salad (page 87), or try it with a chilled cooked chicken salad or mixed greens. We also like to toss it with steamed green beans, asparagus, or broccoli for a quick side dish.

1½ tablespoons Dijon-style mustard
¼ cup fresh lemon juice
¼ cup red wine vinegar
½ cup plus 1 to 2 tablespoons olive oil
⅓ cup packed chopped scallions (white and green parts)

3 ounces crumbled Roquefort or other blue cheese (¾ cup)
2 tablespoons minced fresh tarragon leaves (optional)
Salt and freshly ground black pepper

Whisk the mustard, lemon juice, and vinegar together in a small bowl. Add ½ cup of the olive oil in a slow, steady stream, whisking until all of the ingredients are combined. Stir in the scallions, cheese, and tarragon, and season to taste with salt and pepper. If the dressing is too tart, add an additional tablespoon or two of oil.

refreshing herbs

One of the best ways to revive and refresh herbs that are starting to wilt is to place the fresh herbs in a bowl and cover with cold water and a few ice cubes. Let the herbs soak for about 5 minutes, then drain, and blot dry with paper towels. You can also spin them dry in a salad spinner.

the key to making the perfect vinaigrette

When we make salads at home people always ask us why our salads taste so good. The answer is so simple that we've been accused of holding back, keeping secret ingredients to ourselves. But the truth is there are only a few basic elements that make a really good vinaigrette and thus a really good salad.

This master recipe will make enough vinaigrette to coat (and not drench) about 3 cups lettuce leaves, mixed greens, or salad ingredients.

In the bottom of a salad bowl (preferably made of wood), sprinkle about ⅛ teaspoon fine sea salt. If desired, add 1 small garlic clove and, using the back of a kitchen spoon, crush the garlic in the salt until it's mashed to a paste. Stir about 1 teaspoon to 1 tablespoon of Dijon-style mustard into the garlic paste. Next, stir in a handful of chopped scallions (white and green parts) and/or chopped fresh herbs (chives, basil, rosemary, thyme, oregano, mint, lemon verbena, or lavender). Mix in a good grinding of black pepper.

Choose a good-quality red or white wine vinegar, or for salads with strong flavors or particularly sweet flavors, try well-aged balsamic vinegar. We also love sherry vinegar and herb-flavored vinegars. We add about 3 tablespoons vinegar; we find you need to add less when using the fuller-flavored vinegars. Mix the vinegar into the mustard, garlic, and herbs.

Olive oil is the main, and most crucial, ingredient. This is the dish to show off those special olive oils. The flavor of the olive oil—light and fruity, green and grassy, flowery, peppery—will really set the flavor of the vinaigrette apart more than any other ingredient. We use the best extra-virgin olive oil we can afford. Add about double the amount of oil as vinegar. If you add 3 tablespoons of vinegar, you want to start by adding 5 tablespoons of olive oil and then taste the vinaigrette. You will most likely need the extra tablespoon of oil—making the formula 1 part vinegar to 2 parts oil—but depending on the type of vinegar and the type of oil you choose the equation can change. Using a fork or whisk, slowly mix the oil into the vinaigrette to emulsify. Taste for seasoning. That's the recipe. The magic comes in using the best quality ingredients you can find.

Once you've mastered the perfect vinaigrette, there is only one other crucial element to making great salads: **freshness.** Always use the very freshest greens (or any other ingredient) you can possibly find. Growing or buying salad greens at a farmers' market is your best choice, but there are now many good options available in grocery stores. Whether you buy exotic greens, bagged mesclun mix, hydroponically grown lettuce, or regular old iceberg, all greens should look crisp and firm, and not have wilted or brown leaves. Any soggy, watery, or pale greens are a sign that the greens are old. Always wash greens in several rinses of cold water, and then drain and dry thoroughly. Salad dressings and vinaigrettes will not adhere to greens with any moistness.

favoritevariations

In addition to the basic recipe, we sometimes add a touch of soy sauce; orange juice; grated orange, lemon, or lime zest; lemon or lime juice (instead of, or in combination with, the vinegar); a tablespoon of milk, buttermilk, or cream for a creamy consistency; a dash of sesame oil and/or chopped fresh ginger; a teaspoon or two of tapenade for an olive-flavored vinaigrette; a crushed anchovy fillet with the garlic and a touch of the anchovy oil; about a teaspoon of miso paste; a dash of Worcestershire sauce; a dash of hot pepper sauce or chile paste for a vinaigrette with a bite; pesto; salsa; roasted garlic instead of raw garlic for a sweeter, mellower flavor; a tablespoon of yogurt, sour cream, or crème fraîche for a thicker, creamy texture; chopped ripe fruit such as mango, papaya, pear, apple, peach, or berries; grated or crumbled blue cheese, goat cheese, Parmesan cheese, or just about any kind of cheese. The variations are endless.

sandwiches

4

11 p.m. **thanksgiving night sandwich**

MAKES 2 SANDWICHES

This is the classic. You've polished off the better part of a turkey, you've cleaned the dishes, and the guests have gone home, bellies full, hearts happy. Now it's time for the real feast: the first leftovers. We look forward to this sandwich almost more than the Thanksgiving Day meal itself. This recipe describes what you'll need for two whole sandwiches, which will feed two very hungry people or four moderately hungry ones.

4 slices bread
About ¼ cup leftover gravy (page 183)
1 tablespoon mayonnaise
2 Romaine lettuce leaves, or any other crisp
   lettuce

½ cup leftover stuffing (page 162)
4 thick slices cooked leftover turkey
   (page 183)

Place the bread in the toaster and toast until a light golden color.

Pour the gravy in a small saucepan and heat on low until simmering.

Lay the toast on a work surface. Divide the mayonnaise between 2 slices of the toast and top with the lettuce. Divide the stuffing between the other 2 slices of toast and top with the turkey slices. Spoon the warm gravy over the turkey. Place the 2 slices of bread with the lettuce and mayonnaise on top of the turkey and cut the sandwiches in half. Eat immediately.

favoritevariations

■ Add a tablespoon or two of leftover cranberry sauce to each sandwich.

■ Pile everything onto a single slice of toast per sandwich and serve open-faced, drizzled with the warm gravy.

■ Make a cranberry mayonnaise: Mix 1 tablespoon chopped cranberry sauce into 1 tablespoon mayonnaise.

■ Add a third piece of bread between the turkey and stuffing to make a turkey club.

■ Heat up all the other Thanksgiving leftovers and serve on the side.

chicken salad sandwich with
watercress mayonnaise

MAKES 4 SANDWICHES

The bright, tangy flavor of watercress mayonnaise gives this chicken salad a delicious lift. Pile it on toasted bread with whole watercress, or serve it on a bed of baby greens.

Use leftover cooked chicken, or poach two large chicken breast halves following the instructions for the Asian Pulled Chicken Salad (page 78).

$2^1/_2$ cups chopped cooked chicken (about 1 pound)
3 tablespoons finely chopped red onion
1 cup loosely packed stemmed watercress
$^1/_3$ cup mayonnaise

Salt and freshly ground black pepper
8 slices bread
Watercress or lettuce leaves for the sandwiches

Place the chicken and the onion in a large bowl.

Puree the watercress in a food processor or blender until finely chopped but not pureed, scraping down the sides to incorporate any stray greens. Add the mayonnaise, and whirl again until well blended and very green. Season the watercress mayonnaise with salt and pepper and add it to the chicken mixture. Stir to coat all of the pieces with the mayonnaise.

Lightly toast the bread and divide the salad between 4 slices. Add the watercress leaves to the remaining 4 slices and invert the bread with the watercress on top of the bread with the chicken salad. Cut in half and serve.

favoritevariations

- Substitute arugula or radicchio for the watercress.
- Add 1 teaspoon grated lemon zest and 1 tablespoon fresh lemon juice to the mayonnaise.
- Substitute $2^1/_2$ cups chopped cooked turkey for the chicken (page 183).
- Spread 1 tablespoon mango churtney on each slice of bread.
- Substitute pickled onions (page 239) for the red onion.

trio of **grilled cheese panini**

Grilled cheese, in all its infinite possibilities, is the sandwich we crave no matter how we're feeling. We like it plain and we like it fancy. Here we offer a trio of our favorite combinations—from a basic grilled cheddar sandwich to grilled Emmenthaler and sun-dried tomato to goat cheese with grilled asparagus and roasted red pepper. We love serving all three together, cut into triangles, as hors d'oeuvres, or for a simple, comforting lunch or dinner with a crisp green salad.

Each of these recipes makes one sandwich; they can easily be multiplied.

If you don't have a panini press, see page 99 for information on creating a makeshift panini press. See photograph on page 92.

■ classic cheddar cheese panini

MAKES 1 SANDWICH

2 slices good bread, such as sourdough or whole wheat

1 to 2 teaspoons unsalted butter, softened
2 ounces sliced extra-sharp cheddar cheese

Preheat a panini press or indoor grill on high heat.

Butter the pieces of bread on one side with a thin layer of butter, spreading it all the way to the edges of the bread. Place a piece of bread butter side down on a plate. Add the cheese slices, and place the other piece of bread on top, butter side up.

When the panini press is hot, add the sandwich, close the press, and cook for about 3 minutes, or until the bread is toasted and crispy and the cheese has melted. Serve immediately.

■ emmenthaler and sun-dried tomato panini

MAKES 1 SANDWICH

Prepare Classic Cheddar Cheese Panini, substituting $1/2$ cup lightly packed grated Emmenthaler or other Swiss-style cheese (about $1 1/2$ ounces) for the cheddar, layering on 2 tablespoons chopped sun-dried tomatoes (packed in oil), and seasoning with salt and pepper. Proceed as described in the recipe above.

■ goat cheese, asparagus, and roasted red pepper panini

MAKES 1 SANDWICH

Trim the tough ends off of 2 asparagus stalks. Cut each asparagus in half lengthwise, and place the 4 halves directly onto the hot panini press. Close the lid, and grill the asparagus for $1 1/2$ to 2 minutes, or until the spears have grill marks and are bright green.

Prepare Classic Cheddar Cheese Panini, substituting 2 ounces soft fresh goat cheese for the cheddar and layering on ½ roasted red pepper (from a jar), sliced into ¼-inch-thick strips. Add the cooked asparagus to the sandwich. Season the ingredients with salt and pepper, and place the other slice of bread on top, butter side up, and proceed as described above.

favoritevariations

You can substitute any type of cheese for any of the sandwiches listed above, or add any of the following ingredients:

- Add 1 to 2 slices cooked bacon or pancetta.
- Add 1 tablespoon Pickled Red Onions (page 239).
- Add 1 to 2 tablespoons Four-Onion Confit (page 212).
- Add thin slices of fresh tomatoes.
- Add a tablespoon of tapenade or olive puree.
- Add ⅛ cup lightly sautéed or raw baby spinach leaves.
- Add a few leaves of fresh basil.
- Add thinly sliced cooked steak, chicken, or turkey.
- Add 1 tablespoon of pesto to the bread before you top with the cheese.
- Add thin slices of raw or lightly sautéed pear, apple, or fig.

a makeshift panini press

Panini grills are great (though somewhat costly) pieces of kitchen equipment. They look like large waffle irons, but the grill is ribbed instead of waffled and can be used to cook sandwiches, meats, fish, and vegetables. They make the best grilled cheese sandwiches we've ever tasted (see page 98), breakfast sandwiches (see page 42), and are also great for grilling vegetables.

You can also use a preheated waffle grill or indoor/electric grill instead of a panini press.

But you don't have to run out and buy a panini press to make these recipes. A quick, simple, makeshift way to create a panini press is as follows: Heat a large, heavy skillet (cast iron is ideal) over moderately high heat. Add the sandwich to the skillet and top the sandwich with a smaller skillet or saucepan (make sure the bottom is clean!), and weigh the top skillet down with a large can of soup or beans. Cook the sandwiches until golden on the bottom, about 3 to 4 minutes, gently flip them over, and repeat on the other side.

egg salad, chive, and shallot sandwiches with pancetta

MAKES 4 SANDWICHES

Egg salad, enlivened with fresh chives and shallots, piled onto lightly toasted bread makes a great sandwich. But when you add a slice of salty, crunchy pancetta or bacon (see page 205) it becomes a dish you find yourself craving.

8 large eggs
¾ pound pancetta (about 8 slices), or
    ¾ pound bacon (about 12 slices)
3 tablespoons mayonnaise
3 tablespoons minced shallots (about 2 small
    shallots)

2 tablespoons minced fresh chives
Salt and freshly ground black pepper
8 slices bread
2 cups baby watercress

Hard boil the eggs (see page 85). Peel and finely chop the eggs.

Meanwhile, heat a large skillet over medium-low heat. Add the pancetta and cook, turning occasionally, until crispy, about 12 minutes (10 minutes if using bacon). Drain the pancetta on a paper towel–lined plate.

Mix the chopped eggs, mayonnaise, shallots, and chives together in a medium bowl. Season with salt and pepper to taste.

Lightly toast the bread. Divide the egg salad among 4 slices of the toast. Add 2 slices of pancetta and some watercress to each sandwich, and top with the remaining 4 slices of toast. Serve sandwiches cut into halves or quarters.

favoritevariations

- Substitute fresh dill, basil, or parsley for the chives.
- Use sliced scallions instead of shallots.
- Omit the pancetta and add thin slices of avocado.
- Serve the egg salad on a bed of greens.
- Add a dash of curry and cumin powder to the egg salad.
- Spread 1 tablespoon of mango chutney onto 4 slices of the bread.

grilled chicken "hero" with garlic aïoli

MAKES 4 SANDWICHES

This is a sandwich you can truly sink your teeth into. Piled high with grilled or broiled chicken, warm red bell peppers, pickled onions, goat cheese, garlic aïoli, and fresh greens, this sandwich deserves the best baguette you can find. Don't be scared off by the long list of ingredients; you can prepare almost everything ahead of time and assemble the sandwich just before serving. The sandwiches also hold up really well; they can be assembled up to 6 hours ahead of time and chilled until ready to serve.

1 pound boneless, skinless chicken breast halves (about 2 large)
1½ tablespoons olive oil
Salt and freshly ground black pepper
1 large red bell pepper, cut into ½-inch strips
1 baguette

4 ounces soft fresh goat cheese
¼ to ½ cup Garlic Aïoli (page 243)
1 cup Pickled Red Onions (page 239)
2 cups greens, such as watercress, arugula, or mixed baby greens

Preheat the broiler. Place the chicken breasts in a broiler pan or ovenproof skillet. Add the oil and season with salt and pepper, tossing to coat. Broil the chicken for 8 minutes. Flip the chicken, add the bell pepper to the pan, and broil for another 5 minutes. Flip the peppers strips over and broil for another 5 to 10 minutes, or until the chicken is completely cooked through and the peppers are tender. Transfer the chicken and the peppers to a plate to cool.

Alternatively, you can grill the chicken and the peppers over a hot charcoal, gas, or wood fire. Grill the chicken for 8 minutes. Flip the chicken over and add the pepper strips to the grill. Cook for another 6 to 8 minutes, turning the peppers over after a few minutes, until the chicken is well browned and cooked through, and the peppers are soft. The recipe can be made a day ahead of time up to this point. Do not slice the chicken but cover and refrigerate until ready to assemble the sandwiches.

Cut the baguette into 4 sections. Cut each section in half lengthwise. Spread half of each baguette section with a quarter of the goat cheese, and spread the other half with 1 to 2 tablespoons Garlic Aïoli. Slice the chicken into ¼-inch-thick strips and layer the chicken, the peppers, the pickled red onions, and the greens onto one side of each piece of baguette. Top with the other bread halves.

favoritevariations

■ Substitute thinly sliced regular red onions for the pickled onions.
■ Use sliced Brie or blue cheese instead of goat cheese.
■ For a warm sandwich, toast the bread lightly and assemble the sandwiches while the chicken and peppers are still warm.

lobster blt

MAKES 2 VERY GENEROUS SANDWICHES

When people travel to Maine they want to eat lobster, and this sandwich—created by chef Cheryl Lewis—has become the number-one-selling dish at the Stonewall Kitchen Café. You can prepare the basil aïoli, the lobster salad, and the bacon up to 8 hours ahead of time and assemble the sandwiches at the very last minute.

On a hot summer day or night, this sandwich makes an elegant and easy main course, accompanied by Tangy Coleslaw (page 73) or potato salad.

The recipe can easily be doubled or tripled for a crowd. This recipe makes two *very generous* sandwiches; you will easily have enough for three to four more modest sandwiches.

for the lobster salad and sandwich
Two 1¼-pound live lobsters, or 1¾ cups
    cooked lobster meat (see page 121)
Salt
4 ounces great-quality thick-sliced smoked
    bacon (3 to 4 slices)
1 stalk celery, finely diced
1 tablespoon fresh lemon juice
Sea salt and freshly ground black pepper

4 slices brioche bread, white bread, a crusty
    roll, or your favorite bread
4 Romaine or Buttercrunch lettuce leaves
2 to 4 thick slices vine-ripened tomato

for the basil aïoli
1 cup mayonnaise
¼ cup thinly sliced basil leaves
2½ teaspoons olive oil
Salt and freshly ground black pepper

To cook the lobsters: Fill a large pot with enough water to come about 2 inches up the sides of the pot. Bring to a boil over high heat. Add a pinch of salt. Add the lobsters, shell side down, cover, and let steam for 12 minutes. Drain the lobsters and let cool.

When the lobster is cool enough to handle, remove the meat from the tails and claws and very coarsely chop. You should have between 1⅔ and 1¾ cups of meat. Set aside in a medium bowl. (Save the bodies and shells for snacking on or for making a lobster broth.)

Cook the bacon in a skillet until crisp on both sides, about 10 minutes. Drain on paper towels and set aside.

To make the basil aïoli: In a small bowl, whisk together the mayonnaise, basil, and oil. Season to taste with salt and pepper. Cover and refrigerate; the aïoli will keep for several days. (You will have more aïoli than you need here; save for use in chicken sandwiches, chicken salad, roast beef and cheddar cheese sandwiches, and more.)

Add the celery to the lobster. Fold in 2 tablespoons of the aïoli and the lemon juice to lightly coat the ingredients. Season with salt and pepper. Store in the refrigerator for up to 6 hours if not making the BLTs at once.

To assemble a BLT: Lightly toast the bread. Spread the toast with a light dollop of the basil aïoli, just under a tablespoon on each piece of bread. Divide the bacon, lettuce leaves, tomato slices, and lobster salad between 2 slices of the toast. Cover with the remaining 2 slices toast. Slice the sandwiches in half on the diagonal.

favoritevariations

- Substitute cooked crabmeat for the lobster.
- You can omit the bacon.
- Serve this as a Lobster BLT Salad: Line a plate with a mixture of good greens, pile on the lobster salad and surround with the tomatoes and the bacon, cut into 1-inch pieces. Drizzle lightly with olive oil and vinegar.

the caper of caperberries

Caperberries are the size of a medium-small green olive, with the stem still attached. An oval berry forms if the flower buds of the caper bush (which grows throughout the Mediterranean) are allowed to open and set fruit, creating the caperberry. We love their tart flavor and fabulous crunchy texture, and like to add them to sautéed fish, chicken dishes, salads, sauces, tartar sauces, and mayonnaise (see page 107). We also love serving them alongside a good collection of olives as part of an antipasti platter (see page 217).

fillet of sole piccata sandwiches

SERVES 2 TO 4

Piccata refers to a classic Italian dish, usually made with veal or chicken, sautéed in a hot pan and deglazed with lemon, wine, and sometimes capers. Here we use this technique to make one of the most satisfying sandwiches we know of—tender fillet of sole is sautéed with paper-thin slices of lemon, piled onto slices of lightly toasted baguette, and topped with a caperberry-lemon mayonnaise.

Make the mayonnaise ahead of time and the sandwiches can be put together in about 10 minutes!

for the caperberry-lemon mayonnaise
1/4 cup plus 2 tablespoons mayonnaise
1/4 cup plus 2 tablespoons thinly sliced
   caperberries (see page 106)
1/8 cup fresh lemon juice
Freshly ground black pepper

for the sandwiches
Two to four 5-inch long pieces baguette
1/2 cup all-purpose flour
Salt and freshly ground black pepper
8 ounces fillet of sole
2 tablespoons unsalted butter
2 teaspoons olive oil
1 lemon, preferably organic, washed and
   cut into paper-thin slices

To make the mayonnaise: In a small bowl, mix the mayonnaise, caperberries, lemon juice, and pepper until smooth. Cover and refrigerate until ready to serve or for up to 2 days.

Cut each piece of baguette in half lengthwise and lightly toast in the toaster or under a broiler.

Place the flour on a plate and season liberally with salt and pepper. Lightly dredge the fish fillets in the seasoned flour.

In a large, heavy skillet set over high heat, add half of the butter and half of the oil and let it get hot. Add half of the fish fillets, being careful not to crowd the pan, and cook for 2 minutes. Gently flip the fish over, add half of the lemon slices to the pan and cook another 2 minutes, or until the fish is golden brown and cooked through. Repeat with the remaining butter, oil, fish, and lemon slices.

Place a baguette half on a plate, and spread about 1 tablespoon of the mayonnaise on top. Place a hot fish fillet and a few of the sautéed lemon slices on top of each half. Top with a dollop of mayonnaise and serve open-faced, or topped with another slice of baguette.

favoritevariations
- Use fillet of lemon sole, flounder, haddock, cod, salmon, or any other white fish instead of the sole.
- Use a Meyer lemon or lime instead of the regular lemon.
- Use coarsely chopped capers instead of caperberries.

lamb, feta, mint, and cucumber
sandwiches

MAKES 2 SANDWICHES

Whenever we make Grilled Herbed Butterflied Leg of Lamb (page 198) we make sure to leave leftovers so we can thinly slice the meat and layer it on good bread with feta, mint, and cucumber. You can use leftovers from lamb chops, rack of lamb, or any roasted lamb dish.

4 slices crusty bread, from a loaf of
    sourdough, white, wheat, baguette, or
    Italian bread
½ cup crumbled feta cheese
1 tablespoon chopped fresh mint leaves
½ cucumber, peeled or unpeeled, halved
    lengthwise and cut into ¼-inch-thick
    slices

4 ounces leftover roasted lamb
    (page 198 or 201), 6 to 8 slices
Salt and freshly ground black pepper
2 teaspoons fresh lemon juice
2 teaspoons olive oil

Place 2 slices of the bread on a clean surface. Divide the feta between them, scattering it evenly over each piece. Sprinkle the cheese with the mint and top the mint with the cucumber slices. Add the lamb slices to the cucumbers and season the lamb with salt and pepper. Drizzle the lemon juice and olive oil evenly over the other 2 slices of bread. Place that bread, oil side down, on top of the lamb. Cut in half and serve.

favoritevariations
■ Use leftover roast beef (page 195), chicken (page 173), or turkey (page 183) instead of lamb.
■ Use soft goat cheese instead of feta cheese.

sandwiches

a few of our favorites

We could write an entire volume on our favorite sandwiches. What follows is a short list of a few of our most adored combinations:

- Slices of fresh mozzarella with basil leaves, thick slices of ripe tomato, and Garlic Aïoli (page 243) on a crusty baguette.
- Roasted vegetable sandwich (leftovers from page 59) on sourdough drizzled with Green Sauce (page 241).
- Ultimate Lemon Caesar Salad (leftovers from page 72) on crusty bread or rolled in a tortilla.
- A classic PB and J on good white bread.
- Tuna salad on rye bread with sliced cheddar cheese and a layer of potato chips.
- Shrimp salad (leftovers from page 133) with capers, celery, and lime juice on toasted white.
- Fresh Asian Tuna Salad (leftovers from page 80) with wasabi, mayonnaise, thinly sliced radishes, and crisp lettuce leaves on whole wheat.
- Tuna sandwich with anchovies, pitted olives, and thinly sliced raw fennel on a crusty baguette.
- Chicken salad mixed with mayonnaise and mango chutney on whole wheat.
- Chicken salad mixed with grapes and toasted walnuts on a whole-wheat tortilla.
- Chicken sandwich (leftovers from page 103) with Garlic Aïoli (page 243), lettuce, and tomatoes on ciabatta.
- Roast turkey (leftovers from page 183), bacon, and Pickled Red Onions (page 239) on rye bread or ciabatta.
- Roast turkey (leftovers from page 183) with Tangy Coleslaw (page 73) and Russian dressing (mayonnaise, ketchup, and chopped capers) on Bacon and Chive Biscuits (page 27).
- Fried egg and bacon sandwich on Bacon and Chive Biscuits (page 27).

- Pulled pork sandwiches with Sweet and Spicy BBQ Sauce (page 242) on Bacon and Chive Biscuits (page 27).
- Roast pork (leftovers from page 204) with thinly sliced cheddar cheese and Pickled Red Onions (page 239) on a baguette.
- Meatball sub (leftovers from page 145) on crusty Italian bread.
- Cheddar, bacon, and apple slices on brown bread.
- Gruyère, prosciutto, and roasted red pepper panini on white bread.
- Thinly sliced rare roast beef with watercress, thin slices of cheddar cheese, and Roasted Garlic and Horseradish Sauce (page 233) on pumpernickel.
- Steak sandwich (leftovers from page 187) with Pickled Red Onions (page 239), tomato, avocado, lettuce, and grainy mustard on a baguette.
- Steak sandwich (leftovers from page 187) with Chipotle Cream (page 241) and frisée lettuce on crusty Italian bread.
- Salami, Parmesan shavings (see page 71), arugula, sun-dried tomatoes with oil, and vinegar on a crusty roll.
- A collection of tea sandwiches: goat cheese or cream cheese and thinly sliced peeled seedless cucumbers on crustless brown bread; cream cheese, chopped nuts, and arugula or watercress on seedless multigrain; open-face smoked salmon slices with scallion cream cheese (page 44) on crustless white bread with paper-thin lemon slices; butter and thinly sliced radish sandwiches on dark crustless bread; thinly sliced cheddar cheese and mango chutney on brown bread; and mascarpone and jam with sliced strawberries on crustless white bread.

chocolate and raspberry panini
sandwiches

Bread and chocolate are high on our list of favorite combinations, and few dishes satisfy our inner child better than this gooey chocolate sandwich. We make ours by buttering round slices of fresh baguette, filling them with dark chocolate and fresh berries, and crisping them in a panini press. If you don't have a panini press, see page 99.

Serve this sandwich as dessert, or as a fabulous snack with a bottle of Champagne.

8 round slices baguette (about ¼-inch thick) or your favorite bread

2 tablespoons unsalted butter, softened

4 heaping tablespoons dark chocolate chips (or about 2 ounces chopped chocolate)

½ cup fresh or frozen and thawed raspberries

Preheat a panini press or indoor grill on high heat.

Place the baguette slices on a plate and spread a thin layer of butter on each. Turn 4 slices over and divide the chocolate evenly among the 4 nonbuttered sides. Divide the raspberries over the chocolate and top the remaining slices of bread, butter side-up. Place the sandwiches in the panini press and cook for 2 minutes, or until the bread is golden and the chocolate has melted. Serve immediately.

favoritevariations

- Cut 2 marshmallows into 4 slices each, add 2 slices of marshmallow to each sandwich along with the chocolate, and omit the raspberries.
- Add ¾-inch-thick banana slices to each sandwich and omit the raspberries.
- Substitute fresh or frozen blueberries or blackberries for the raspberries.
- Substitute thin slices of ripe peaches or white peaches for the raspberries.
- Use white or milk chocolate instead of dark or use a combination.
- Spread 1 tablespoon maple syrup or honey on the bread before topping with the chocolate.
- Spread 1 tablespoon peanut butter—chunky or smooth—on the bread before topping with the chocolate.

flavored **bubbly fruit waters**

SERVES 6

Imagine a glass pitcher filled with sparkling water and wedges of melon, kiwi, lemons, and fresh mint leaves. The fruit slowly infuses the water with its essence. Fanciful and aesthetic, these flavored waters are refreshing and elegant to serve at any gathering. Make several pitchers using different herbs, fruit, and berries and serve as-is or accompanied by vodka, light rum, or gin. Don't make the water more than 30 minutes or so before serving or the bubbles will go flat.

These fruit waters make great accompaniments to any of the sandwiches in this chapter; they are a great way to dress up any lunch or dinner.

6 cups sparkling water or seltzer, chilled
½ ripe cantaloupe, rind removed and flesh
    cut into 1-inch pieces
½ lemon, skin scrubbed clean and cut into
    thin slices

¼ cup fresh raspberries
¼ cup fresh mint leaves
3 to 4 bamboo skewers
Ice cubes or flavored ice cubes (see page
    113)

Place the water in a large glass pitcher.

Arrange the cantaloupe, lemon slices, raspberries, and half the mint leaves on the skewers, interspersing colors and types of fruit. Place the skewers in the pitcher and add ice.

favoritevariations

- Use a melon baller to cut melon balls.
- Use lemon verbena instead of mint.
- Use honeydew instead of, or in addition to, the cantaloupe.
- Use lime instead of, or in addition to, the lemon.
- Add ¼ cup pomegranate juice or unsweetened cranberry juice.
- Add a tablespoon or two of any of the sweet syrups on page 20.
- Add 1 orange cut into wedges or clementine sections.
- Add ½ cup fresh orange or grapefruit juice.
- Add 1 kiwi, peeled and thinly sliced
- Add organic rose petals.

frozen essence

making flavored ice cubes

Ice cubes made of coffee, tea, flowers, herbs, citrus, juices, and more are all the rage in our kitchens. We love adding little cubes of frozen espresso to summer iced coffees, or popping a few ice cubes made with mint syrup into an iced tea or lemonade or any alcoholic drink. Instead of diluting your drink, the cubes add a whole new flavor dimension.

Most new refrigerators come with automatic ice cube machines, which means that many kitchens these days are without old-fashioned ice cube trays. Pick up a few inexpensive plastic ice cube trays to have on hand for making these flavored cubes.

The only limit on the flavor combinations is your imagination. The basic recipe is as follows: Fill each ice cube compartment a little more than halfway (about 1 tablespoon liquid or puree) and freeze for about 2 hours, or until frozen. The ice cubes can then be popped out of the tray and kept in a tightly sealed plastic container or bag in the freezer for about a week. You can mix and match and freeze several flavors in one tray, but make sure to keep them in separate plastic bags once they're frozen.

Here are a few of our favorite flavored ice cubes:

- **Iced Tea:** Add to iced tea for extra tea flavor or to lemonade.
- **Iced Coffee or Espresso:** Add to iced coffee for an extra coffee flavor, to milk, or chocolate milk (for mocha drinks).
- **Iced Sugar Syrups** (page 20): Add to iced tea, iced coffee, cocktails, fruit salads, fruit drinks, lemonade or limeade.

- **Edible Flowers:** Place an organically grown edible flower—violet, marigold petals, nasturtium, lavender, chive blossoms, and so on—into each ice cube tray compartment and cover with about a tablespoon of water. Use in cocktails, iced tea, sparkling water, or any drink or punch.
- **Juices:** Freeze orange, grapefruit, pink grapefruit, cranberry, apple, pomegranate, blood orange, tangerine, or any juice. Mix and match flavors in virgin or alcoholic drinks—particularly martinis and Champagne. Or serve to kids to cool off on a hot summer day.
- **Lemon or Limeade:** Freeze lemon or limeade. Use in iced tea, alcoholic drinks, or add to a tall glass of sparkling soda.
- **Berries:** Place a berry—raspberry, blueberry, blackberry, or strawberry—into each ice cube compartment and cover with sugar syrup (page 20) or water. Add to fruit punch, lemonade, alcoholic drinks, or sparkling or plain water.
- **Chocolate Milk:** Chocolate milk frozen into ice cubes makes a great mocha drink when added to iced coffee.
- **Tonic:** Freeze tonic for refreshing summery gin and tonics.
- **Herbs:** Puree fresh summer herbs—basil, mint, chervil, thyme, rosemary, oregano, lavender, or chives—with a touch of olive oil and freeze. Use the herbal cubes thawed in soups, stews, tarts, quiches, and so on, particularly in the winter when really fresh herbs are difficult to find.

5

seafood and fish

salmon and ginger cakes

MAKES ABOUT TEN 2-INCH CAKES

We coat these fish cakes—chopped fresh salmon, mixed with ginger, scallions, cilantro, sweet red pepper, and a dash of sesame oil—in panko breadcrumbs before lightly pan-frying them. The result is a fish cake that's light in texture but bursting with fresh flavors.

1 pound skinless salmon fillet, cut into
    ¼-inch dice
½ cup finely chopped red bell pepper
¼ cup chopped scallions (white and green
    parts)
¼ cup minced fresh cilantro leaves
½ tablespoon finely peeled, grated fresh
    ginger
1⅓ cups panko bread crumbs (see below)

1 large egg, lightly beaten
1 tablespoon Asian sesame oil
1 tablespoon soy sauce
Salt
Freshly ground black pepper
About ⅓ cup canola oil
Lemon and lime wedges
Orange-Miso Dipping Sauce (page 238)

In a large bowl, gently mix the salmon, pepper, scallions, cilantro, ginger, ⅓ cup of the panko bread crumbs, egg, sesame oil, and soy sauce until blended. Season with ¼ teaspoon salt and pepper to taste.

Place the remaining cup panko bread crumbs in a shallow bowl, and season with salt and pepper. Using a ¼-cup measuring cup, form the salmon mixture into ten 2-inch cakes, flattening them slightly to make a 1-inch-thick round. Press each cake into the bread crumbs on both sides, patting extra bread crumbs into the edges of the cakes with your hands. Set aside, and repeat with the remaining salmon mixture. The salmon cakes can be made about 6 hours ahead of time; wrap in plastic and refrigerate until ready to cook.

Heat a large, heavy 10-inch skillet over medium heat. Add the oil (larger pans may require more oil; the oil should be about ⅛ inch deep). When the oil is hot, add half of the salmon cakes. Cook for 3 minutes on each side, or until golden brown. If necessary, tilt the pan during cooking to distribute the oil evenly. Drain on paper towels, and repeat with the remaining salmon cakes. The salmon cakes may be made a day ahead and reheated for 5 to 10 minutes in a preheated 350°F oven, or until warmed through.

Serve the salmon cakes with the lemon and lime wedges and orange-miso dipping sauce.

NOTE: Panko (Japanese bread crumbs) have a coarser texture than regular bread crumbs and lend an excellent crunchy texture to foods. Look for panko in Asian food stores or the specialty food aisle of your supermarket.

favoritevariations

- Add 1 tablespoon liquid chile sauce, such as the Thai chile-garlic sauce sriracha or Chinese chile paste, to the mixture.
- Add 1 to 2 tablespoons chopped smoked salmon to the mixture.
- Substitute ¾ to 1 pound cooked crab (preferably lump crabmeat) for the salmon.
- Serve with the Asian Dipping Sauce (page 238) or Mango Salsa (page 236) instead of the Orange-Miso Dipping Sauce.

scallop "chips"

SERVES 6 TO 8

The inspiration for these crisp, savory "chips" came from an episode of the wildly entertaining TV show *Iron Chef America* on the Food Network. The "secret" ingredient was scallops, and Iron Chef Morimoto thinly sliced them and served them with a dipping sauce. That idea reminded us how much we love an old New England favorite—deep fried scallops. These scallop chips are a combination of East meets West—very thinly sliced sea scallops are coated in panko bread crumbs and fried so that they are crisp on the outside and tender inside—and they cook in about 2 minutes! We like making them in a wok because the oil sits at the bottom and none of it splatters.

Serve the scallops as an appetizer with Orange-Miso Dipping Sauce (page 238), Classic Cocktail Sauce (page 236), Garlic Aïoli (page 243), Asian Dipping Sauce (page 238), or lemon and lime wedges.

1 pound sea scallops, tabs removed (see Note, page 54)
About 2 cups safflower or vegetable oil
One 1-inch piece fresh, peeled ginger

2 cups panko bread crumbs (see Note, page 116), or homemade bread crumbs
1 lemon, cut into wedges

Place the scallops in the freezer for 30 to 45 minutes to make them much easier to slice.

In a wok or a large, heavy skillet, heat the oil over high heat about 20 seconds. Add the ginger to the oil and let it heat up for about 2 minutes. The oil is hot enough when you drop a tiny bit of panko into it and it sizzles immediately.

Meanwhile, thinly slice the scallops horizontally. You should get 3 to 4 slices from each large scallop. Place the panko in a bowl and lightly coat each slice of scallop with panko on all sides. Place on a plate.

Preheat the oven to 200°F.

Remove the ginger from the oil with a slotted spoon. Cook the scallops in batches in the hot oil. Add enough scallops to fit in a single layer in the pan. Cook for 30 seconds; gently flip them over and cook for another 30 seconds. Drain on paper towels. (If you're making a double batch and need to keep the scallops warm, place them on an ovenproof plate and place in the oven while you fry the remaining batches). Serve immediately.

favoritevariations

Substitute any of the following for the scallops:

- Thinly slice large peeled shrimp lengthwise and fry for about 1 minute.
- Thinly slice boneless, skinless chicken breast and fry for 3 to 4 minutes, or until cooked through.
- Use whole shucked oysters or clams, and fry about 1 minute.
- Add 2 to 3 tablespoons black or white sesame seeds to the panko.
- Add 2 to 3 tablespoons chopped fresh cilantro leaves or other herbs to the panko.

lobster salad with lime and ginger

SERVES 2 AS A MAIN COURSE OR 4 AS AN APPETIZER

In Maine, nothing says summer like a good lobster roll. The basic recipe is pretty much the same throughout the state: plump lobster meat mixed with mayonnaise and, usually, chopped celery. Our version is spiked with fresh ginger, lime zest, and crunchy scallions. Serve it New England–style in a lightly toasted split-top hot dog bun, or on a bed of watercress for an elegant appetizer or a light summer dinner. See photograph on page 114.

1½ cups cooked lobster meat (see page 121)
1 teaspoon grated lime zest
1 teaspoon fresh lime juice
1 teaspoon grated, peeled fresh ginger

1 tablespoon mayonnaise
1 scallion (white and green parts), chopped
Salt and freshly ground black pepper

Mix together the lobster, lime zest and juice, ginger, mayonnaise, and scallion in a small bowl until well combined. Season to taste with salt and pepper.

favorite variations

- Top cucumber rounds, radish rounds, or endive spears with a spoonful of the salad for a colorful hors d'oeuvre.
- Substitute lump crabmeat for the lobster.

learning lobster

For a Mainer, cooking lobster is about as difficult as making toast. Well, not exactly, but it's no big deal. Here's how we do it: Fill a large pot with about 2 inches cold salted water. Bring the water to a rolling boil over high heat. Place the lobsters on their backs, shell side down, into the boiling water. The idea is that all those delicious juices will get trapped in the shell instead of leaching out into the water, lost forever. Cover and steam the lobster for about 12 to 20 minutes—12 minutes for a 1-pounder and about 20 minutes for a 2-pounder. To test for doneness, simply pull off one of the small legs; if it comes off easily, the lobster is ready.

Drain the lobsters and let cool. Twist the tail from the body. Using a fork, pull the meat from the tail and remove. It should come out in one piece; if it doesn't pull out easily, turn your fork around, place it in the tail backward, grab ahold of the meat, and pull it out. Remove the claws from the body and, using a nut or lobster cracker, crack the claw shells. Remove the meat from the claws. The body contains all kind of sweet juices and meat and, quite frankly, the best way to eat the body is to rip it apart and suck on the feelers and the meat in between, extracting all the deliciousness in your mouth. Just be sure to remove and discard the sac at the top of the head first. The tomalley, the green-colored liver, is a matter of taste—some love it, others steer clear. A 1½-pound lobster will only yield about ½ pound, or 1½ cups, of actual lobster meat.

tuna tartare on cucumber rounds

MAKES ABOUT 2 DOZEN HORS D'OEUVRES

This refreshing, elegant appetizer seems to be on the menu in nearly every restaurant. What makes our tartare special is the combination of Asian flavors—crunchy scallions, fragrant soy, sesame oil, and fresh ginger mixed with high-grade (often referred to as sushi-grade) tuna all piled on cucumber slices. Garnish it with whole cilantro leaves or a tiny dollop of wasabi.

8 ounces fresh sushi-grade tuna (about
   1 large steak), cut into 1/2-inch cubes
2 sliced scallions (white and green parts)
1 tablespoon chopped fresh cilantro leaves
1 tablespoon grated, peeled fresh ginger

1 tablespoon soy sauce
1 tablespoon Asian sesame oil
1 seedless cucumber, sliced diagonally into
   1/4-inch-thick rounds

Place the tuna, scallions, cilantro, ginger, soy sauce, and sesame oil in a medium bowl and mix gently until well blended.

Arrange the cucumber slices on a large serving tray, and pile a generous tablespoon of the tuna mixture on each cucumber slice. Serve immediately.

favoritevariations

- Add 1 small tomato, seeded and finely chopped.
- Serve the tartare on endive spears instead of cucumber slices.
- Top each cucumber slice with a tiny dollop of salmon caviar.
- Top each cucumber slice with a tiny dollop of prepared wasabi.

crab, asparagus, and lemon **risotto**

SERVES 4

We love just about any kind of risotto, but there's something about the combination of asparagus, fresh crabmeat, lemon, leeks, and chives that is particularly appealing. It's light and full of fresh flavors but also provides the feeling of comfort we look for in this classic Italian rice dish.

3 cups fresh or frozen fish stock (available in many fish stores), or two 8-ounce bottles clam juice plus 1 cup water, or 3 cups chicken broth, homemade (see page 63) or low-sodium canned

1 pound medium asparagus, ends trimmed and reserved, cut into ¾-inch pieces

1½ tablespoons olive oil

1 leek (white and light green parts only), cut in half lengthwise, and thinly sliced

Salt and freshly ground black pepper

1 garlic clove, thinly sliced

2 tablespoons chopped fresh chives or parsley leaves

1 cup Arborio or Spanish Bomba (risotto short-grain) rice

1 cup dry white wine

12 ounces fresh crabmeat (preferably lump crabmeat; if frozen, thaw before using)

1 teaspoon grated lemon zest

1 tablespoon fresh lemon juice

1 teaspoon unsalted butter

In a small saucepan, heat the fish stock (or clam juice) over low heat until simmering. Add the reserved asparagus ends and simmer for 10 minutes. Use a slotted spoon to remove the asparagus ends and discard. Keep the stock warm over very low heat.

In a medium heavy pot, heat 1 tablespoon of the olive oil over a low flame. Add the leeks and cook for 5 minutes, stirring frequently. Season with salt and pepper. Add the garlic and 1 tablespoon of the chives and cook for 30 seconds. Add the rice and cook for 2 to 3 minutes, stirring well to coat all the rice kernels with the oil and leeks. The rice will take on a pearly white color and be slightly translucent along the edges. Add half of the wine, stirring until the liquid has been absorbed. Add the remaining wine, and stir until all of the liquid has been absorbed. Slowly add the warm broth, ½ cup at a time, again stirring until the liquid has absorbed before adding additional broth. You can make the risotto a few hours ahead of time and cook in the last ½ cup of liquid just before guests come.

When all but the last ½ cup of the liquid has been added, the risotto should be almost tender. Mix in the asparagus and the remaining ½ cup liquid, and cook for 4 to 5 minutes, or until the asparagus is just tender and the liquid is almost absorbed. Gently stir in three-quarters of the crabmeat, the lemon zest, and lemon juice and cook for another minute until warmed through. Season to taste with salt and pepper.

In a small skillet, heat the remaining ½ tablespoon olive oil and the butter over moderate heat. Add the remaining crabmeat and a good grinding of pepper and cook for 1 to 2 minutes, or until just warmed through.

Divide the risotto in 4 plates or soup bowls and sprinkle with the cooked crab and the remaining tablespoon chives.

favoritevariations

■ Use cooked chopped lobster meat instead of the crab.

■ Use 1 pound sea scallops, cut in half, tabs removed (see Note, page 54), instead of the crab.

■ Although seafood risotto is not traditionally served with cheese, you can serve ½ cup freshly grated Parmesan cheese on the side, if you like.

baked swordfish with a
mustard-caper-lemon sauce

SERVES 2 TO 4

When we tell people that this swordfish is marinated in milk we always get the same reaction: "Did you say *milk*?" Here's how it works: The milk not only tenderizes the swordfish, but it is then used as the basis for a very simple, creamy sauce. This is an ideal dish for a weeknight, served with Cardamom Creamed Spinach (page 218) and roasted or baked potatoes. You can double or triple the recipe to serve a larger crowd.

One 1-pound swordfish steak, about 1 inch thick
½ cup milk (see Note)
2 tablespoons unsalted butter
2 tablespoons drained capers

1 teaspoon Dijon-style mustard
Juice of 1 lemon
Freshly ground black pepper
1 lemon, cut into wedges

Place the fish in a medium ovenproof skillet or gratin dish, pour on the milk, and let "marinate" for at least 15 minutes at room temperature or up to several hours, covered and refrigerated.

Place a rack in the middle of the oven and preheat the oven to 400°F.

In a small saucepan, melt the butter over low heat. When it begins to sizzle, add the capers, mustard, lemon juice, and pepper and stir to create a smooth sauce. Cook for 5 minutes, or until the sauce is slightly thickened.

Bake the fish for 10 minutes. (If you have a thicker steak, you will need to bake it for 12 to 14 minutes, or until almost tender.)

Remove from the oven and preheat the broiler. Spoon the sauce over the fish (do not drain off the milk) and place under the broiler for 3 to 5 minutes, or until the fish begins to turn golden brown and is opaque and tender when tested in the center with a small, sharp knife.

Serve hot with the lemon wedges.

NOTE: The sauce is delicious made with low-fat milk, but you can also make it creamier by using whole milk or a touch of heavy cream.

favoritevariations

- If you can't find really fresh swordfish, substitute a cod, salmon, or haddock steak.
- Add 1 tablespoon chopped fresh thyme leaves, or 1 teaspoon dried, to the sauce.
- Omit the capers and add anchovy fillets crisscrossed on top of the fish.

roasted salmon with peas and edamame beans with a raw pea pesto

SERVES 4

Salmon and peas are an old New England tradition. Even though peas are harvested in the spring, it's the standard Fourth of July meal (the idea being that peas are just ready for harvesting in the beginning of July and salmon is almost always plentiful). We decided to play a bit with this classic combination by searing the salmon in a hot pan, surrounding it with fresh peas and edamame (soy) beans, dousing it with lemon juice, and roasting it in a hot oven. We make a quick pesto using fresh raw peas, olive oil, garlic, and almonds and serve it on the hot salmon. (The pesto can be made ahead of time, or while the salmon roasts.) Best of all, the entire dish takes less than 30 minutes!

The pea pesto is also delicious served with raw vegetables, chicken dishes, or tossed with pasta.

for the raw pea pesto
½ cup shelled fresh English peas (from about 8 ounces peas in the pod)
1 small garlic clove, chopped
Salt and freshly ground black pepper
⅓ cup olive oil
2 tablespoons slivered or chopped almonds

for the salmon
1½ tablespoons olive oil
1⅓ to 1½ pounds salmon fillet, skin on, cut into 4 pieces
1 garlic clove, very thinly sliced
Salt and freshly ground black pepper
¼ cup shelled fresh English peas (from about 4 ounces peas in the pod)
1 cup shelled edamame beans (see Note)
Juice of 1 small lemon (about 2 tablespoons)

To make the pesto: In a food processor or blender, pulse the peas, garlic, and salt and pepper several times until coarsely chopped. Add the olive oil and pulse a few more times. Add the almonds and pulse until the pesto is coarsely but not fully blended. Taste for seasoning. The pesto can be made several hours ahead of time; cover and refrigerate.

Place a rack in the middle of the oven and preheat the oven to 450°F.

To prepare the salmon: Heat a large, heavy, ovenproof skillet (cast iron is ideal) over high heat for about a minute. Add the olive oil and let it heat up for about 10 seconds, until hot. Add the salmon pieces, skin side down. Sprinkle the garlic on top, season with salt and pepper, and cook for 2 minutes. Using a wide spatula, gently flip the salmon over, and scatter the peas and edamame around the fish. Pour the lemon juice over the fish, peas, and beans, and season everything with salt and pepper. Roast in the oven for 7 to 10 minutes, depending on the thickness of the salmon, or until opaque and tender when poked in the center with a small, sharp knife.

Remove the fish from the oven. Use a spatula to gently flip the fish over and place each piece in the center of a serving plate. Spoon the peas and edamame around the fish, with a thick stripe of pesto down the length of each piece of salmon; serve the remaining pesto on the side.

NOTE: Edamame, or green soy beans, can be found fresh or frozen in many supermarkets.

trio of **fish en papillote** (fish cooked in paper)

We tried many versions of wrapping fresh fish with a few simple flavorings inside parchment paper and baking them (or wrapping them in aluminum foil and grilling them) and offer our three favorites. We hope they'll inspire you to create your own combinations. Each of these recipes serves a different number of people; they can easily be doubled or tripled for a party.

Serve any of these with the Asian Dipping Sauce (page 238), Orange-Miso Sauce (page 238), or Garlic Aïoli (page 243).

■ **asian-style cod** with ginger and two peppers

SERVES 4

Parchment paper or aluminum foil
1 yellow bell pepper, cut into thin strips
1 red bell pepper, cut into thin strips
1 pound skinless cod fillet

One 2-inch piece peeled, fresh ginger, cut into julienne slices (about ¼ cup)
2 tablespoons soy sauce
2 tablespoons Asian sesame oil
Salt and freshly ground black pepper

Place a rack in the middle of the oven and preheat the oven to 425°F, or light a charcoal, gas, or wood fire until red hot.

Cut four 12 × 12-inch pieces of parchment paper or 15-inch-long pieces of aluminum foil. Fold the paper in half, crease, and unfold. Place one-fourth of each of the peppers in the center of the paper and top with the fish; sprinkle the top with the ginger, soy, and sesame oil. Season with salt and pepper. Bring the bottom edge up to the top edge of the paper to enclose the package. To seal, roll the top of the paper over 2 to 3 times and crease, making ¼-inch folds over each other. Repeat on each side to enclose the ingredients thoroughly. You can also use a metal paper clip to attach the paper. Repeat the filling and folding with the remaining ingredients and parchment.

(If using foil, to seal the packets, simply pull the two sides up into the center, fold the foil over itself a couple of times to seal, being careful not to fold the foil so close that it touches the fish. Fold the sides of the foil shut tightly.)

To bake, place all four packets on a cookie or baking sheet. Bake for 10 minutes. To grill, place the foil packets directly on the grill rack, cover the grill, and cook for 10 minutes. The paper will puff up as the packets cook. For a fillet that is about 1 inch thick at the thickest part, cook 10 minutes; cook 12 minutes for thicker fillets. To serve, place a packet on each serving plate and, with a small, sharp knife, tear the packet open to expose the fish, being careful of the steam that will be released.

RECIPE CONTINUES ▶

■ **salmon** and asparagus with chives

SERVES 3

Parchment paper or aluminum foil
1 pound skinless salmon fillet, cut into
   3 pieces
2 scallions (white and green parts), cut into
   1-inch pieces
12 ounces medium asparagus, ends trimmed,
   and cut into 1-inch pieces

One 1-inch piece peeled, fresh ginger, cut
   into julienne slices (about 2 tablespoons)
3 tablespoons chopped fresh chives
3 tablespoons unsalted butter, cut into
   3 pieces
Salt and freshly ground black pepper

Prepare and cook as for the Asian-Style Cod above (page 131), dividing the ingredients among three packets as follows: Surround each piece of salmon with one-third of the scallions, asparagus, ginger, and chives. Top the fish with 1 tablespoon butter and season to taste with salt and pepper.

Follow the directions for sealing the packets and cooking them as described on page 131.

■ **shrimp, scallops,** and thyme-lemon butter

SERVES 2

Parchment paper or aluminum foil
1 tablespoon unsalted butter, at room
   temperature
1 tablespoon minced fresh thyme leaves
1 tablespoon fresh lemon juice

Salt and freshly ground black pepper
12 large shrimp, peeled and deveined
6 large sea scallops, tabs removed (see Note,
   page 54)
Lemon and lime wedges

Prepare and cook as for Asian-Style Cod above (page 131), dividing the ingredients between two packets as follows: In a small bowl, mix the butter, thyme, lemon juice, salt, and pepper to taste. Place the shrimp and scallops in the packets and divide the butter on top of the shellfish.

Follow the directions for sealing the packets and cooking them as described on page 131.

shrimp cocktail with two sauces

SERVES 8 TO 10 AS AN HORS D'OEUVRE

For an eye-catching party appetizer, we like to layer our Classic Cocktail Sauce (page 236) and our Orange-Miso Dipping Sauce (page 238) in a favorite glass. You can present the shrimp in individual small glasses (as shown below), or use a wide-rimmed glass, draping many shrimp over the rim.

Salt
2 pounds large raw shrimp, peeled and
    deveined

Classic Cocktail Sauce (page 236)
Orange-Miso Dipping Sauce (page 238)

Bring a large pot or skillet of lightly salted water to a simmer and add the shrimp. Once the water has come to a boil again, cook for 2 to 3 minutes, or until completely pink throughout. Drain the shrimp and place on a paper towel–covered plate to cool completely. Chill the shrimp until ready to serve.

Place about three-quarters of the Classic Cocktail Sauce in the bottom of a large margarita glass (or divide it between 4 small martini glasses). Pour the Orange-Miso Dipping Sauce onto the cocktail sauce, and top with the remaining cocktail sauce. Hook the shrimp over the sides of the glass holding the sauce.

sautéed shrimp with garlic, lime, and chile sauce

SERVES 4

Fast, simple, and bursting with flavor, these spicy, pleasingly tart shrimp can be served as an appetizer with cold beer, as part of our antipasti platter (see page 217), or as a main course accompanied by couscous, pasta, or rice. We also like to serve the shrimp on top of 2 cups of mixed greens or baby arugula and pour the warm sauce on top to slightly wilt the greens.

1 to 2 tablespoons olive oil
2 garlic cloves, thinly sliced
1 pound large shrimp, shelled and deveined
Juice from 2 limes

¼ to 1 teaspoon Chinese chile paste or hot pepper sauce
½ cup Vermouth or dry white wine
1 lime, cut into wedges for garnish

In a large skillet, heat 1 tablespoon of the oil over medium-high heat. Add the garlic and, stirring, cook for 1 minute. Add the shrimp, in one layer if possible, and cook for 2 minutes. Using tongs, flip the shrimp over and cook for 1 minute.

Add the lime juice and chile paste to taste (¼ teaspoon will provide a hint of spice and 1 teaspoon will sock-it-to-ya!). Raise the heat to high and add the Vermouth. Cook for 1 minute. Remove the shrimp to a platter.

Add the remaining tablespoon oil if you like and boil the juices down in the pan over high heat for another minute. Pour the sauce on top of the shrimp and garnish with the limes.

favoritevariations

Add any or all along with the garlic:

- Roasted or steamed asparagus, cut on the diagonal into 1-inch pieces.
- 2 chopped scallions (white and green parts).
- 2 tablespoons julienne strips peeled, fresh ginger.
- Roasted cippoline or pearl onions, halved (page 222).
- Very thin strips of red bell pepper.
- Roasted garlic cloves (page 161) in place of the thinly sliced garlic.
- ½ cup chopped peanuts or cashews added during the last minute of cooking, or sprinkled on as a garnish.

roll, roll, roll

a hint for citrus

There's nothing more frustrating than cutting open a lemon or lime, smelling the promise of its exotic, vibrant juice, only to find that the citrus is dried out and won't yield more than a drop or two of juice. When shopping, always look for citrus that feels heavy in your hand; it's usually the juiciest. And, once you're home, roll the lemon or lime on a countertop under the palm of your hand to help release the juice. Then cut the fruit in half and squeeze out the juice. You'll find that juices flow much easier and you end up with more juice.

baked haddock with lemon
bread crumbs, and a tomato-olive sauce

SERVES 3 TO 4

While the flavors in this dish are sophisticated enough for a weekend dinner party, this is one of our favorite weeknight dinners since it can be on the table in 30 minutes. Surround the haddock with chopped tomatoes and olives, sprinkle with a simple lemon–bread crumb topping, and bake for just about 10 minutes. While the fish bakes, throw together a big green salad, and cut up some good crusty bread for mopping up the haddock's delicious juices.

3 tablespoons olive oil
1 pound skinless haddock fillet, or salmon, striped bass, bluefish, cod, or any firm white fish fillet
1 pound ripe red or yellow tomatoes (about 2 medium), chopped
1 cup chopped Kalamata, green, or cured black olives (or a combination)

¼ packed cup chopped fresh parsley or basil leaves
Salt and freshly ground black pepper
¼ cup plain bread crumbs or crushed crackers
1 tablespoon grated lemon zest
1 tablespoon fresh lemon juice
1 tablespoon unsalted butter, cut into small cubes

Place a rack in the middle of the oven and preheat the oven to 425°F.

Use 1 tablespoon of the olive oil to grease the bottom of a shallow roasting pan or rimmed baking sheet. Place the fish in the center of the pan.

Combine the tomatoes, olives, and parsley in a large bowl and season with salt and pepper. Surround the fish with the tomato and olive mixture, leaving the top of the fish bare.

Mix the bread crumbs and lemon zest together in a small bowl, using your hands to separate the lemon zest and incorporate it evenly into the breadcrumbs. Season the mixture with salt and pepper, and set aside.

Drizzle the lemon juice over the fish. Sprinkle the bread crumb mixture evenly over the fish, then drizzle the remaining 2 tablespoons olive oil over the bread crumbs and the tomato mixture. Scatter the butter pieces over the bread crumbs.

Bake the fish for about 10 minutes (for a fillet about 1 inch thick at the thickest part, cook 8 minutes; cook 12 minutes for thicker fillets), and serve immediately.

favoritevariations

- Add ½ cup chopped bell pepper, ¼ cup drained capers, and 2 chopped garlic cloves to the vegetable mixture.
- Pour ¾ cup dry white wine over the vegetables before baking to make a light sauce at the bottom of the pan.

6

pasta, potatoes, and bread

asian-style **cold soba noodles** with cucumber-cashew salad

SERVES 4 TO 6

We find Asian-style cold noodles with sesame sauce positively addictive. In this version we take soba noodles (Japanese buckwheat noodles) and toss them with a thick chile-enhanced peanut butter and sesame paste sauce. The noodles are served cold, surrounded by a refreshing cucumber and cashew salad, lightly tossed with sesame oil and rice wine vinegar.

This is ideal picnic fare, or the perfect accompaniment to roasted or grilled foods. The noodles can be made several hours ahead of time; cover and refrigerate until ready to serve.

for the sauce and noodles
Salt
3 garlic cloves, minced
3 tablespoons finely chopped, peeled fresh ginger
4 scallions (white and green parts), thinly sliced
1/2 cup chunky-style peanut butter
1/4 cup tahini (sesame paste made from raw sesame seeds)
2 teaspoons Chinese chile paste
1/4 cup soy sauce
1/4 cup minced fresh cilantro leaves plus several sprigs for garnish

One 8.8-ounce package soba noodles (Japanese buckwheat pasta)

for the cucumber-cashew salad
1 large European (or seedless) cucumber, cubed (about 3 cups)
3/4 cup coarsely chopped lightly salted cashews
2 tablespoons Asian sesame oil
2 tablespoons rice wine vinegar (or white wine vinegar)
Freshly ground black pepper

Bring a large pot of lightly salted water to a boil over high heat.

To make the sauce: In a large bowl, mix the garlic, ginger, and scallions. Using a spoon, mix in the peanut butter and the tahini. Add the chile paste and soy sauce and stir well. Add 1/2 cup hot (or almost boiling) water from the pot of water and stir into the sauce. Stir in cilantro.

To make the salad: In a small bowl, mix the cucumbers, cashews, sesame oil, and vinegar and season to taste with pepper. Set aside.

Add the noodles to the pot of boiling water and stir well. Cook for about 6 minutes, or until just tender. Drain the noodles in a colander and place under cold running water. Toss the noodles around until they are chilled. Drain again.

Toss the noodles with the peanut butter sauce, making sure that the noodles are well coated. If making the noodles ahead of time, cover and chill for several hours until ready to serve.

To serve, place the noodles on a large serving plate and surround with the cucumber and cashew salad. Garnish with a sprig or two of cilantro.

favoritevariations

- Substitute pistachios, walnuts, or almonds for the cashews.
- Chop 1 small red or yellow bell pepper and add to the cucumber salad.
- Add 1 small chopped chile pepper to the salad.
- Serve with wedges of lime.

mediterranean **orzo salad**

SERVES 6 TO 10

This pasta salad—loaded with Kalamata olives, sweet grape tomatoes, capers, and a twist of lemon—bursts with summer flavor. You can serve it warm as a side dish or chilled at a picnic with roast chicken and a green salad.

Salt

1 pound orzo pasta (about 1¼ cups), or other small pasta

¼ cup olive oil

⅓ cup plus 1 tablespoon red wine vinegar

2 tablespoons grated lemon zest

¼ cup freshly squeezed lemon juice

2 cups chopped Kalamata olives

2 pints grape tomatoes, halved lengthwise, or 1 large yellow or red tomato, cubed (about 4 cups)

1 cup finely chopped red onion

½ cup drained capers

½ cup lightly packed chopped fresh parsley leaves

Freshly ground black pepper

Bring a large pot of lightly salted water to a boil. Add the orzo, and cook until al dente, about 9 minutes, stirring occasionally. Use a fine-mesh strainer to drain the pasta well. Transfer the pasta to a large mixing bowl.

While the pasta is still hot, add the olive oil, vinegar, lemon zest, and lemon juice and stir to combine. Let the pasta cool for about 5 minutes, stirring occasionally.

Add the olives, tomatoes, red onion, capers, and parsley, and stir to combine. Season with salt and pepper to taste (you probably won't need much salt). Serve warm, at room temperature, or cold.

favoritevariations

■ Increase the olives to 1½ cups and mix Kalamata, green, and black olives.

■ Double the lemon zest and lemon juice.

■ Substitute ¼ cup thinly sliced caperberries for the capers (see page 106).

■ Add ¼ cup finely shredded fresh basil leaves, or chopped fresh oregano.

■ Add ¼ cup chopped sun-dried tomatoes.

■ Add 1 cup chopped seedless cucumbers or chopped red bell pepper.

■ Add 1 cup crumbled feta cheese.

■ Substitute 1 pound of another cooked grain, such as Israeli couscous, barley, or quinoa, for the orzo.

spaghetti carbonara with basil swirl

SERVES 4

This is comfort food, the kind of dish we crave after a long, hard day. Eggs are whisked with grated Parmesan cheese, cooked bacon or pancetta, and a touch of cream and then are tossed with hot pasta. A dollop of basil puree is swirled into the pasta just before serving. The heat from the pasta "cooks" the egg, creating an irresistible, creamy sauce. Since the eggs in this dish are not completely cooked we advise that you use really fresh, organic eggs (see page 38).

Real Parmigiano-Reggiano is a must in this recipe. The pasta begs for the cheese's nutty, full flavor (see page 150 for more on cheeses). See photograph on page 138.

8 ounces thick-sliced pancetta or bacon
Salt
1 pound spaghetti or linguine
2 large organic eggs

1¾ cups freshly grated Parmesan cheese
¼ cup heavy cream
Salt and freshly ground black pepper
½ cup Basil Swirl (page 233)

Heat a large, heavy skillet over moderately low heat. Working in batches and being careful not to crowd the skillet, cook the pancetta, turning occasionally, until crispy, 12 to 15 minutes. Drain on paper towels and repeat with the remaining pancetta. Coarsely chop the pancetta.

Bring a large pot of salted water to a boil. Add pasta and cook until *al dente* according to package directions, 10 to 12 minutes. Drain well in a colander.

In a large serving bowl, whisk the eggs, 1¼ cups of the Parmesan cheese, and the cream. Season with salt and pepper. Add all but 1 tablespoon of the pancetta along with the hot pasta and toss. Top with the remaining tablespoon of pancetta and the remaining ½ cup Parmesan cheese. Place 2 tablespoons of the basil puree on top of each bowl of pasta. Serve immediately.

favoritevariations

■ Add 1 cup defrosted frozen peas to mixture when you add the pancetta.

■ Drain the skillet you cook the pancetta in of all but 1 teaspoon grease. Place over high heat, add ½ cup dry white wine and a garlic clove, thinly sliced, and cook for about 5 minutes, or until the wine has reduced somewhat. Let cool for 1 or 2 minutes and whisk into the egg mixture.

spaghetti and **three-meat meatballs**

SERVES 4 TO 6

We don't like to boast, but when it comes to meatballs you'd be hard-pressed to find better ones than these. A combination of ground beef, pork, and veal mixed with grated Parmesan cheese and herbs, these large meatballs are coated in bread crumbs and cooked in hot olive oil until a crisp, crunchy crust forms on the outside and the meatball is tender and juicy inside. We then make a simple tomato sauce right in the meatball pan, and serve the meatballs and sauce poured over spaghetti or linguine.

The meatballs and sauce can be made up to a day ahead of time and refrigerated. Reheat over a low gentle flame while you boil the water for the pasta. You can also make the meatballs and sauce and simply serve them as an appetizer with crusty Italian bread, or make a meatball hero sandwich.

for the meatballs

2 large eggs
8 ounces ground beef, preferably ground round
8 ounces ground pork
1/2 pound ground veal
1 cup packed freshly grated Parmesan cheese
3 garlic cloves, very thinly sliced
1/2 cup finely sliced fresh basil leaves
1 3/4 cups plain bread crumbs
1/2 cup milk
2 tablespoons minced fresh rosemary leaves
Salt and freshly ground black pepper
1/4 cup olive oil

for the tomato sauce and pasta

1 cup dry red wine
One 26-ounce can whole peeled tomatoes, preferably with basil
1/2 cup thinly sliced fresh basil leaves
2 garlic cloves, very thinly sliced
1 tablespoon tomato paste
1/2 cup finely chopped fresh parsley leaves
1 bay leaf
Salt and freshly ground black pepper
1 pound spaghetti or linguine
1 cup freshly grated Parmesan cheese

To make the meatballs: In a large bowl, whisk the eggs. Using your hands (see page 190) or, if you insist, a large metal spoon, mix in the ground beef, pork, and veal until well combined into the egg. Add the cheese, garlic, basil, and 3/4 cup of the bread crumbs and mix until well incorporated. Add the milk, rosemary, a generous dash of salt, and pepper and make sure the meatball mixture is fully integrated.

Place the remaining 1 cup of bread crumbs on a large plate or in a bowl. Using your hands, form the meat mixture into 16 meatballs, each about 2 inches across. Roll each meatball in the bread crumbs to coat on all sides.

Heat two large skillets over medium-high heat. Divide the olive oil between the skillets and let it get hot, but not smoking. Divide the meatballs between the two skillets and cook for

RECIPE CONTINUES ▶

6 minutes until browned. Using tongs, gently flip the meatballs over and cook for another 6 minutes to brown the other sides. (If just making the meatballs without the sauce, cook another 6 to 10 minutes, or until the meatballs are crusty on the outside and there is no sign of pink inside.)

To make the sauce: Remove excess grease from both skillets. Divide the wine and pour into the skillets; let simmer for 2 minutes. Meanwhile, break up the tomatoes with your hands (see page 61), or use a small, sharp knife and divide between the skillets. Divide the basil, garlic, tomato paste, 1 cup of water, and half the parsley into both skillets and mix well. Add the bay leaf to one skillet and season both with salt and pepper to taste; let simmer over very low heat, stirring occasionally, for 1 hour. Remove the bay leaf and taste for seasoning. The meatballs and sauce can be made a day ahead of time; cover and refrigerate until ready to serve.

Bring a large pot of lightly salted water to a boil over high heat. Add the pasta and cook for about 10 to 12 minutes, depending on the thickness of the pasta, until al dente, or almost tender. (Reheat the meatballs and sauce over low heat if you made them ahead of time. Add about $^1/_4$ cup of the pasta water if the sauce seems too thick.) Drain the pasta and place in a large serving plate or bowl. Top with the meatballs and sauce and toss gently. Sprinkle with the remaining $^1/_4$ cup parsley. Pass the cheese separately.

favoritevariations

- Add $^1/_2$ pound ground lamb instead of the beef, pork, or veal.
- Add $^1/_2$ cup toasted chopped pine nuts (see page 260) to the meatball mixture.
- Add 2 tablespoons chopped fresh thyme leaves instead of rosemary to the meatball mixture.

cleaning and storing herbs

give it a whirl

One of the best ways to clean a bunch of fresh herbs is to remove the stems from the herbs and soak the leaves in a bowl of cold water to remove any dirt clinging to the leaves. Rinse the herbs under cold water and drain. Place the herbs in a salad spinner and spin until totally dry. Moisture causes herbs to deteriorate quickly.

To store herbs, place them on several sheets of paper towel and gently roll them up into a loose fat cigar shape. Then place the herbs in a plastic bag and store in the refrigerator for several days, depending on the freshness of the herbs. You can then use the herbs whole or chopped, or tie the stems into bundles with kitchen string and add to soups, stews, and sauces. Don't store fresh herbs directly in plastic bags or they will "sweat" and won't stay fresh nearly as long.

four-cheese macaroni with
thyme-parmesan crust

SERVES 6 TO 8

Trust us, this is not your ordinary mac and cheese. When you add fresh mozzarella, Fontina, Parmesan, and mascarpone cheeses to pasta something out of the ordinary happens. We also add a layer of fresh mozzarella in the middle of the pasta dish, for the ultimate cheese experience, and scatter a mixture of grated Parmesan, thyme, and bread crumbs on top for a crunchy topping. You can make the dish in one large skillet, or baking dish, or make it in individual ramekins, but you'll need to reduce the baking time. The dish can be assembled up to 2 hours ahead of time and baked just before serving.

1 pound short, textured pasta, such as
   macaroni, cavatappi, ziti rigate, or penne
   rigate
1 tablespoon unsalted butter
2 tablespoons olive oil
3 tablespoons all-purpose flour
3 cups milk, warmed
12 ounces fresh mozzarella cheese, half
   grated and half very thinly sliced
   (about 3 cups total)

1 cup freshly grated Parmesan cheese
8 ounces Fontina cheese, grated (about
   2 cups)
¼ cup mascarpone cheese
Salt and freshly ground black pepper
2 tablespoons plus 2 teaspoons chopped
   fresh thyme leaves
½ cup plain bread crumbs

Place a rack in the middle of the oven and preheat oven to 400°F.

Bring a large pot of lightly salted water to boil over high heat. Add the pasta and cook until barely al dente, 7 to 9 minutes. Drain, return to the pot, and set aside.

Meanwhile, melt the butter in a medium saucepan with 1 tablespoon of the olive oil over low heat. When the butter has melted completely and begins to sizzle, add the flour and whisk until combined. Cook, stirring constantly, until the mixture begins to bubble, about 1 minute. Add half of the warm milk in a slow, steady stream, whisking until the mixture is smooth and begins to thicken, about 2 minutes. Add the remaining milk, whisk again until smooth, and increase the heat to medium high, stirring frequently, until the mixture comes to a boil. Remove the sauce from heat and add the grated mozzarella and half of the Parmesan, and all of the Fontina and mascarpone, whisking constantly to prevent the cheese from becoming lumpy. When the sauce is completely smooth, add salt and pepper to taste and 2 tablespoons of the thyme.

Pour the sauce over the pasta in the pot and stir to combine completely. Spoon half of the pasta into a large ovenproof skillet, or a roughly 9 × 12-inch baking dish or several smaller dishes (ramekins work really well) and arrange the mozzarella slices evenly over the pasta. Pour the remaining pasta over the cheese layer and spread evenly.

Mix the remaining Parmesan cheese, the remaining 2 teaspoons thyme, and the bread

crumbs together in a small bowl. Sprinkle the mixture evenly over the top of the pasta. Drizzle the remaining tablespoon olive oil evenly over the crust.

Bake the pasta for 30 to 40 minutes (smaller dishes will bake in 15 to 20 minutes), or until the cheese is bubbly and the crust is golden brown. Serve hot.

favoritevariations

- Substitute Gruyère, Emmenthaler, or Swiss cheese for the Fontina.
- Substitute crumbled fresh goat cheese for the mascarpone.
- Add 1 cup chopped cooked ham or chicken to the sauce before pouring over the pasta.
- Add $\frac{1}{2}$ cup chopped scallions (white and green parts) or finely chopped yellow onion to the cheese sauce.
- Add $\frac{1}{4}$ cup chopped parsley leaves, $\frac{1}{4}$ cup chopped chives, and 2 tablespoons chopped rosemary leaves to the cheese sauce.
- Add the Basil Swirl (page 233) to the middle of the casserole along with the mozzarella for a gorgeous green layer and vibrant basil flavor.

a few of our favorite cheeses

There are few cheeses that we don't like. In fact, we use cheese just about every day in every imaginable dish—over eggs and in omelets, melted on toast, sprinkled into savory muffins and pancakes, dips, sandwiches, casseroles, tacos, burritos. . . . Well, you get the point. What follows are just a few of our favorite varieties:

ASIAGO Some call this "the poor man's Parmesan," but we think it has its own special qualities. A hard, cow's milk cheese made in Italy, Asiago has a slightly sharp, fruity flavor and a dry, granular texture. It's a great choice for grilled cheese or panini sandwiches (page 98), grated and tossed with salads, or for grating over soups and stews.

BLUE CHEESE Who would think we could be so passionate about a cheese that is riddled with mold? These blue-veined cheeses are actually inoculated or sprayed with spores of the mold *Penicillium roqueforti* or *Penicillium glaucum*. Holes are formed that allow the spores to penetrate the cheese during the aging process, causing a blue or green mold to form. Whether it's Roquefort, Maytag Blue, Stilton, or Gorgonzola, we adore the full flavor, creamy, and often tangy, spicy flavor that blues offer. Roquefort is considered "king of the blues," made only from the milk of specially bred sheep and ripened in limestone caves. All blues become stronger and drier in texture as they age. Crumbled over greens (page 91), in salad dressings (page 90), sandwiches (pages 94–109), or served with pears, apples, figs, melon, walnuts, and almonds are among our favorite ways to eat blue cheese. We also love making a dip with it to serve with Baked Buffalo Chicken Wings (page 237) and drizzle over crisp Romaine or Buttercrunch lettuce leaves.

BRIE A wedge of truly ripe French brie with its white rind and its almost oozing interior is something we find hard to resist. Brie offers complex flavors (some say there is a definite hazelnut aftertaste) and that famous creamy texture, making it the ideal choice for any cheese plate. We like to thinly slice it and serve it with salads, on croûtes (page 165), in panini sandwiches (page 98), egg dishes, on top of polenta and with burgers (both melted on top and chopped into the ground meat mixture). We love serving a whole wheel or large wedge of Brie lightly sprinkled with dried cranberries, cherries, raisins, and golden raisins, and with toasted nuts such as walnuts, hazelnuts, almonds, pine nuts, and pistachios. The dried fruit offers a chewy texture and a kick of acidity, creating a great contrast to the rich Brie, and the nuts provide a fresh crunch.

CAMEMBERT This cow's milk cheese, with its white rind and creamy Brie-like interior, can be used much like Brie. A really ripe Camembert practically oozes and can be spread on crackers, French bread, apple and pear slices, and so much more. Try baking a small Camembert directly in the wooden box it arrives in: Remove the cheese from the paper coating. Cut off the top rind and place the cheese back into the wooden box. Place the box on a doubled-over sheet of aluminum foil and bake at 350°F until the center is soft and gooey, about 15 minutes. Serve this Camembert "fondue" with cubes of French bread, Polenta Croutons (page 164), and assorted raw vegetables.

CHEDDAR Although we associate cheddar with New England, its origins are found in the village of Cheddar in the Somerset region of England. This firm cow's milk cheese is just about the most versatile we know—not to mention the fact that it's the most popular cheese in the world. It can be grated, shredded, eaten in slices, melted into sauces or a soup, used to make amazing grilled cheese sandwiches (page 98), and so much more. Ranging in color from pale

(CONTINUED) ▶

white to a deep yellow (and artificially colored to be bright orange), its flavor span goes from mild and creamy to bitingly sharp and dry.

EMMANTHALER OR EMMENTHAL This traditional Swiss-made cheese (named for the Emmenthal Valley in the central part of Switzerland where it's made) has a wonderful fruity flavor and sweet aroma that some compare to hay. Its beige-yellow rind is hard and thin and protects a pale-colored cheese that comes with holes the size of a nickel. Its mellow, nutty flavor goes with all sorts of foods, and it's delicious melted. It's also produced in France.

FETA This well-known Greek cheese can be so good when it's fresh and well handled and so bland and tasteless when it's not. Traditionally made from sheep's milk (often mixed with goat's milk), it is now often prepared with pasteurized cow's milk cheese. We think sheep's milk feta has a far superior flavor. Feta often comes sold floating in salted water (brine) which keeps it fresh and moist. You should always drain the water before using to avoid a cheese that tastes overly salty. The texture and flavor of feta varies widely. It is a white-as-snow cheese without a rind that can be creamy or crumbly and soft or semidry. It has a rich, tangy flavor and is the classic ingredient in a Greek salad (see page 88 for our version).

FONTINA One of Italy's prized cow's milk cheeses, Fontina comes from the Val d'Aosta region of the Italian Alps. Prized for its semifirm texture and smooth, dense, slightly creamy interior, its flavor is hard to pin down. Some of the more common descriptions of Fontina are honey-like and nutty with a subtle essence of mushrooms. Fontina is also made in this country, France, and Denmark, but the Italian variety is considered the most flavorful. Serve with ripe fruit, crusty bread, or in panini sandwiches (page 98).

GOAT CHEESE (CHÈVRE) The smooth, tangy flavor of goat cheese has turned us into addicts. We sprinkle it on salads, breakfast eggs, omelets, in quiche and vegetable tarts, and even mac and cheese (Variations on page 149). We make a quick dip for raw vegetables by blending soft goat cheese with fresh herbs and a touch of milk and olive oil. Other days we surround a whole log with sun-dried tomatoes and thin slices of leek or onion and pop it in a 350°F oven until it just starts to melt and serve it with a crunchy baguette. And we also use it to stuff chicken (see page 175) and crumble into soups; we even like to make cheesecake with goat cheese (see Variations on page 266).

GOUDA The famed Dutch cheese was named for the eponymous town located outside Rotterdam. A hard, cow's milk cheese with a smooth texture and sweet, fruity flavor, like all cheeses, it becomes more intense and sharp as it ages. Mild Goudas are aged for just a few months, while extra-aged Goudas can be aged for up to 5 years! Gouda is delicious melted in sandwiches and panini (page 98), on burgers (page 193), layered in scalloped potatoes, or served with a selection of ripe fruit.

GRUYÈRE Made in the French-speaking region of Switzerland, Gruyère is a hard, cow's milk cheese with a grainy texture and nutty, complex flavor. We love eating it with fruit (particularly pears), putting it in grilled cheese sandwiches (page 98), or using it for cheese croûtes (page 165). Gruyère is also a great base for a fondue, soufflé, savory tart, omelet, or frittata (page 33).

MANCHEGO A new Spanish favorite of ours, Manchego is named for the Spanish region of La Mancha, home of Don Quixote. Made from pasteurized sheep's milk, Manchego offers a briny, nutty flavor that develops a kind of peppery bite as it ages. When it's 13 weeks old or younger it's sold as *curado*, or cured; Manchego aged over

3 months is referred to as *viejo* (aged). Traditionally paired with quince paste (*membrillo*), we eat this cheese for breakfast on toast, drizzled lightly with a flowery honey and served with fresh fruit.

MOZZARELLA Fresh, smooth mozzarella, the classic pizza ingredient, has become something of a superstar in this country. Its elastic texture (we mean that in the kindest sense of the word) and creamy, briny flavor makes it equally good served fresh or cooked. We like to thinly slice fresh mozzarella and layer it between slices of eggplant, ripe tomato, and basil leaves, and bake at 400°F until the vegetables are brown and tender and the cheese is bubbling, about 1 hour. We thinly slice it and layer it on pizza and in grilled cheese (page 98), tarts, macaroni and cheese (page 148), lasagna, and so much more. Buffalo mozzarella is a particularly soft, flavorful mozzarella made from buffalo's milk.

MONTEREY JACK (OR JACK CHEESE) This semisoft, mild cheese is a true American—made by the Vella family since 1931. Made from cow's milk, primarily in the Sonoma region of California, it is sold unaged and aged (or dry). Unaged Jack is soft and moist and excellent for melting in sandwiches, panini (page 98), macaroni and cheese (page 148) and sauces. Aged Monterey Jack is firm with a shaper, nutty flavor.

PARMESAN As far we're concerned, this is one of the world's greatest cheeses. If you've only experienced pregrated Parmesan cheese you really haven't tasted Parmesan. While costly, there are few cheeses as full flavored and nuanced as a piece of authentic cow's milk Parmigiano-Reggiano. When we call for Parmesan cheese in this book, we are hoping you will seek out the real thing. Look for the words "Parmigiano-Reggiano" stenciled on the rind. There are imitations of Parmesan made in Argentina, the United States, and Australia, and while some of them are quite tasty, none can truly compare. Real Parmigiano-Reggiano, which comes from the region around Parma, Italy, is aged for several years until it obtains its unique granular texture and sweet, delicate, nutty flavor. We eat chunks of it with fresh figs, prosciutto, crusty bread, and a good Italian olive oil. We even save the rind to flavor soups.

RICOTTA Most of us know ricotta as the soft, mild cheese you layer in lasagna. Ricotta (which means "recooked") has a fabulous creamy flavor and smooth, slightly grainy texture and is great used for grilled cheese (page 98), mac and cheese (page 148), and for stuffing crepes or pasta. Ricotta salata is a hard, sheep's milk cheese that is excellent thinly sliced and paired with beets, salads, or fruit and bread.

SWISS Many cheeses are sold under the heading "Swiss cheese," but most of them are fairly flavorless and have the texture of wax. Modeled after Swiss-made Emmenthal, the term *Swiss cheese* refers to a large, generic category of cheese made in the United States. It's pale yellow, made from cow's milk, and has distinctive large holes. Good Swiss cheese has a sweet, mild, nutty flavor that makes it an ideal choice for any sandwich or for melting.

cheese

buying, storing, and serving tips

You buy a wedge of cheddar, a small wheel of Brie, and a chunk of Parmesan cheese, bring it home, and pop it in the cheese drawer of your refrigerator. But within a week the cheese has lost its fresh taste and there are signs of mold on the cheddar. Shouldn't cheese last longer than a week? Is there a right way to store cheese that you don't know about?

BUYING It all starts at the store. Always shop for cheese from a reputable cheese shop or a food store that sells lots of cheese and won't have it sitting around for a long time. Ask for cheese freshly cut from the wheel or block, as opposed to precut cheese that has been wrapped in plastic for an indefinite amount of time.

STORAGE The most important thing to remember about cheese is that it continues to age even after you bring it home so having the right storage conditions can make the difference between perfect cheese and moldy, overripe cheese.

Cheese can be successfully stored in the refrigerator for several weeks, ideally at 45° to 60°F. If you bought the cheese at a grocery store chances are good that it's tightly wrapped in plastic. Wrapping cheese directly in plastic doesn't allow it to breathe. Unwrap the cheese and wrap it tightly in parchment (or wax) paper and then double wrap it in aluminum foil. If you are worried about keeping stinky odors away from other foods in your refrigerator (as in blue cheese and ultraripe triple-crème cheeses), place the wrapped cheese in a lidded plastic container. The cheese should be stored in your refrigerator's cheese or vegetable compartment.

MOLD ISSUES If mold appears on any firm, semifirm, or semisoft cheese (as opposed to blue cheese or any other cheese that is supposed to be covered in an edible mold), do not throw it away. You can simply cut away the offending portion (plus a little extra) and discard. Any mold seen on fresh or soft-ripened cheese, however, signals that it should be thrown out.

FREEZING CHEESE This is possible but not a great idea. Frozen cheese tends to lose its unique texture, and in some cases its flavor as well. We sometimes freeze small pieces of cheese (usually leftover grated hard cheese) and find it's best to thaw the cheese thoroughly and use it cooked, rather than raw.

SERVING TEMPERATURE When serving cheese be sure to bring it to room temperature about 30 minutes to an hour before serving so all the flavors will have a chance to shine.

PUTTING TOGETHER A CHEESE PLATTER Think about serving 2 to 4 cheeses (unless you're having a really big party or a cheese and wine party in which case you could serve 8 to 10 types of cheese). Offer a good mix of hard cheeses along with soft cheeses: balance cow's milk with goat and sheep's milk cheeses. You could also think about offering a selection of all American-made cheeses, an exclusive French or Italian cheese selection, or a tasting of all goat cheeses or all blue cheeses. Arrange cheeses on grape leaves or a wooden or marble board, accompanied by slices of apples, pears, figs (fresh or dried), or melon wedges. Serve an assortment of nuts and dried fruit (cranberries, cherries, raisins, and apricots), assorted crackers, breadsticks, crusty bread, and biscuits and let everyone taste and discover new favorites, encouraging them to go for the stronger cheeses such as Roquefort and Gorgonzola last.

potato pancakes with horseradish-dill crème fraîche and smoked trout

MAKES ABOUT 12 TO 15 PANCAKES

This unusual appetizer combines small, bite-size potato pancakes with an herb-cream sauce and slivers of smoked fish. Make the potato pancakes ahead of time and reheat in a low oven. These pancakes are also delicious served at a brunch with Champagne mixed with fresh squeezed orange or pomegranate juice.

for the pancakes
2 large baking potatoes, peeled
1 large egg
Salt and freshly ground black pepper
1 cup vegetable oil or shortening

for the crème fraîche and smoked trout:
½ cup crème fraîche, sour cream, or plain yogurt
1 tablespoon drained prepared horseradish
1½ teaspoons minced fresh dill plus dill sprigs for garnish
Freshly ground black pepper
4 ounces smoked trout, flaked

Using the small holes of a box-style grater, grate the potatoes into a large bowl. Let the grated potatoes sit for about 15 minutes so they release their water. Pick up a handful of the potatoes and, using your hands, squeeze the potatoes to release all the moisture from them. Place the squeezed out potatoes in a separate bowl. Pour off all the water remaining from the potato bowl, making sure *not* to discard the thick brown substance at the bottom of the bowl; this is potato starch and it is the secret to delicious, light, fluffy potato pancakes.

To make the crème fraîche and trout: Mix the crème fraîche, horseradish, chopped dill, and pepper to taste in a small bowl; cover and refrigerate until ready to serve. Separate the trout into small flakes.

Add the egg to the bowl with the remaining potato starch and beat well. Season with salt and pepper. Add the squeezed out potatoes and mix until well incorporated.

In a large, heavy skillet, heat the oil over high heat. Let it get hot; it's ready when you add a tiny bit of the potato mixture and it immediately sizzles. Using a tablespoon, form 1½-inch-wide pancakes and carefully add them to the skillet, making sure not to crowd the pan. You may need to turn the heat down a bit so the pancakes don't burn. Use a spatula to push down on the pancakes to flatten them out a bit. Cook for 2 to 3 minutes on each side, or until golden brown and cooked through. Drain on paper towels. Repeat until you've used all of the potato mixture.

The pancakes can be served immediately or made several hours ahead of time and reheated on a cookie sheet in a 275°F oven until hot, about 10 minutes. To serve, sprinkle some trout and a dollop of crème fraîche on top of each pancake. Garnish with a dill sprig.

favoritevariation
■ Use smoked salmon, bluefish, or mackerel instead of smoked trout.

twice-baked potatoes with
chive-scallion-pancetta stuffing

SERVES 4 TO 8

All three of us grew up with this favorite of the 1950s—a baked potato with the filling scraped out, mixed with sour cream and spices, and then restuffed back into the potato shell. This modern adaptation combines the potato with sour cream, tangy blue cheese, crunchy green scallions, chives, and smoky Italian pancetta or bacon. What we love most about these potatoes is that they can be made entirely ahead of time (making them classic party food) and reheated just before serving. And the ideas for flavor variations are endless; see below.

2¾ pounds baking potatoes (about 4 large)
5 ounces thinly sliced pancetta or thick slab bacon (about 5 slices)
¾ cup sour cream
½ cup plus ⅓ cup crumbled good-quality blue cheese

½ cup plus 2 tablespoons milk
4 scallions (white and green parts), finely chopped
2 tablespoons minced chives
2 tablespoons olive oil
Salt and freshly ground black pepper

Place a rack in the middle of the oven and preheat the oven to 400°F.

Poke several holes in the potatoes and place on a cookie sheet. Bake for about 1 hour, or until just soft when pierced with a small, sharp knife. Remove from the oven and set aside until cool enough to handle.

Meanwhile, cook the pancetta in a large skillet over medium heat until crisp on both sides, 10 to 12 minutes depending on the thickness of the meat. Remove and drain on paper towels. Crumble the pancetta or bacon and set aside.

Cut the potatoes in half lengthwise and using a small spoon, remove the flesh from each potato half, leaving the skin intact to act later as a container for the filling. Place the potato flesh in a small bowl and mash it with a fork or potato masher. Add the sour cream, ½ cup of the blue cheese, the milk, scallions, chives, half of the pancetta, the olive oil, and salt and pepper to taste. Mix well.

Place the potato skins in a large shallow baking dish. Spoon the filling back into the potato shells, mounding it up. Top each potato half with some of the remaining pancetta and blue cheese. Sprinkle the top with a good grinding of pepper. The dish can be covered and refrigerated for several hours before baking.

Bake for 30 to 35 minutes, or until the stuffing is hot throughout.

favoritevariations

- Substitute goat cheese for the blue cheese.
- Substitute grated Parmesan or cheddar for the blue cheese.
- Add buttermilk instead of regular milk.
- Omit the pancetta or bacon.
- Add a dash of hot sauce or chopped chile peppers to the stuffing.
- Add roasted or chopped raw garlic cloves to the stuffing.
- Add ½ cup finely chopped roasted red pepper to the stuffing.
- Add chopped fresh herbs such as basil, thyme, rosemary, chervil, or lavender to the stuffing.

grown-up **potato puffs**

MAKES 25 TO 30 POTATO PUFFS; SERVES 6 TO 8

We have particularly strong memories of Tater Tots as a childhood favorite—those little frozen potato treats with soft, creamy mashed potatoes on the inside and a crunchy outside. Our mothers would take them out of the box, pop them in the oven for 10 minutes, and we had instant comfort food.

Our version is just a bit more sophisticated, and just a touch more labor intensive, but guaranteed to bring back a rush of warm childhood feelings and a deep sense of comfort. Here mashed potatoes are mixed with tangy Roquefort cheese (you could use virtually any cheese you like) and shaped into little nuggets, dipped in a seasoned egg mixture, and then lightly coated in Japanese panko flakes (bread crumbs). Then we bake them until golden brown and slightly crunchy on the outside.

The good news is that these potato treats can be made up to a day ahead of time, placed on a cookie sheet, and baked 15 minutes before you're ready to eat them. Alternatively, you can also freeze these on a cookie sheet until hard and then transfer them to an airtight container and keep them in the freezer for up to 2 weeks. To cook the frozen ones, increase the baking time to 20 to 25 minutes, turning them once.

Serve with Tenderloin of Beef with a Horseradish Crust (on page 195), Best Roast Chicken (page 173), on top of a frisée or mixed green salad, or as an hors d'oeuvre with cocktails.

1½ pounds baking potatoes (about 2 large), peeled and quartered
2 tablespoons unsalted butter
½ cup milk
3 ounces Roquefort cheese, crumbled (about ⅓ cup)

Salt and freshly ground black pepper
2 large eggs
2 cups panko (see Note, page 116), or plain bread crumbs
Flour for your hands (if needed)

Bring a medium pot of water to boil over high heat. Add the potatoes and cook for 14 to 16 minutes, or until just tender when tested with a fork. Drain the potatoes.

Place the potatoes back into the pot and mash with a potato masher until smooth (or use a ricer). Over very low heat, add the butter and milk and mash until light and creamy, about 2 minutes. Remove from the heat, add the cheese, and season with salt and pepper. Let cool slightly. You can also transfer the mixture to a bowl and let cool in the refrigerator for about 30 minutes if you're in a rush.

In a shallow bowl, whisk the eggs until blended, and season them with salt and pepper. Place the panko on a large plate.

Lightly flour your hands and form a heaping 2 tablespoons of the mashed potato mixture into a cylindrical shape and place on a cookie sheet. Set aside and repeat with the remaining potato mixture. You should have 25 to 30 potato puffs.

Dip one of the potato puffs into the egg mixture, coating lightly on all sides. Then dip the potato in the panko until coated on all sides. Place on a cookie sheet, and repeat with the remaining potato puffs. Cover loosely, and refrigerate for at least 1 hour and up to 8 hours before baking.

Preheat the oven to 400·F.

Bake the potato puffs for about 15 minutes, gently turning the potatoes once during baking, or until light golden brown, crisp, and hot throughout.

favoritevariations

- Substitute grated or cubed Parmesan, Manchego, sharp cheddar, or your favorite hard cheese, or a soft crumbled goat cheese for the Roquefort.
- Add 1 tablespoon minced fresh herbs to the potato mixture.
- Add 2 minced garlic cloves and ¼ cup chopped fresh chives to the potato mixture.
- Sprinkle the potato puffs with coarse sea salt before baking.

ultimate **mashed potatoes**

Mashed potatoes should win some sort of award for withstanding every culinary trend that has passed through the decades. This recipe is for the rich, classic, creamy, buttery kind of mashed potatoes, the ultimate comfort food that goes with nearly everything. Eat them plain, enjoy them with roasts and grilled foods, or serve them with holiday or everyday meals. We also like to top pot pies (made with beef, chicken, lamb, seafood, or simply vegetables) with a "crust" of mashed potatoes rather than pastry.

You'll notice the amounts of milk and cream in this recipe vary. The amount you add will depend on exactly how creamy and decadent you like your potatoes to be. Start with the low measures, taste, and then add more.

3 pounds medium Yukon gold potatoes (5 to 6 large), peeled and cut in half

¼ cup (½ stick) unsalted butter

1 to 1½ cups milk

½ to ¾ cup heavy cream

Salt and freshly ground black pepper

Bring a large pot of water to a rolling boil over high heat. Add the potatoes and cook for 20 to 25 minutes, or until the potatoes feel tender when tested in the center with a small, sharp knife. Drain the potatoes thoroughly.

Place the potatoes back into the pot over very low heat and add the butter. Using a potato masher, mash the potatoes working in the butter. (Alternatively, use a ricer to puree the potatoes, place them back into the pot and then add the butter.) Slowly add 1 cup of the milk and ½ cup of the cream, mashing and stirring. We are of the strong belief that mashed potatoes should have some lumps, so mash until *almost* smooth. Add salt and pepper to taste and add additional milk and cream as needed.

favoritevariations

- **Bacon-Chive Mashed Potatoes:** At the very end, add 4 to 6 crumbled pieces of crisp, cooked bacon or pancetta (see page 205 for more on bacon and pancetta) and ⅓ cup minced fresh chives.

- **Wasabi Mashed Potatoes:** At the very end, add 1 to 2 teaspoons prepared wasabi (Japanese green horseradish) to taste. The potatoes will be spicy.

- **Scallion-Herb Potatoes:** At the very end, stir in ½ cup thinly sliced scallions (white and green parts) and ½ cup chopped fresh herbs such as basil, rosemary, oregano, chervil, thyme, or chives.

- **Roast Garlic and Olive Oil Potatoes:** Add roasted garlic (see page 161) and mash the potatoes. Substitute olive oil for the butter.

- **Cheesy Potatoes:** Add ½ to 1 cup grated cheese or crumbled goat, feta, or blue cheese at the end.

roasting garlic

When you roast garlic it becomes sweet and mellow rather than assertive, and there are few better scents in the world than a head of garlic roasting in your oven. Use roasted garlic mashed into potatoes (page 160); in pasta dishes and sauces; spread on crusty bread; and in dips, stews, casseroles, and sandwiches—virtually anywhere you'd like a garlic flavor without the power of raw garlic.

Place a rack in the middle of the oven and preheat the oven to 400°F. Cut an eighth of an inch off the top of the garlic and place in a small ovenproof skillet. Drizzle the garlic with 1 to 2 teaspoons olive oil and a grinding of pepper. Roast for about 25 to 45 minutes, depending on the freshness and size of the garlic. The garlic is done when it is very soft. Let cool and then squeeze the garlic out of its skin.

herbed **bread and celery stuffing**

SERVES 8 TO 10

There is enough stuffing here to fill a 10- to 12-pound turkey (or several chickens) and have enough leftover to fill a good-size baking dish. The stuffing can be made several hours ahead of time, but you should *never* stuff a bird until just before you are ready to roast it.

The most important element in this stuffing is the bread. This is the time to use up those small bits and pieces hiding out in the refrigerator or freezer or sitting around in bakery bags. The better the quality bread you use, the better the final stuffing will be. We like to use a wide variety of bread for this stuffing—bits of chopped up baguette, sourdough, pumpernickel, white bread, whole wheat, ciabatta—quite literally anything and everything we have around. Do keep in mind that there is a big difference between bread that has been sitting around a few days and is beginning to dry out and bread that is way past its prime; avoid any bread that is moldy or smells off.

2 tablespoons unsalted butter

1 tablespoon olive oil

3 medium onions, chopped

6 garlic cloves, thinly sliced

2 tablespoons chopped fresh thyme leaves, or 2 teaspoons dried, crumbled

Salt and freshly ground black pepper

5 stalks celery, chopped

½ cup very thinly sliced fresh basil leaves

1½ cups chopped fresh parsley leaves

10 cups cubed bread

1 cup milk

In a large skillet, heat 1 tablespoon of the butter and the olive oil over medium-low heat. When the butter has melted and begins to sizzle, add the onions and garlic and cook, stirring, for about 8 minutes, or until the onions are soft. Season with half the thyme and some salt and pepper. Add the celery, and half of the basil and half of the parsley, and cook for 5 minutes, stirring frequently, or until the celery is just beginning to soften. The celery should still have somewhat of a crunch.

Meanwhile, place the bread in a large bowl, and mix in the remaining thyme, basil, and parsley. Pour the celery mixture from the skillet on top of the bread and gently toss to mix all of the ingredients. Place the skillet back over a low heat and add the milk and the remaining tablespoon butter and simmer for 2 to 4 minutes, using a spatula to scrape up any bits and pieces clinging to the bottom of the skillet. Pour the hot milk mixture over the bread and toss; the stuffing should be somewhat moist. Season to taste.

If making the stuffing more than an hour ahead of time, cover and refrigerate until you are ready to stuff the bird. The stuffing can also be placed in a lightly greased baking dish or casserole and baked at 350°F. for 15 to 20 minutes, or until hot throughout. If possible, baste with some of the turkey juices from the bottom of the turkey pan to keep the stuffing moist.

favoritevariations

- Add 1 pound coarsely chopped shucked fresh oysters to the skillet when the celery is nearly done and cook for about 2 minutes. They will add a rich, subtle, briny flavor.
- Add 1 cup toasted chopped walnuts (see page 260) or your favorite nuts when you add the celery.
- Add 1 cup thinly sliced peeled fresh water chestnuts when you add the celery.
- Add ½ cup coarsely chopped dried cranberries, cherries, or raisins when you add the celery.
- Add 1 pound sausage meat, removed from the casing, when you add the onions to the skillet.
- Substitute cubed cornbread for regular bread.

polenta **croutons**

Where is it written that all croutons must be made from leftover bread? Why not experiment with squares of polenta to make a cornmeal crouton to serve with salads, soups, stews, or to top a casserole? We spread cooked instant polenta into a pan, let it chill for an hour or so, and then cut the cold polenta into little squares. (This, we discovered, can all be done hours ahead of time.) We then brushed the squares with olive oil and placed them under the broiler until they were golden, crisp, and hot. The consensus: Why didn't we think of this years ago?

We love these croutons served on top of Coq au Vin with Cippoline Onions (page 181), on top of salads, New England Five-Onion Soup (page 64), or dipped into cheese fondue. You also might want to consider cutting the polenta into 2- to 3-inch squares and topping with a good, simmering tomato sauce.

Salt	1½ cups instant polenta
4 tablespoons olive oil	Freshly ground pepper

Bring 5¼ cups water to a boil over high heat in a large saucepan. Add 1 teaspoon salt and 1 tablespoon of the olive oil. Pour the polenta into the boiling water in a slow, steady stream, using a whisk to stir the polenta as you add it. Reduce the heat to low, and cook the polenta, whisking, for 3 minutes. Remove the polenta from the heat, cover, and let sit for 5 minutes.

Grease a 12 × 8-inch rimmed baking sheet or a 9 × 13-inch baking pan with 1 tablespoon of the olive oil. Transfer the polenta to the pan, and use a large, flat spatula to spread the polenta evenly into the pan. Let the polenta cool to room temperature, then refrigerate until chilled, about 1 hour.

Preheat the broiler.

Cut the polenta into 1-inch cubes and place on a baking sheet. Drizzle the polenta with the remaining 2 tablespoons olive oil, and season with salt and pepper, turning the squares gently to cover all sides in the oil and seasonings. Broil for 3 to 5 minutes, or until the polenta squares are light golden brown and crisp. Gently flip over and broil for another 3 to 5 minutes, until golden and hot. Serve immediately or chilled for up to 3 days and reheat for 5 minutes in a 400°F oven just before serving.

favoritevariations

- Add 2 tablespoons minced garlic to the water with the salt and olive oil when you cook the polenta.
- Add 1 cup freshly grated Parmesan cheese to the polenta just before you pour it onto the baking pan.

cheese croûtes

When we use the term *croûtes* we are referring to toasted slices of crusty bread in the shape of an oversize crouton. These crisp, cheesy croûtes are the perfect accompaniment to our Ultimate Lemon Caesar Salad (page 72). We also love to serve them with soups, stews, or roasts. They make a great side dish to salads, particularly those made with sharp greens like watercress and arugula. In fact, they are so tasty you could serve them as a snack with cocktails.

MAKES 12 CROÛTES

12 slices bread from a baguette, sourdough, ciabatta, or any loaf of crusty bread, ¼ inch thick
¼ cup olive oil
¾ cup packed freshy grated Parmesan, cheddar, Swiss, Manchego, soft goat, blue cheese, Gruyère, or any one of your favorite cheeses (see page 150)
Freshly ground black pepper

Place a rack in the middle of the oven and preheat the oven to 350°F.

Place the bread slices on a cookie sheet. Using a pastry brush or the back of a spoon, brush the toasts with half of the olive oil. Bake for 5 minutes. Sprinkle with half of the cheese and bake for another 3 to 4 minutes or until the cheese is melted.

Gently flip the toasts over and brush with the remaining oil. Bake for 5 minutes. Sprinkle with the remaining cheese and sprinkle the top of the toasts with pepper. Serve warm or at room temperature.

The croûtes can be made a day ahead of time; cover and place in a tightly sealed tin or plastic bag.

olive and anchovy toasts

MAKES 16 TOASTS

Wonderfully pungent, these toasts are not for the faint of heart. These flavors are the essence of Mediterranean cooking—lusty anchovies mixed with full-flavored briny olives. Serve these toasts with our Chopped Greek Salad (page 88) or on their own as an hors d'oeuvre. You can also use the anchovy toast as the basis for sandwiches or just make the topping (without the bread) and mix it with linguine for a quick pasta dish.

8 slices white bread
5 tablespoons extra-virgin olive oil
4 to 6 anchovy fillets

1 cup finely chopped Kalamata olives
Freshly ground black pepper

Preheat the oven to 400°F.

Trim the crusts off the bread, and cut each square in half diagonally to form 2 triangles. Place 3 tablespoons of the olive oil in a small bowl. Place the bread on a baking sheet, brush with the olive oil, and bake until the bread is lightly browned, flipping the bread halfway through, for a total of 8 to 10 minutes.

While the bread is toasting, make the spread. Mash the anchovies into a paste with the back of a spoon in a small bowl. Add the olives and the remaining 2 tablespoons olive oil, and mix well to combine. Season with pepper.

Spread the olive and anchovy mixture onto the toasts with the back of a spoon or a small knife. The toasts can be made up to 1 hour ahead.

favoritevariations

- Use a hearty olive bread in place of the white bread.
- Substitute green olives for the Kalamata olives.
- For non–anchovy-lovers, substitute 1/4 cup finely chopped roasted red peppers for the anchovies.

pita crackers

When you split open pita bread, lightly brush it with olive oil, sea salt, and freshly ground pepper, and bake it in a hot oven, it transforms into the most delicious crackers. Not only are these crackers simple to make, but they are very low in fat and excellent for serving with dips, salsas, or to accompany a tuna, egg, chicken, or green salad. These crackers also keep for several days in a tightly sealed plastic bag.

MAKES 16 CRACKERS

2 pita breads, white or whole wheat
About 1/2 cup olive oil
Sea salt and freshly ground black pepper

Place a rack in the middle of the oven and preheat the oven to 350°F.

Using a serrated knife, cut the pita bread in half horizontally, slitting apart the two layers. Cut each half in 4 triangles and place on a cookie sheet. You should have 16 pieces.

Using a pastry brush or the back of a small spoon, lightly brush each triangle with some olive oil. Sprinkle with salt and pepper. Bake for about 10 minutes; the crackers should be golden brown. Remove from the oven and let cool. The crackers will harden a bit, making them ideal for dipping.

favoritevariations

- Add 1 teaspoon crushed fennel or coriander seeds with the salt and pepper.
- Add 1/2 to 1 teaspoon spices like cayenne, curry, cumin powder, or herbs like thyme, basil, rosemary, or oregano.

7

poultry and meat

baked buffalo chicken wings with
blue cheese dipping sauce

SERVES 4 TO 6

This is classic bar food, the kind of dish you see everywhere these days. But let's face it: Most Buffalo wings are not only greasy and heavy, they leave you feeling like you made a mistake ordering them in the first place. We admit a weakness for these spicy wings, so we toyed with the recipe a bit and came up with something we *really* like.

The first thing that distinguishes these wings is that they are baked, not fried, and lightly coated (not glopped) with a tart, spicy sauce. Also, because the wings are baked at a high temperature, the skin gets crispy, and the hot pepper and vinegar sauce soaks in perfectly. Served with celery sticks and a fabulous Blue Cheese Dipping Sauce (page 237), these wings make great party food. Ice cold beer seems to be the drink of choice, and don't forget to pass plenty of napkins.

If you're serving these for a party, you can bake the wings up to 24 hours ahead, cover, and refrigerate overnight. Just before serving, simply reheat the wings for 5 to 10 minutes in a pre-heated 400°F oven, until hot, and then toss with the spicy sauce.

¼ cup olive oil
3 small garlic cloves, minced
¼ teaspoon cayenne pepper
1 teaspoon salt
¼ teaspoon freshly ground black pepper
2½ pounds chicken wings, small legs
  (drumettes), or boneless thighs, skin on
  (about 16 pieces)

¼ cup ketchup
3 tablespoons red wine vinegar
½ to 1 tablespoon hot pepper sauce
4 stalks celery, cut into 3-inch-long strips
2 carrots, cut into 3-inch-long strips
  (optional)
Blue Cheese Dipping Sauce (page 237)

Place a rack in the middle of the oven and preheat the oven to 475°F.

Mix the oil, garlic, cayenne, salt, and pepper together in a large bowl. Pat the chicken wings dry using paper towels; then toss them in the oil mixture to coat.

Place the wings on a large baking sheet and bake for 15 minutes (20 minutes for legs). Carefully flip the chicken over and cook for another 10 minutes, or until the chicken is well browned and cooked through.

Meanwhile, whisk the ketchup, vinegar, and hot pepper sauce until blended in a large bowl. Remove the chicken from the oven, drain off the excess oil, and pour the ketchup sauce over the wings, making sure to coat them thoroughly. Place the wings on a platter and serve hot or at room temperature accompanied by the celery, carrots, and Blue Cheese Dipping Sauce.

favoritevariations

■ Use sriracha (Thai chile-garlic sauce) or Chinese chile paste instead of (or in addition to) the hot sauce.
■ Add a pinch of ground dried chiles to the oil and garlic mixture.

best **roast chicken**
with roasted garlic–herb butter

SERVES 4

There are some recipes that are just so good we don't even try to make them better. Roast chicken is one such dish. This recipe originally appeared in a somewhat different version in our book *Stonewall Kitchen Harvest*. Here the amount of fresh herbs is increased and the chicken is surrounded by onions and fingerling potatoes to make this a whole meal in one pan.

What makes this recipe unique is the roasted garlic–herb butter that is tucked *under* the skin of the breast meat and then massaged on the outside of the bird, creating crisp skin and flavorful, moist meat.

for the garlic-herb butter
5 large garlic cloves, left whole
1 tablespoon olive oil
3 tablespoons unsalted butter, at room
  temperature
1 tablespoon chopped fresh sage, or
  ¼ teaspoon dried, crumbled
1 tablespoon chopped fresh rosemary, or
  ¼ teaspoon dried, crumbled
1 tablespoon chopped fresh thyme leaves, or
  ¼ teaspoon dried, crumbled
Salt and freshly ground black pepper

for the chicken and vegetables
One 3- to 4-pound chicken, preferably
  organic
4 medium onions, quartered
1½ pounds fingerling or new potatoes
  (cut in half if large)
Salt and freshly ground black pepper
2 tablespoons olive oil
1½ cups dry red or white wine

To make the garlic-herb butter: Place a rack in the middle of the oven and preheat the oven to 350°F. Place the garlic in a small roasting pan or ovenproof skillet and pour the oil on top. Roast for 15 minutes, tossing the garlic cloves once or twice until they are tender when tested with a small, sharp knife. (If the garlic cloves are small they will be tender and ready after about 11 minutes.) Remove from the oven and let the garlic cool for about 5 minutes.

In a small bowl, mash the butter with the back of a spoon. Add the sage, rosemary, and thyme. Season with salt and pepper and mix well. Finely chop the roasted garlic (it will become a paste, which is fine) and add it to the butter along with any oil from the garlic roasting pan. (The butter can be made 24 hours ahead of time, covered and refrigerated.)

To roast the chicken and vegetables: Place a rack in the lower third of the oven in order to fit the bird and a large roasting pan and preheat the oven to 450°F.

Remove the bag of giblets from the cavity of the chicken. Rinse the chicken and cut off any excess fat near the flaps of the cavity. By wiggling your fingers under the skin, gently loosen the

RECIPE CONTINUES ▶

breast skin from the meat to create a small pocket. Distribute half of the garlic-herb butter under both sides of the breast skin, massaging it into the breast meat. Rub the remaining butter over the outside of the bird, massaging it onto the skin of the breast, wings, and drumsticks. Place the bird in the middle of a large roasting pan. Surround the chicken with the onions and potatoes and season with salt and pepper. Drizzle the oil over the onions and potatoes and toss them with a spoon or by shaking the pan.

Roast the chicken for 25 minutes. Pour half of the wine over the bird and gently toss the potatoes and vegetables. Reduce the oven temperature to 375°F. Roast for another 20 minutes, and pour the remaining wine on top of the bird. Gently toss the vegetables again so they brown and cook evenly. Roast for another 20 to 25 minutes, or until the drumstick feels loose when you gently wiggle it, or the juices run clear and not pink when you pierce the meat under the wing or the thickest part of the thigh with a knife.

Remove from the oven and let cool for 5 to 10 minutes before carving. Serve the meat with the potatoes and vegetables on the side and spoon any pan juices on top of the chicken.

favoritevariations

- You can substitute (or add) any of the following vegetables to the roasting pan for the onions and potatoes: 4 medium parsnips, peeled and cut into pieces about 2 inches long and $\frac{1}{2}$ inch wide; 2 to 3 large carrots, peeled and cut into pieces about 2 inches long and $\frac{1}{2}$ inch wide; 1 pound medium asparagus, ends trimmed, stalks cut into 2-inch pieces; 2 medium fennel bulbs, quartered; 2 whole heads of garlic.
- For other flavored butter ideas to use in place of the garlic-herb butter, see page 244.

chicken breasts with
mediterranean stuffing

SERVES 4

This is one of those dishes that looks (and tastes) like it took hours to prepare, but it is deceptively simple. A "pocket" is made in a chicken breast by slicing it almost in half. We then stuff it with a mixture of Mediterranean flavors—spinach, goat cheese, sun-dried tomatoes, and olives—before quickly sautéing it in a large skillet; a touch of white wine transforms the pan juices into a fast, simple, and irresistible sauce.

2 tablespoons olive oil

1 garlic clove, chopped

5 ounces baby spinach, or regular spinach, stemmed

Salt and freshly ground black pepper

1½ pounds boneless, skinless chicken breast halves (about 4 medium)

4 ounces soft goat cheese or mascarpone cheese

¼ cup chopped sun-dried tomatoes, packed in oil

2 tablespoons black olive tapenade, available in specialty food stores

1 tablespoon plus 1 teaspoon unsalted butter

½ cup dry white wine

Heat a large skillet over medium-high heat. Add 1 tablespoon of the olive oil. When hot, add the garlic, and stir for about 15 seconds. Add the spinach and season with salt and pepper. Cook, stirring, until the spinach has wilted completely and excess liquid has evaporated, 4 to 5 minutes. Remove the spinach to a small plate and set aside to cool slightly.

Using a small, sharp knife, cut one chicken breast almost in half horizontally so it opens like a book—the breast meat should still be held together on one long side. Repeat with the remaining chicken pieces. Season the outside of each breast with salt and pepper and open the chicken breasts up on the cutting board.

In a small bowl, mix the goat cheese and sun-dried tomatoes until well blended.

Using your hands, squeeze the excess moisture out of the sautéed spinach. Chop it and spread a quarter of it on one half of each chicken breast. Spread equal amounts of the cheese mixture over the spinach. Then, using a small spoon, spread some of the tapenade on the empty side of each chicken breast. Close the tapenade side of the chicken breast over the cheese, and press gently to adhere.

Heat a large skillet over medium heat (you can use the spinach pan; just wipe it out with a paper towel). Add the remaining olive oil and about 1 teaspoon of butter. When the butter has melted, gently place each chicken breast in the pan. Cook for about 6 to 8 minutes per side, depending on the thickness of the breast, or until chicken is golden and cooked through and the

RECIPE CONTINUES ▶

cheese has melted. (Lift up the pocket flap to check to see if the chicken is thoroughly cooked; there should be no signs of pinkness.) Remove the chicken to a serving plate and cover loosely with foil to keep warm.

Raise the heat to high. Add the wine to the skillet. Let the wine cook off for 2 to 3 minutes, scraping the browned bits off the bottom of the pan with a spatula or a wooden spoon. Add the remaining tablespoon butter to the pan, stir until the butter melts, and then pour the sauce over chicken. Serve the chicken whole or sliced.

favoritevariations

- Replace the tapenade with Winter Parsley Pesto (page 232) or store-bought pesto.
- Substitute chopped roasted red peppers for the sun-dried tomatoes.
- Omit the goat cheese and add a thin slice of Brie or Camembert to each chicken breast.
- Add a thin slice of prosciutto to the layers in addition to, or instead of, one of the other ingredients.
- Substitute Swiss chard, arugula, or kale for the spinach.
- Use sherry or a fairly dry red wine instead of white wine.
- Add 1 teaspoon grated lemon zest to the sauce when you add the butter.
- Substitute 4 ounces herbed spreadable cheese (such as Boursin) for the goat cheese, and $\frac{1}{4}$ cup chopped, seeded, ripe tomatoes for the sun-dried tomatoes.
- For an entirely new stuffing: substitute $\frac{1}{4}$ pound crumbled Gorgonzola cheese (1 cup), $\frac{1}{4}$ cup chopped toasted walnuts (page 260), and $\frac{1}{4}$ cup Four-Onion Confit (page 212) or caramelized onions.

delicious deglazing

You see the word *deglaze* in recipes a lot these days. Sounds like a fancy term, but it really refers to a very basic cooking technique. After you have sautéed chicken, meat, seafood, or vegetables in a hot skillet there are all kinds of delicious little bits that cling to the bottom of the pan. Deglazing—adding some sort of liquid to the pan and heating it—removes those bits to make a flavorful sauce.

Here's the step-by-step process: After you finish cooking your foods in a skillet, remove the food to a dish. Do not wash the skillet! If there's more than a teaspoon of fat in the skillet, remove it by tilting the juices in the pan to the side and spooning off the fat. Be sure not to remove any of the natural juices in the pan; they'll add a lot of flavor. Place the skillet over high heat and add a good splash (the amount depends on how big the skillet is, how much meat, poultry, or fish you have cooked, and how much sauce you want) of liquid to the pan. Wine, sherry, alcohol, fruit juice (apple cider is particularly good with pork), stock or broth (chicken, beef, seafood, or vegetable), or water are all good choices. Bring to a boil, scraping the bottom of the pan with a spatula or wooden spoon as the liquid heats. Let the liquid boil away and reduce a little to create an instant sauce. Season with salt and pepper and any herbs or spices you like. If you want to enrich or round out the sauce, remove it from the heat and stir in a touch of butter, cream, milk, yogurt, sour cream, or crème fraîche and place back over a very low heat for a minute or two.

portuguese-style **chicken stew**

This hearty chicken stew combines many of our favorite Mediterranean ingredients—spicy chorizo sausage, tender chicken, garlic, leeks, red wine, and briny black olives. We love serving the stew over Israeli or plain couscous, rice, risotto, or wide egg noodles. It's also excellent spooned over Mashed Parsnips (page 228).

As with all stews, you can make this dish several hours, or the night, ahead of time and reheat over low heat until simmering before serving.

1 pound chorizo, linguica, or a spicy Italian sausage, cut into ¾-inch rounds

One 3- to 4-pound chicken, cut into 8 pieces

About ½ cup all-purpose flour

Salt and freshly ground black pepper

2 tablespoons olive oil

2 medium leeks (white and light green parts only), halved lengthwise and cut into ½-inch pieces

7 garlic cloves, peeled, 5 left whole and 2 finely chopped

2 large green bell peppers, sliced into ½-inch strips

2 tablespoons chopped fresh thyme leaves

⅓ cup chopped fresh parsley leaves

½ teaspoon sweet Hungarian paprika (see page 179)

1 cup dry red wine

1 cup chicken broth, low-sodium canned or homemade (see page 63)

1 cup pitted black Niçoise olives

Place a rack in the middle of the oven and preheat oven to 350°F.

Heat a large, heavy, ovenproof soup pot or Dutch oven with a well-fitting lid over medium heat. When hot, add the chorizo in an even layer and cook until the pieces are browned on both sides, 8 to 10 minutes. Transfer the chorizo to a paper towel-lined plate to drain. Remove the pan from the heat and spoon off all but 1 tablespoon fat.

Pat the chicken pieces dry with paper towels. Place the flour on a large plate or in a plastic bag and season liberally with salt and pepper. Lightly coat the chicken pieces with the flour. Heat the same large pot over medium-high heat. When hot, add the chicken pieces, a few at a time, skin side down. Cook until browned, about 3 minutes, reducing the heat if the chicken starts to brown too quickly. Gently flip the chicken over and brown on the other side, another 2 to 3 minutes. Transfer the chicken to a clean plate and repeat until all of the chicken pieces have been browned. Wipe out the pot with paper towels.

Add the olive oil to the pot and heat over medium heat. Add the leeks, and sauté, stirring frequently, for 5 minutes, until soft. Season the leeks with salt and pepper and stir in the whole and the chopped garlic, the peppers, thyme, parsley, and paprika. Add the reserved chorizo and chicken, the red wine, and broth and raise the heat to high. Bring the mixture to a vigorous simmer, remove from the heat, and cover with the lid. Bake for 45 minutes, stirring gently every 15 minutes to ensure even cooking. Add the olives, and bake for an additional 15 minutes.

- Substitute Kalamata or green Spanish olives, or a mixture of a few different kinds of olives for the Niçoise olives.
- Use 3 pounds chicken thighs instead of whole chicken parts.
- Add 2 chopped ripe tomatoes or 1 cup canned peeled whole tomatoes to the stew with the red wine.
- Use a combination of red, green, and yellow peppers instead of just green peppers.
- Add a few dashes of hot pepper sauce to the stew during the last 5 minutes of cooking.

paprika

not just some pretty red stuff

Many of us grew up believing that paprika was just some pretty pinkish-red spice that Mom sprinkled over deviled eggs and party food. It was thought of as a garnish, something vaguely sophisticated, like parsley—there to add color and flair. But it turns out that paprika lends great flavor to soups, stews, egg dishes, roasts, and more when used properly.

Paprika is made from the dried, ground pods of sweet red peppers, *Capsicum annumn.* They are larger and milder than chile peppers and are famous for their bright red color and mild, sweet flavor. Paprika is grown and made in Spain, South America, California, and Hungary, where it's an important part of the cuisine.

Spanish paprika comes in three varieties: *dolce,* or sweet; *agridulce,* or semisweet; and *picante,* or hot. The recipes in this book call for sweet Hungarian or Spanish paprika.

Smoked paprika, a Spanish favorite which has become more common in specialty food stores, adds a smoky, spicy depth to foods and is used in many Spanish rice and seafood dishes. Unlike Hungarian paprika powder, which is made by drying chiles in the sun, the Spanish smoked version is prepared by roasting the peppers over smoldering oak fires before being ground to a velvety powder.

Store paprika in a tightly sealed container in a cool, dark spot for up to 6 months.

coq au vin with cippoline onions

SERVES 4 TO 6

There are few stews that satisfy like a good coq au vin. We think you'll agree that this version—chicken browned in bacon fat and then simmered with a whole bottle of red wine, sweet cippoline onions, carrots, button mushrooms, and fresh parsley—is about as good as it gets. Since wine is such a key ingredient in this stew it's worth it to find something better than your plain old cooking wine. Look for a good Côte du Rhône, Burgundy, or Bordeaux. You might want to cook the stew with the same wine you will be drinking.

The stew can be made a day ahead of time (in fact, like most stews, the flavors come together beautifully as it sits) and reheated just before serving. Serve topped with Polenta Croutons (page 164).

4 ounces bacon (about 4 slices)
1 cup plus 2 tablespoons all-purpose flour
Salt and freshly ground black pepper
One 3- to 4-pound chicken, cut into 8 pieces
1 tablespoon olive oil
1 pound cippoline or baby or pearl onions, left whole
4 medium carrots, peeled and cut into 1-inch pieces
5 garlic cloves, peeled, 4 left whole and 1 finely chopped

3 tablespoons fresh thyme leaves, chopped
One 750 ml bottle dry red wine
1 bay leaf
1 tablespoon tomato paste
3 tablespoons unsalted butter
10 ounces button mushrooms, quartered (about 2 cups)
1/2 cup chopped fresh parsley leaves

Place a rack in the middle of the oven and preheat to 325°F.

In a large ovenproof pot with a tight fitting lid, cook the bacon, uncovered, on the stove over low heat until mostly crisp on both sides, about 10 minutes. Drain on paper towels, leaving about 2 tablespoons of the bacon fat in the pan; discard the rest. Cut the bacon into 1-inch pieces and reserve.

Place 1 cup of the flour on a large plate or in a plastic bag, and season liberally with salt and pepper. Dredge the chicken pieces on all sides in the seasoned flour.

Heat the bacon fat in the pan over moderately high heat and brown the chicken, a few pieces at a time, until golden brown on all sides, about 5 minutes. Remove from the pot, and repeat with the remaining chicken.

Use a paper towel to wipe out the bottom of the pot. Add the olive oil and heat over low heat. Add the onions, carrots, whole and chopped garlic, and half of the thyme and cook, stirring, for 3 to 4 minutes, or until the onions just begin to turn golden brown. Season with salt and pepper

RECIPE CONTINUES ▶

and stir in the remaining 2 tablespoons flour. Cook for 3 minutes, stirring frequently. Raise the heat to high, add the wine, and bring to a boil. Reduce the heat to low, add the bay leaf, and whisk in the tomato paste making sure to incorporate it into the sauce. Add the browned chicken pieces and gently spoon some of the vegetables and wine over the meat. Cover the stew, place in the oven, and bake for 1 hour.

In a medium saucepan, heat 1 tablespoon of the butter over low heat. When the butter is sizzling, add the mushrooms, and cook for 3 minutes, stirring frequently. Add the remaining thyme and the reserved bacon and cook for 2 more minutes. Add the mushrooms and bacon to the stew, stir gently, and bake for another 20 to 30 minutes, or until the chicken is quite tender; it should be almost falling off the bone.

Remove from the oven, season to taste, and stir in the remaining 2 tablespoons butter to finish the sauce. Sprinkle in the parsley and serve hot.

favoritevariations

- Add a variety of wild mushrooms to the stew instead of button mushrooms for an earthier, wilder mushroom flavor.
- Add 1 pound parsnips, peeled and cut into 1-inch pieces. If you add extra vegetables you'll also need to add 1 to 2 cups additional wine, broth, or water to the stew, just enough to cover all of the ingredients.

roast stuffed turkey with vegetables

SERVES 8 TO 10

It seems a pity to relegate the roasting of a turkey—an exceedingly flavorful, moist bird—to one day a year. We eat turkey sandwiches year-round, and we never think twice about roasting a chicken throughout the seasons, but turkey has a bad rap as a complicated, time-consuming bird to prepare. Not true. We like to find a smallish bird and roast one up in mid-February when we could all use a little celebration. And the leftovers make many great meals. Be sure to check out our 11 p.m. Thanksgiving Night Sandwich (page 94) for the ultimate turkey leftovers.

We stuff our bird with a simple bread stuffing flavored with lots of herbs, sautéed onions, garlic, and crunchy celery and surround it with chunks of peeled carrots, parsnips, and onions.

for the turkey
One 10 to 15-pound pound turkey, preferably organic
1 tablespoon vegetable oil
Salt and freshly ground black pepper
Herbed Bread and Celery Stuffing (page 162)
1 slice bread
¼ cup (½ stick) unsalted butter
12 garlic cloves, peeled, left whole
About 1 teaspoon sweet Hungarian paprika (see page 179)

for the roasted vegetables
8 medium carrots, peeled and cut into 2-inch pieces

8 medium parsnips, peeled and cut into 2-inch pieces
8 medium yellow or red onions, halved
Salt and freshly ground black pepper

for the gravy
Turkey gizzard, heart, and neck
1 medium carrot, chopped
1 medium onion, quartered
1 stalk celery, chopped
A few sprigs fresh parsley leaves
1 bay leaf
6 peppercorns
Salt and freshly ground black pepper
2 to 3 tablespoons all-purpose flour

Remove the turkey from the refrigerator about 1 hour before roasting while you make the stuffing.

Arrange the racks in the oven so the bird will fit on the middle shelf. Preheat the oven to 450°F.

To prepare the turkey: Rinse the bird under cold water and remove the neck, gizzard, and heart, and set aside to make the gravy. Remove the liver and save for another use. (The liver is delicious lightly coated in flour and then sautéed with 1 teaspoon butter in a skillet over medium-high heat for 5 to 6 minutes per side.) Pat the bird dry with paper towels.

Use the vegetable oil to lightly grease the bottom of a large roasting pan. Season the turkey with salt and pepper, inside the cavity and on the outside. Loosely stuff both the body and neck cavities of the turkey with the stuffing, pressing down but being careful not to overstuff the bird. Press the slice of bread into the cavity at the wide opening to keep the stuffing inside so it won't fall out while the turkey roasts. Place the bird in the roasting pan, breast side up.

RECIPE CONTINUES ▶

In a medium skillet, heat the butter over low heat. Add the garlic cloves and cook for 5 minutes until the butter has completely melted, and the garlic is just beginning to turn light golden brown. Remove from the heat. Using a spoon or a barbecue or pastry brush, brush the skin of the turkey with *some* of the garlic butter, reserving the rest to baste with later, and scatter at least half the garlic cloves around and on top of the bird. Sprinkle the top of the bird with the paprika. Using a piece of kitchen string, tie the legs together to keep them from touching the sides of the roasting pan. (Tying the legs also makes for a "neater" looking roasted turkey.)

Place the pan in the oven and roast for 15 to 20 minutes per pound, depending on the freshness of the bird, or 2 hours 30 minutes to 3 hours 20 minutes for a 10-pound bird or 3 hours 45 minutes to 5 hours for a 15-pound bird. (Fresh turkey tends to cook much faster than those that have been frozen.) After 30 minutes, reduce the heat to 350°F. Baste the bird every hour or so with the remaining garlic and butter and with the liquids that have accumulated on the bottom of the roasting pan.

To make the roasted vegetables: When you've estimated that the turkey has about 1 hour remaining to roast, place the carrots, parsnips, and onions in a bowl and season with salt and pepper. Scatter the vegetables around the bird. (If there isn't a lot of room left in your roasting pan, place the vegetables in a well-oiled baking pan and place on the rack below the turkey.) Roast for 1 hour, stirring the vegetables once or twice so they brown evenly on all sides. If the turkey skin appears to be browning too quickly, cover the bird very loosely with aluminum foil.

Test for doneness: The bird should be a gorgeous golden brown; when you wiggle a drumstick, it should feel slightly loose; and when you pierce the skin directly above the wing, the juice should run clear yellow, not pink. Gently remove the bird from the roasting pan and place on a serving platter; cover loosely with aluminum foil.

While the bird is roasting, make the gravy: Place the reserved gizzard, heart, and neck in a medium saucepan. Add the carrot, onion, celery, parsley, bay leaf, peppercorns, 1/8 teaspoon salt and pepper to the pot and cover with about 6 cups of cold water. Bring to a boil over high heat, reduce the heat to low, and simmer for about 1 to 2 hours to make a light turkey stock that will be the basis of your gravy.

To finish the gravy, once you've removed the bird from the pan, remove any excess fat from the pan by tilting it to one side and spooning off the fat, being careful not to remove any of the natural juices. Place the roasting pan over two burners over moderate heat. Use a spatula to loosen any bits clinging to the bottom of the roasting pan. Sprinkle on the flour and, using a whisk, mix the flour with the juices in the bottom of the pan. Cook for 1 minute, stirring, until the paste has come together and is beginning to turn a pale golden color. Pour a little more than half of the turkey stock through a sieve into the pan and whisk to create a smooth gravy. Simmer for 5 to 10 minutes, until slightly thickened and flavorful. Thin the gravy by adding additional stock as needed. Season to taste with salt and pepper. Keep the gravy warm over low heat, stirring occasionally, until ready to serve.

Remove the stuffing from the bird and place in a serving bowl. Carve the bird and serve with the roasted vegetables and hot gravy.

burrito party

This is one of our favorite parties to pull together for a small crowd—it's festive, and with a bit of preparation in the morning, everything comes together at the last minute without much effort at all. Don't be intimidated by the length of the recipe; if you take a close look you'll see it's really just a bunch of small steps.

Several hours before the party, marinate the flank steak (in a lime-cumin-cinnamon marinade), the chicken (with tequila, garlic, and jalapeños), and the shrimp (with chipotle peppers). Make up a batch of Fresh Tomato Salsa (page 236), Mango Salsa (page 236), Chunky Guacamole (page 234), Black Bean Salad (page 74), and Chipotle Cream (page 241). Don't feel that you need to make all these sauces and salads (though they will be greatly appreciated), but pick and choose what appeals to you, depending on how much time and energy you have. Make up and refrigerate platters of fresh cilantro, chopped ripe tomatoes, wedges of lime, and crunchy lettuce.

When the crowd arrives, light the grill, wrap the tortillas, and plan on spending no more than about 30 minutes grilling the meat and fish. Set out your condiments and side dishes, and let the party begin!

If you make the steak, chicken, and shrimp, and all the sauces you'll have more than enough to feed 8 to 10 people. You can also easily double any of these recipes to feed a larger group. Pitchers of margaritas, cold beer, or minted iced tea are the ideal drinks to serve with this spicy feast.

for the flank steak
1½ pounds flank steak
3 tablespoons soy sauce
1 tablespoon grated lime zest
Juice of 1 lime
¼ teaspoon ground cumin
⅛ teaspoon ground cinnamon
Freshly ground black pepper

for the chicken
1½ pounds boneless, skinless chicken breast
   halves (about 3 large)
¼ cup tequila or dry white wine
2 garlic cloves, thinly sliced
½ fresh jalapeño pepper, minced, or
   1 tablespoon chopped, drained, pickled
   jalapeños

for the shrimp
1 pound shrimp, peeled and deveined
2 tablespoons olive oil

¼ cup adobo sauce from a can of chipotle
   pepper in adobo sauce (save the rest of
   the can and the pepper for making the
   Chipotle Cream)

for the sauces, tortillas, and garnishes
Fresh Tomato Salsa (page 236)
Mango Salsa (page 236)
Chunky Guacamole (page 234)
Chipotle Cream (page 241)
Black Bean Salad (page 76)
Ten 6-inch corn tortillas
Ten 9-inch flour tortillas
2 limes, cut into wedges
1 cup fresh cilantro leaves
1 medium red onion, finely chopped or
   thinly sliced
1 small head Romaine or crisp lettuce,
   chopped
Hot pepper sauce (optional)

RECIPE CONTINUES ▶

To marinate the beef: Place the steak in a medium nonreactive bowl and add the soy sauce, lime zest, lime juice, cumin, cinnamon, and a good grinding of pepper, and mix well. Cover and refrigerate for at least 2 hours, or up to 8 hours.

To marinate the chicken: Place the chicken in a medium nonreactive bowl and add the tequila, garlic, and jalapeño, and mix well. Cover and refrigerate for at least 2 hours.

To marinate the shrimp: Place the shrimp in a medium bowl and add the oil and adobo sauce and mix well. Cover and refrigerate for at least 2 hours, or up to 8 hours.

Make any or all of the following: the salsas, Chunky Guacamole, Chipotle Cream, and Black Bean Salad.

About an hour before the party, wrap the corn and flour tortillas separately in moist, clean tea towels and then wrap in aluminum foil.

Arrange the lime, cilantro, onion, and lettuce on a serving platter or in individual bowls. Set out the hot pepper sauces, if desired.

Light a charcoal, gas, or wood fire until red hot. (The beef, chicken, and shrimp can also be cooked indoors in a broiler or in hot skillets with about a teaspoon of oil in each pan. If you're cooking in a skillet, follow the cooking times below and add the marinade to the pan during the last 2 to 3 minutes of cooking so it can cook down to a glaze.)

Remove the beef, chicken, and shrimp from the refrigerator about 20 minutes before grilling to bring it to room temperature.

Remove the beef, chicken, and shrimp from their respective marinades. Place the marinades in small saucepans and bring to a boil over high heat. Reduce the heat and let simmer 5 minutes.

Grill the chicken for 10 minutes, brushing with the marinade. Flip over, brush with the remaining marinade, and cook for another 5 to 10 minutes until cooked through with no signs of pinkness when you cut into the center of a breast.

Grill the beef for 5 minutes, brushing with the marinade. Flip the beef over, brush with the remaining marinade, and cook for another 4 to 5 minutes, or until medium rare. Add the shrimp to the grill and cook for 2 minutes, flip them over, brush with the marinade, and cook for another 2 minutes, or until firm and cooked through. Transfer the chicken, beef, and shrimp to a foil-covered plate and let rest for a few minutes.

Place the tortillas on the grill or in a warm 350°F. oven for about 5 minutes, or until warmed through.

Thinly slice the chicken and beef; leave the shrimp whole. Arrange all the sauces, salads, and garnishes with the tortillas and the grilled foods and let everyone create their own burritos.

three moms' **meat loaf**

Each one of us has distinct childhood memories involving meatloaf. We all grew up eating it in one form or another, and each of us had a kind of a love-hate relationship with the dish. But we decided it was time to take a new look at this American classic. This recipe, a sophisticated, much-improved version of what we remember from days past, combines elements from each of our mother's best meat loaves.

Three Moms' Meat Loaf combines ground beef, pork, and veal, fresh rosemary, thyme, and parsley and is baked free-form on a baking sheet. The meat loaf stays moist and flavorful thanks to a few strips of bacon placed on top and a simple tomato sauce that forms in the pan. If you are lucky enough to have any leftovers, the meat loaf makes a fabulous sandwich the next day.

1 tablespoon olive oil
1 small onion, chopped
2 garlic cloves, minced
1 pound ground beef chuck (see Note)
12 ounces ground pork (see Note)
12 ounces ground veal (see Note)
2 large eggs
1 cup plain bread crumbs

1 tablespoon tomato paste
¼ cup chopped fresh parsley leaves
2 tablespoons chopped fresh thyme leaves
1 tablespoon chopped fresh rosemary leaves
2 teaspoons salt
Freshly ground black pepper
One 16-ounce can crushed tomatoes
4 ounces thick-sliced bacon (about 4 slices)

Place a rack in the middle of the oven and preheat oven to 375°F.

Heat the olive oil in a medium skillet over medium-low heat. When hot, add the onion and garlic and cook, stirring occasionally, until the onion is soft, about 10 minutes.

In a large bowl, combine the onion mixture, beef, pork, veal, eggs, bread crumbs, tomato paste, parsley, thyme, rosemary, salt, and a generous grinding of pepper, mixing well with your hands or a wooden spoon. Turn the meat out onto a rimmed baking sheet, a roasting pan with high edges, or a large 11 × 15-inch or a 9 × 13-inch glass dish and form the meat mixture into a loaf approximately 5 × 8 inches and 3 to 4 inches tall. Mix the tomatoes with $1^1/_2$ cups water in a small bowl and pour the sauce over the top of the meat loaf, allowing some of it to fall into the pan. Drape the bacon strips over the meat loaf widthwise.

Bake for 30 minutes, basting with the pan juices several times. Increase the oven temperature to 400°F, and bake an additional 30 to 40 minutes, basting every 10 minutes or so, for a total cooking time of 60 to 70 minutes. The bacon should be cooked through and a thermometer inserted into the center of the meat loaf should measure 165°F. Remove from the oven and let the meat loaf rest for 10 minutes, then cut into slices and serve with the bacon and the tomato juices from the bottom of the pan.

RECIPE CONTINUES ▶

NOTE: If you can't find all three meats (often found premixed with the label "meat loaf mix" in supermarkets), try a mixture of whatever ground red meats you can find, totaling $2^{1}/_{2}$ pounds. For the best flavor, make sure the meat has at least 10 percent fat. Each meat generally lists the amount of fat on the label.

favoritevariations

- Add $^{3}/_{4}$ cup freshly grated Parmesan cheese for a richer meat loaf.
- Finely chop 1 small red or green bell pepper and add it to the pan with the onions and garlic.
- Substitute fresh basil for the parsley.

it takes a hand

We live in a world of food processors, blenders, mixers, microwaves. . . . Sometimes it seems there's a machine to do just about everything. But we've found that there are times when there's just no better way to mix ingredients than with your own two hands. There's something sensuous and old-fashioned about forming and creating foods using your hands. We'd venture to say it's a lost art.

We use our hands to make pastry, pie crusts, meatballs, and many other foods. For Three Moms' Meat Loaf (page 189) and the meatballs (page 145), for example, you can really work in the herbs and different types of meat and make sure they get combined evenly by working them together with your fingers. (When dealing with raw meat it's crucial that your hands are clean to begin with and that you make sure to clean them well with warm water and soap at the end of the cooking process.)

grilled **stilton burgers**

SERVES 4

There's not much involved in distinguishing a good burger from a great one, but if you follow the Great Burger Tips on page 194 you'll learn a few of our secrets. At the *Stonewall Kitchen Café*, where this is one of the most popular items, the burger is topped with imported Stilton cheese, but you could use any good-quality blue cheese (see page 150 for more on cheese).

1½ pounds ground beef (see page 194)
Salt and freshly ground black pepper
2 ounces Stilton cheese, or any good-quality blue cheese, cut into four ½-inch-thick slices

4 crusty burger rolls, split
4 tomato slices
4 crisp Romaine lettuce leaves

Preheat a charcoal, gas, or wood fire until red hot, or preheat the broiler for 4 to 5 minutes.

Form the ground beef into 4 burgers, each about ¾ inch thick, being careful not to over-handle the meat or your burgers will be dense. Sprinkle both sides of the burgers with a generous amount of salt and pepper.

When the fire, broiler, or pan is hot, cook the burgers for 7 minutes without moving the burger or pressing it down. Using a wide spatula, gently flip the burger over and press down *only once.* Cook for 5 minutes. Add the cheese to the top of the burger and grill or broil until it melts, about 2 minutes. The burger will be medium rare.

Meanwhile, grill or broil the buns until warmed through. Place the burgers on the rolls and top each with a slice of tomato and a Romaine leaf.

favoritevariations

- Add 1 tablespoon chopped fresh tarragon, basil, rosemary, oregano, chives, or thyme to the ground meat.
- Serve the burgers with sautéed portabella mushrooms.
- Serve the burger with grilled or sautéed yellow or red onions, or Four-Onion Confit (page 212).
- Top the burger with 1 or 2 slices of crisp, cooked smoked bacon.
- Top the burger with a flavored butter (see page 244).
- Top the burger with chopped fresh or sautéed chile peppers or a few drops of hot pepper sauce.
- Top with a few tablespoons of Chunky Guacamole (page 234) and Fresh Tomato Salsa (page 236).
- Substitute a good sharp cheddar, Monterey Jack, Parmesan, Brie, goat cheese, or your favorite cheese for the Stilton. (See page 150 for more on cheese.)
- Spread a tablespoon or two of roasted garlic (see page 161) on each of the hamburger buns.

Making a great burger isn't rocket science, but if you want yours to be a notch above here are a few tips that will make a real difference:

- We like to use a mix of 85 percent ground sirloin (ask your butcher to grind it fresh for you) and 15 percent ground round or chuck for a good balance of flavor, fat, and texture. (For the burger recipe on page 193, that's 1¼ pounds ground sirloin and ¼ pound ground chuck.) Ground sirloin generally has 5 percent or less fat, while ground chuck is usually 15 percent to 20 percent fat and ground round is around 10 percent. Some insist that for the ultimate juicy burger, mix half ground beef (your choice) with ground pork, which is generally 40 percent fat. You can make a leaner burger by using less chuck or pork, but keep in mind that you don't want your burger to be too lean (don't go below 15 percent) or it will end up pretty dry.
- You can make burgers from virtually any type of meat, fish, or vegetables. Consider ground turkey, lamb, or pork, ground or chopped fish (such as salmon, tuna, scallops, or lobster), or vegetables and grains (lentils, mushrooms, tofu, grated carrots, and more).
- One of the keys to a successful burger is to make it thick (about ¾ inch) so the burger can get brown and crusty on the outside and remain juicy and somewhat rare on the inside. If you make your burgers too thin, they won't have a chance (or the time) to achieve that great glazed crust on the outside before they're overcooked inside.
- Never prod or cut a burger open as it cooks; you will loose precious juices.
- *Don't overhandle burgers.* Imagine the kind of light touch you need when you're handling buttery pastry. Mix the ingredients gently and quickly, or your burgers may turn dense.
- Burgers are infinitely adaptable and mix well with virtually any type of spices, herbs, vegetables, cheeses, chiles, and more. See Favorite Variations on page 193 for ideas.

beef tenderloin with horseradish crust

This recipe is what we like to call a no-brainer. All you need to do is look for the best-quality beef you can afford, season it with salt and pepper, place it in a hot oven, and let the high heat work its magic. Just before it's done, coat the beef with drained horseradish to form a spicy crust and make an easy red wine sauce right in the pan. Since the recipe calls for so little you may want to cook with whatever wine you are serving the beef with.

Beef tenderloin is made up of several filet mignons attached at the hip—the center cut, the primest, most velvety, tender, melt-in-your-mouth meat you can buy. This is ideal dinner party food, served with Grown-Up Potato Puffs (page 158), Cardamom Creamed Spinach (page 218), and Roasted Garlic and Horseradish Sauce (page 233).

One 1¾ pound beef tenderloin
   (9 × 3½ inches wide)
1 tablespoon olive oil
Fine sea salt

Coarsely ground black pepper
2 tablespoons well-drained horseradish
½ cup dry red wine

Place a rack in the middle of the oven and preheat the oven to 450°F.

Place the beef in a roasting pan or large ovenproof skillet. If your cut of beef is thick and then tapers off on either or both ends, tuck the narrow ends under the thicker main part of the tenderloin. Coat the beef with the oil and season generously with salt and pepper.

Roast for 10 minutes. Remove from the oven and spoon the horseradish on top, patting it down to help it adhere. Roast for another 20 to 25 minutes, or until the internal temperatures is 120°F. for rare or 130°F. for medium rare; remember the beef will continue to cook even after you take it out of the oven. Place the beef on a cutting board or serving plate and let rest for 4 minutes before slicing and serving with the pan sauce. Immediately pour the wine into the bottom of the pan, using a spatula to help scrape up any bits and pieces clinging to the bottom of the pan, and cook over medium heat for about 2 minutes.

beef short rib stew with bok choy in an orange-hoisin-ginger sauce

SERVES 4

Short ribs are exceptionally flavorful, have the distinct advantage of standing up to long slow cooking, and produce meat so tender and buttery it practically falls off the bone. Here short ribs are cooked in a velvety Asian-flavored sauce made with red wine, orange juice, hoisin, ginger, garlic, and onion.

Because short ribs tend to be fatty it's best to make this stew a day (or at the very least the morning) ahead of time and refrigerate it for several hours. That gives the fat time to rise to the surface where it becomes quite easy to spoon off and remove. The stew can then be reheated 30 minutes before serving over low heat when the crunchy green bok choy (Chinese cabbage) is added. Serve with steamed rice, noodles, or Israeli or plain couscous.

½ cup plus 2 tablespoons all-purpose flour
Salt and freshly ground black pepper
4 pounds beef short ribs
¼ cup vegetable oil
2 tablespoons olive oil
1 large red onion, thinly sliced
1 Vidalia onion, thinly sliced
8 scallions (white and green parts), cut into 1-inch pieces
4 garlic cloves, thinly sliced

2 tablespoons grated or minced, peeled fresh ginger
One 750 ml bottle red wine
1 cup orange juice, preferably fresh-squeezed
2 tablespoons hoisin sauce
2 tablespoons soy sauce
1 large bok choy (white and green parts), cut into 1-inch pieces, or 4 baby bok choy, left whole
1 tablespoon unsalted butter (optional)

Place a rack in the middle of the oven and preheat the oven to 350°F.

Place ½ cup of the flour on a plate or in a plastic bag and season liberally with salt and pepper. Lightly coat the ribs on all sides in the seasoned flour.

In a large pot, heat the vegetable oil over medium-high heat for about 1 minute. When hot (to test, add a drop of flour; it should sizzle), add the ribs and brown them on all sides for 6 to 8 minutes. Remove the ribs to several sheets of paper towel and blot dry. Clean out the pot with paper towels.

Add the olive oil to the pot and heat over low heat. Add the red and Vidalia onions, half of the scallions, garlic, and ginger and cook, stirring frequently, for 10 minutes. The onions should be light golden brown. Add the remaining scallions, garlic, and ginger and cook for 10 seconds. Sprinkle in the remaining 2 tablespoons flour and cook for 2 minutes, stirring. Add the wine, raise the heat to high, and bring to a boil. Reduce the heat to low, add the orange juice, hoisin sauce, and soy sauce and stir well, making sure all the ingredients are incorporated and the sauce is smooth. Add the ribs to the sauce, spooning some of the onions on top, and simmer for 5 minutes. Cover the pot.

Bake in the oven for 1 1/2 hours, stirring once or twice. Remove from the oven and let the stew come to room temperature. Cover and place in the refrigerator for at least 4 hours, or overnight.

Using a spoon, remove all of the congealed fat that has risen to the surface.

About 30 minutes before you are ready to serve the stew, add the bok choy. Add the butter if desired; the butter gives the sauce a creamy feel. Place the stew over low heat or in a preheated 350°F. oven for 30 minutes, until the stew is bubbling and the meat is tender. The bok choy should still have a slight crunch to it. Serve hot.

favoritevariation

■ **Add 1 teaspoon grated orange zest with the bok choy.**

grilled **herbed butterflied leg of lamb**
with mint–red wine sauce

SERVES 8

A butterflied leg of lamb is a poetic name for a leg of lamb that has had the bone removed—the two flaps of meat that surround the bone open up and create the shape of a "butterfly." This is one of the all-time great cuts of meat for outdoor grilling. Have your butcher butterfly the lamb for you (be sure to call ahead and order it and ask the butcher to save the bone for stock, soup, or your favorite dog!). The lamb, though tender, greatly benefits from an hour or more in a marinade before it's grilled.

We have two tricks to share: The first is the marinade. We soak the meat in red wine, loads of fresh chopped mint, garlic, rosemary, soy sauce, and balsamic vinegar to tenderize and flavor the meat. The second tip: When the charcoal, gas, or wood fire is red hot, we add a big bunch of herbs to the grill rack and cook the meat directly on top of the herbs. This keeps the lamb from burning by elevating it a bit from the direct fire, and infuses it with a gorgeous herbal smoky flavor. Look for organic or unsprayed herbs.

The marinade simmers while the meat grills to make a simple sauce. Serve this with roasted or steamed potatoes, Ultimate Mashed Potatoes (page 160), Fennel Gratin "Lite" (page 226), Cardamom Creamed Spinach (page 218), or a big salad tossed with a few mint leaves.

If you're lucky you'll have plenty left over to make Lamb, Feta, Mint, and Cucumber Sandwiches (page 108).

One 7-pound leg of lamb, butterflied
2 cups dry red wine
1/2 cup soy sauce
1/2 cup balsamic vinegar
8 cloves garlic, coarsely chopped
1 cup coarsely chopped fresh mint leaves
  plus extra whole leaves for garnish

1/2 cup chopped fresh rosemary leaves
Generous grinding of black pepper
1 large bunch of fresh rosemary sprigs,
  preferably organic
2 tablespoons unsalted butter

Place the lamb in a large nonreactive bowl. Add the wine, soy sauce, vinegar, garlic, mint, rosemary, and pepper and turn to coat on both sides. Marinate the lamb for at least 1 hour or for up to 24 hours in the refrigerator.

Heat a charcoal, gas, or wood fire until red hot. Place a grill rack on top of the fire and scrub it clean of any debris. Place the bunch of rosemary directly on the rack, spreading it out so it covers enough surface to place the meat on top. Remove the meat from the marinade (save the marinade) and place the lamb directly on the rosemary, fat side up. Cover the grill and cook for 15 minutes.

Meanwhile, place the marinade in a small saucepan and simmer it over very low heat while the lamb cooks.

Gently flip the meat over (making sure the rosemary stays under the meat and doesn't flip over with it), and cover the grill again. Cook for another 15 minutes. Flip the meat one last time and cook for another 15 to 20 minutes, depending on the thickness of the meat. A meat thermometer inserted in the thickest part of the meat should read 130°F for medium-rare. Remove the meat to a serving platter, cover loosely with aluminum foil, and let rest for 5 to 10 minutes.

Meanwhile bring the marinade to a boil for 5 minutes and then remove from the heat. Swirl in the butter until it melts. Strain the sauce into a small bowl or gravy boat.

Thinly slice the meat on the diagonal, garnish with mint leaves, and serve hot with the sauce.

favoritevariation

- Add ¼ cup finely chopped fresh oregano leaves to the marinade.

rack of lamb with
walnut-rosemary crust

SERVES 2 TO 4

When you coat a rack of lamb with a simple mixture of chopped walnuts, rosemary, lemon zest, and bread crumbs you have a seriously elegant dish without much effort at all. Prepare the lamb ahead of time and pop it into the oven about 35 minutes before you're ready to serve it. Don't be concerned if some of the crust falls off when you're slicing the chops; simply spoon it on top of each serving.

Accompany the lamb with Cardamom Creamed Spinach (page 218), and Twice-Baked Potatoes (page 156), or Grown-Up Potato Puffs (page 158).

One 1¾-pound rack of lamb (8 ribs)
Salt and freshly ground black pepper
½ cup finely chopped walnuts
2½ tablespoons minced fresh rosemary,
    or 2 teaspoons dried, crumbled

¼ cup plain bread crumbs
2 tablespoons olive oil
1 teaspoon grated lemon zest

Place the lamb in a small roasting pan or ovenproof skillet fat side up and season with salt and pepper.

In a small bowl, mix the walnuts, rosemary, bread crumbs, olive oil, and lemon zest with some salt, and pepper. Using your hands, press the mixture onto the fat side of the rack so it clings to the surface of the meat. The lamb can be prepared several hours ahead of time up to this point; loosely cover and refrigerate until ready to roast.

Place a rack in the center of the oven and preheat the oven to 400°F.

Roast the lamb for 25 to 35 minutes, until the meat reaches an internal temperature of 125°F for rare and 130°F to 135°F for medium rare to medium. Keep in mind that the meat will continue to cook even after it's removed from the oven, so be careful not to overcook. Remove from the oven and let rest for several minutes before cutting the rack into individual chops.

favoritevariation

■ Use finely chopped almonds, pine nuts, or pistachios in place of the walnuts.

dry-rubbed **paper bag pork ribs**

SERVES 6

We dream about these ribs. In the dream there are unlimited racks of them—all dry-rubbed with fragrant spices, grilled slowly over indirect heat on the barbecue, doused with cranberry juice, and when they're so tender that the meat just about falls off the bone, we dip them in a sweet and spicy barbecue sauce. The secret to these tender, juicy ribs is the technique. As soon as they are done grilling we wrap them in foil and place them in a paper bag, which allows all the juices to settle. See photograph on page 168.

4½ pounds baby back pork ribs (three
    1½-pound racks, or two 2¼-pound racks)
⅓ packed cup light brown sugar
¼ cup chile powder
2 teaspoons dried thyme
2 teaspoons dried basil or oregano
1 teaspoon sweet Hungarian paprika
1 tablespoon ground cumin
½ teaspoon ground allspice

½ teaspoon ground dried coriander
Charcoal and 1 cup mesquite or fruitwood
    chips (see page 203), soaked and drained
    (optional)
Kosher salt
¾ to 1 cup cranberry juice or apple cider
Brown paper bag (the kind you get at the
    grocery store)
Sweet and Spicy Barbecue Sauce (page 242)

Pat the ribs dry with paper towels and place them on a large roasting pan or platter. In a small bowl, mix the brown sugar, chile powder, thyme, basil, paprika, cumin, allspice, and coriander until blended. Pat both sides of the ribs with the dry rub, taking care to cover all surfaces with the spice mixture (including the rib ends). Cover the ribs with plastic wrap and refrigerate for 30 minutes to 1 hour.

Meanwhile, preheat a charcoal or wood fire until red hot. Carefully bank the coals to one side of the grill, creating a hot side and a cooler side. You can also add mesquite or special fruit wood chips in a foil packet (see box opposite) to impart a smoky flavor. Open the vents of the grill lid over the cool side of the grill to regulate the temperature; ideally, the inside temperature will hover between 275°F and 325°F. If using a gas grill, cook over very low heat.

Sprinkle the ribs lightly with the salt on both sides. Place them fat side up and bone side down on the cooler side of the grill. Cook for 30 minutes. Rotate the ribs, placing the rack nearest to the edge in the middle and vice versa, to avoid burning. Pour about 2 tablespoons of the cranberry juice into the hollow of each rack of ribs and cook for an additional 15 minutes.

After 45 minutes total cooking time, carefully flip the ribs. Drizzle with a little of the cranberry juice. Cook, basting the ribs with a little more of the juice every 15 minutes or so, for an additional 45 to 75 minutes. We find they generally take around 1 hour 45 minutes total cooking time. The meat should feel tender when pierced with a small, sharp knife.

Transfer the ribs to a large sheet of aluminum foil. Wrap the ribs completely in foil. Place the package inside the paper bag, and fold the bag a few times to seal it. Allow the ribs to sit (at room temperature) for 30 minutes. Remove the ribs from the bag and the foil, and serve immediately with the barbecue sauce. You can make the ribs a day ahead of time, although they are never quite the same. To reheat, place the ribs (in the foil) on a baking sheet in a preheated 350°F. oven for 10 to 15 minutes. You can also reheat them in the foil on a warm grill, but take care not to burn them, as the spices might become bitter.

what's mesquite?

Mesquite is a type of hardwood tree that grows through the southwestern part of the United States and in Mexico. It imparts a sweet, earthy, smoky flavor to foods. You can grill using mesquite charcoal, but we find the mesquite flavor can be overwhelming. For just a little boost of smokiness, soak a handful of mesquite chips in water for 10 minutes. Drain the chips and place them in a packet of aluminum foil, and use a fork to poke holes in a few places on top of the packet. Place the packet (with the holes on top) on top of your hot coals, or in the corner of a gas grill, and the smoke from the chips will escape and flavor your food. We also like using cherry or apple wood chips, or look for a variety of flavored wood chips made specially for grilling in specialty food stores. You can also throw the chips directly onto your regular charcoal.

roast pork loin with honey-thyme glaze

SERVES 4

Look for a really fragrant herb- or flower-scented honey—such as lavender or rosemary honey—for this roast. The honey, mixed with fresh thyme and garlic, creates a simple glaze for the meat. Serve this roast for a family dinner (along with roasted potatoes and a good salad) or a dinner party with Twice-Baked Potatoes (page 156) and the Roasted Vegetable Platter (page 222).

This recipe can also be made with a 2- to 2½-pound boneless pork tenderloin. Reduce the cooking time to a total of 25 to 40 minutes, depending on the size of the roast.

One 2½-pound boneless pork loin roast
2 tablespoons olive oil
Fine sea salt and freshly ground pepper

3 garlic cloves, chopped
3 tablespoons chopped fresh thyme leaves
¼ cup honey

Place a rack in the middle of the oven, and preheat oven to 400°F.

Place the pork roast fat side up in a roasting pan large enough to fit the roast comfortably. Drizzle the olive oil over the roast and then season liberally with salt and pepper. Scatter the garlic and 1 tablespoon of the chopped thyme over the roast, pressing the seasonings into the roast with your hands. Mix the remaining 2 tablespoons chopped thyme with the honey in a small bowl and set aside.

Roast the pork for 20 minutes. Remove from the oven, and spoon or brush the honey-thyme glaze evenly over the top of pork. Return the pan to the oven and roast an additional 15 to 30 minutes, basting occasionally with pan juices, until the pork reaches an internal temperature of 155°F., and the top has turned a golden brown. Let the pork rest for 5 to 10 minutes before slicing.

favoritevariations

■ Substitute fresh sage or rosemary for the thyme.

■ Substitute a good store-bought marmalade or savory jam for the honey.

bacon bits

There's nothing quite like the aroma of bacon. The seductive, smoky scent fills a kitchen with the promise of a good breakfast or sandwich or amazingly flavored stew, casserole, sauce, or roast. Whenever we consider giving up meat (which is, in all honesty, not too often), the thing we know we could never do without is bacon. It's just one of those foods we can't imagine living without.

In recent years buying bacon has become confusing. It used to be that you just went to the grocery store, bought a pack of bacon tightly wrapped in plastic, and that was it. These days there's thick slab bacon and country bacon, Canadian bacon, organic bacon, bacon with and without nitrates, and the list goes on. . . . And when do you use bacon versus pancetta?

A BIT ABOUT BACON The side and back of a pig contain just the right amount of fat and meat to create bacon. The side pork, as it's called, is salted or cured in a brine solution and then smoked. Most of us buy bacon presliced, in thin or thick slices. What's become interesting in recent years is the proliferation of artisanal bacon—that is, bacon made in small batches, from pigs naturally raised on smaller pork farms, smoked and flavored with a variety of wood (such as hickory, mesquite, apple, and other fruit woods), herbs, and flavors. Some companies coat the smoked bacon in brown sugar, molasses, or maple syrup or with garlic, pepper, cinnamon, juniper berries, or other spices and herbs. Many of these artisanally made bacon varieties are smoked slowly for long periods of time, which renders some of the fat out of the meat, resulting in bacon that is lower in fat and shrinks less when you cook it.

Really good bacon has just the right proportion of fat to give the meat its sweet, tender flavor and crisp texture. Many experts claim that great bacon needs the fat to account for at least one-half to two-thirds of the total weight. There are many new brands of bacon sold these days claiming to have less fat, but keep in mind they also have a lot less flavor.

Many inexpensive brands of presliced supermarket bacon have water added. Brine is pumped into the bacon to create the illusion of plumpness, but when you cook it the bacon shrinks to half its original size. Often you are simply left with burnt fat.

WHEN SHOPPING FOR BACON Look for a variety without nitrates (used to preserve the meat) because it is a far more natural, fresh product. Some of our favorite producers are: Nueske's (www.neuskes.com), Harrington's (www.harringtonham.com), North Country Smokehouse (www.ncsmokehouse.com), Nodine's (www.nodinesmokehouse.com), and Niman Ranch (www.nimanranch.com).

Some of the more common types of bacon are:

- **Canadian bacon,** called back bacon in Canada, is prized for its lean, tender meat. Taken from the eye of the pork loin, Canadian bacon is smoked and comes fully cooked. Canadian bacon has the advantage, as well as the disadvantage, of being very low in fat. As a result, it doesn't shrink like regular bacon, but it won't add the rich bacon flavor other varieties offer. In fact, it's more like a round piece of ham than regular American bacon. We use Canadian bacon for sandwiches, classic eggs Benedict and omelets.
- **Country, or country-style bacon,** refers to bacon that has been generously sliced and well cured.
- **Double-smoked bacon** is bacon that has a particularly strong smoky flavor. This is the bacon to use in dishes that can stand up to its full flavor: sauces for pasta, rich stews and casseroles, or an unforgettable BLT sandwich.

(CONTINUED) ▶

- **Slab bacon** is quite literally an unsliced slab of bacon. There are several advantages to buying bacon in this form: you can cut it thick or thin depending on your preference and the dish you are using it for. Slab bacon also tends to be a bit less expensive than presliced bacon. The rind must be removed before cooking.
- **Thick-sliced or thick-cut bacon** is generally cut about twice as thick as slices of supermarket bacon.
- **Pancetta** is Italian bacon, generally sold in a rolled spiral shape. It is cured with salt and herbs, and what distinguishes it from American bacon is that it is not smoked. Made from part lean meat and part fat, pancetta comes from the pig's belly and is seasoned with salt, lots of pepper, and spices. It is rolled into a salami shape and cured.

STORING BACON AND PANCETTA Bacon and pancetta will keep, tightly wrapped in plastic, in the refrigerator for about a week. They can also be tightly wrapped in foil and frozen for several months.

COOKING PRIMER Bacon and pancetta are raw and must be cooked; we like to cook them in a heavy cast-iron skillet or griddle over medium-low heat; it takes longer, but we find there is less shrinkage and the bacon has a better final texture than bacon cooked quickly over high heat. Always drain the fat by placing the cooked bacon on several pieces of paper towel and blotting it dry. Bacon can also be baked in the oven, or cooked in a microwave.

vegetables

8

parsnip chips

SERVES 2 TO 4

We love potato chips for their salty, addictive crunch. But we never like the way they make us feel when we're all done eating. We decided to try making baked chips from parsnips, one of our favorite root vegetables, by lightly brushing them with olive oil, salt, and pepper and putting them in a very hot oven. These are a delicious, healthy alternative to heavy, greasy potato chips!

Serve the chips as is or accompanied by hot pepper sauce, Classic Cocktail Sauce (page 236), Mango Salsa (page 236), Fresh Tomato Salsa (page 236), or Garlic Aïoli (page 243). They are delicious served with burgers, grilled foods, or as a hors d'oeuvre.

2 medium parsnips, peeled (see Note)
About 2 tablespoons olive oil

Coarse sea salt and freshly ground black pepper to taste

Place the rack in the middle of the oven and preheat the oven to 400°F.

Beginning at the fatter end, slice the parsnips about $1/8$-inch thick, like an old-fashioned potato chip. When the rounds become smaller (and when you get to the very skinny end of the parsnip), slice the remainder lengthwise, into long flat pieces. The idea is that all the slices are big enough to enjoy but also of uniform thickness.

Place the parsnips in a bowl and toss with the olive oil, and a bit of salt and pepper.

Place on a baking sheet and bake for 12 to 15 minutes, or until golden brown. Using a small spatula, flip the chips over, and reduce the heat to 350°F. Bake for another 10 to 15 minutes, depending on the thickness of the parsnips, or until crisp on the outside, tender on the inside, and light golden brown. Remove from the oven, let cool on the baking sheet, and serve warm or at room temperature.

NOTE: Look for young, thin parsnips. Older, thicker ones may be woody or fibrous inside and they won't crisp up properly.

favoritevariations

- Try this technique with carrots, sweet potatoes, beets, and eggplants, baking them until crisp on the outside and tender on the inside, about 10 to 15 minutes per side, depending on the thickness.
- Sprinkle the chips with a touch of chile powder during the last 5 minutes of baking.
- Sprinkle with a touch of ground cumin and coriander during the last 5 minutes of baking.
- If you have a mandoline vegetable slicer, or a very thin slicer attachment on your food processor, you can slice the vegetables paper thin, about $1/16$ inch, and bake them for just 5 to 6 minutes per side.

four-onion confit

SERVES 4

Don't let the word *confit* scare you off—this is simply a luscious combination of very slowly sautéed leeks, shallots, red onion, and garlic. The combination of all four onions adds a variety of sweetness, pungency, and earthy flavors. You'll have enough to top about a pound of pan-roasted or grilled steak, pork, lamb chops, fish fillets, or 2 cups sautéed vegetables, such as spinach and zucchini. We also love using it on top of pizza, quesadillas, baked potatoes, polenta, or pasta.

The topping can be made up to 2 to 4 days ahead of time and reheated before serving.

2 tablespoons olive oil
1 large leek or 2 medium leeks (white and
    light green parts only), thinly sliced
1 large red onion, or 2 medium, thinly sliced

2 large shallots, or 4 small ones, thinly sliced
8 garlic cloves, peeled, 6 left whole and
    2 chopped
Salt and freshly ground black pepper

In a large skillet heat the oil over low heat. Add the leek, onion, shallots, whole and chopped garlic, and cook, stirring occasionally for 35 minutes, or until tender and light golden brown. Season with salt and pepper to taste.

favoritevariations

- Add 1 to 2 tablespoons balsamic vinegar to the mixture for the last 10 minutes of cooking.
- Add 1 chopped, peeled Granny Smith apple to the onions after they have cooked for 10 minutes; this is particularly good with pork chops or roasts.
- Add 1 tablespoon chopped fresh herbs at the very beginning of cooking.

cleaning leeks

getting at that stubborn, hidden dirt problem

Leeks grow surrounded by soil; small hills of dirt are mounded up around each leek, so as it grows taller and taller, the dirt protects the tender white bulb from sunlight and exposure. The dirt also gets trapped inside the multiple layers. It's no wonder that leeks are such a mess.

Here's our cleaning tip: Rinse the outside of the leek under cold water. Cut the leek in half lengthwise and then gently rinse the leek under cold running water, using your hands to separate and lift each layer so you can get rid of the soil caught between the layers. Let the leek dry (or pat it with a tea towel or paper towel) and then cut and use as you like.

green beans with tomatoes and kalamata olives

A cross between a side dish and a salad, this colorful bean dish is light, refreshing, and a fabulous combination of flavors and textures. Green beans are lightly steamed, layered with tomatoes, toasted pine nuts, and pitted Kalamata olives, and topped with a balsamic vinegar–olive oil vinaigrette.

1 pound green beans, ends trimmed
1 large ripe heirloom tomato, or any ripe tomato, cored and chopped
½ cup yellow pear tomatoes, cut in half
¾ cup pitted Kalamata olives, cut in half
1 teaspoon Dijon-style mustard

Salt and freshly ground black pepper
2 scallions (white and green parts), finely chopped
3 tablespoons balsamic vinegar
¼ cup olive oil, plus 2 tablespoons
⅓ cup pine nuts, toasted (page 260)

Fill a large pot with 2 inches of lightly salted water and bring to a boil over high heat. Add the beans, cover, and cook for 4 minutes. Immediately drain the beans and place under cold running water to stop the cooking; drain again.

Place the beans in a large serving bowl. Push the beans off to the sides of the bowl to create a hollow in the center. Add the chopped tomato and pear tomatoes to the center. Arrange the olives along the outside of the beans, near the edge of the bowl.

Put the mustard in a small bowl and season with salt and pepper. Add the scallions, vinegar, and oil and mix well. Taste for seasoning.

Pour the dressing over the beans and tomatoes. Sprinkle with the toasted pine nuts. Serve at room temperature or cover and chill for several hours before serving.

favoritevariations

- Substitute walnuts, pistachios, pecans, or almonds for the pine nuts.
- Add 1 cup crumbled soft goat or blue cheese on top.
- Crumble 2 to 3 slices cooked bacon or pancetta on top.
- Add a can of tuna fish (well drained) on top of the tomatoes.
- Add 2 peeled and quartered hard-boiled eggs to the bowl.
- Add 2 to 3 thinly sliced cloves of roasted garlic (page 161).

stuffed eggplant provençal-style

SERVES 4

This is one of our favorite ways to cook eggplant. We make a savory blend of onion, garlic, tomato, herbs, and cheese and use it to stuff small eggplants. The dish can be assembled ahead of time and baked just before serving. Serve the eggplants hot from the oven, or at room temperature as part of a light summer lunch or dinner. A cucumber and mint salad and warm rolls would help round out this dish to make a perfect vegetarian meal.

2 medium-small eggplants, about 6 ounces each
6 tablespoons olive oil
Salt and freshly ground black pepper
1 small onion, finely chopped
1 to 2 fillets of anchovy (optional)
¼ cup pine nuts, coarsely chopped

1¾ pounds ripe red or yellow tomato (about 3 large), finely chopped
½ cup plain bread crumbs
¼ cup finely chopped fresh basil or mint leaves
¼ cup packed freshly grated Parmesan, or crumbled feta cheese

Place a rack in the middle of the oven and preheat oven to 350°F.

Cut the stem ends off of the eggplants. Cut the eggplants in half lengthwise. Using a spoon, remove almost all of the flesh from each of the four eggplant halves leaving a shell made from the eggplant skin and a thin layer of flesh. Finely chop the eggplant flesh and set aside.

Lightly grease the bottom of a medium ovenproof skillet, baking dish, or broiler pan with 1 tablespoon of the olive oil. Place the eggplant shells into the pan and lightly season with salt and pepper.

In a large skillet, heat 2 tablespoons of the olive oil over low heat. Add the onion and cook, stirring occasionally, for 10 minutes. Add the anchovies, if desired, and cook for 2 minutes. Add the chopped eggplant and another tablespoon of the olive oil, and season with salt and pepper. Cook for 5 minutes, stirring frequently. Stir in the pine nuts and cook for another 2 minutes. The mixture should be a nice golden brown. Remove from the heat and let cool for 2 to 3 minutes. Stir in about 1 cup of the chopped tomato, bread crumbs, basil, and cheese and taste for seasoning. Using a spoon, divide the stuffing among the four eggplant shells, pressing down and doming the mixture. (The eggplants can be made several hours ahead of time up to this point. Cover and refrigerate for up to 6 hours. Bring to room temperature before baking.)

Surround the eggplants with the remaining chopped tomatoes, and season the tomatoes with salt and pepper. Drizzle the eggplant and tomatoes with the remaining 2 tablespoons oil. Bake for 40 minutes, or until the eggplant shells are soft and the stuffing is hot. Turn the oven to broil and broil for 5 minutes to brown and crisp up the top. Serve hot or at room temperature.

- Use medium zucchini instead of eggplant.
- For a Middle Eastern flavor, add ¼ cup golden raisins and a dash each of ground cinnamon and cumin along with the pine nuts.
- Sprinkle ¼ cup freshly grated Parmesan or crumbled feta cheese on top of the eggplant just before placing under the broiler.
- Add ½ pound chopped cooked Italian sausage to the skillet with the onions.

down east antipasti platter

Having a variety of good canned ingredients in the pantry is the key to impromptu entertaining. When people stop by or we're looking for a quick party dish, we pull a few items from the pantry or refrigerator and put them together with one or two homemade dishes to create this impressive antipasti platter. Serve with crusty bread, imported crackers, bread sticks, or Parmesan croûtes (see page 165). Serve a combination of the following ingredients, arranged on a large platter.

homemade ideas

- Parsnip Chips (page 210)
- Stuffed Eggplant Provençal-Style (page 214)
- Grilled Asparagus (page 98), drizzled with olive oil, lemon juice, and fresh cracked pepper
- Sautéed Shrimp with Garlic, Lime, and Chile (page 134)
- Tuscan-Style White Bean Salad (page 75)
- Roasted Vegetable Platter with Green Sauce (page 222)
- Pickled Red Onions (page 239)
- Fresh Tomato Salsa (page 236)
- Mango Salsa (page 236)
- Winter Parsley Pesto (page 232)

pantry items

- Assorted olives
- Caperberries
- Tapenade
- Jarred roasted sweet red peppers and sun-dried tomatoes packed in oil

refrigerator items

- Cubes of feta cheese marinated in olive oil and red wine vinegar
- Cubed summer tomatoes with fresh mint or basil, olive oil, and balsamic vinegar
- Chunk of Parmesan cheese or any of your favorite cheeses (see page 150 for more on cheese).
- Hummus
- Thin slices of salami, capicola, Spanish jamon, or prosciutto
- Cubes of fresh mozzarella cheese
- Thin slices of fresh fennel and radishes served with an assortment of sea salt and flavored butters (page 244).

cardamom **creamed spinach**

SERVES 6

This is a standard side dish at our holiday gatherings. The fresh green flavor of spinach, dusted lightly with grated cardamom and nutmeg, and cooked with garlic and cream, is the perfect accompaniment to roast turkey, chicken, duck, pork, or beef. But don't wait for a holiday to try this dish; serve it with pasta, rice, or couscous dishes.

The spinach can be made ahead of time and reheated just before serving.

3 tablespoons olive oil
2 large cloves garlic, minced
Four 5-ounce bags baby spinach
Fine sea salt and freshly ground black
    pepper

About $\frac{1}{2}$ teaspoon ground nutmeg
About $\frac{1}{4}$ teaspoon ground cardamom
$\frac{2}{3}$ cup heavy cream

Heat a large, heavy skillet over high heat. Add half of the olive oil. When hot, add half of the garlic. Begin adding spinach to the skillet by large handfuls, stirring as you go, and adding additional spinach until half of the spinach is in the pan. Season with salt and pepper. Cook, stirring, until all of the spinach is completely wilted, about 5 minutes total. Transfer the spinach to a large plate and repeat with remaining olive oil, garlic, and spinach.

Place a second large plate on top of the spinach. Squeeze the two plates together carefully over the sink to rid the spinach of all of its excess liquid. Chop the spinach and return it to the pan.

Over medium heat, stir the spinach to release any additional liquid. Add the nutmeg, cardamom, and cream, stirring to combine. Bring to a simmer, reduce the heat to low, and cook the spinach, stirring occasionally, for another 5 minutes. Taste for seasoning and add additional nutmeg, cardamom, salt, or pepper as needed.

Creamed spinach may be made up to 4 hours ahead, refrigerated, and reheated in a skillet over medium heat just before serving or placed in a small baking dish or casserole and put in a preheated 350°F. oven for about 10 minutes, or until simmering.

favoritevariation

■ Substitute Swiss chard leaves for the spinach, increasing the cooking time to 10 minutes when wilting the greens. Be sure to remove the rib in the center of the chard leaf before chopping the Swiss chard.

roasted brussels sprouts with pancetta and balsamic glaze

SERVES 4 TO 6

Roasted in a hot oven with pancetta and balsamic vinegar, Brussels sprouts caramelize into an entirely new (and suddenly desirable) vegetable.

1¼ pounds medium Brussels sprouts
1 teaspoon olive oil
Salt and freshly ground black pepper

4 ounces thick-sliced pancetta or bacon, cut into ½-inch pieces
1 tablespoon balsamic vinegar

Place the rack in the middle of the oven and preheat the oven to 450°F.

Using a small, sharp knife, trim the ends from the Brussels sprouts and tear off the loose outer layer of leaves. Place the sprouts in a baking dish. Drizzle the oil over the sprouts, season with salt and pepper, and toss to coat. Sprinkle the pancetta over the top of the sprouts and roast for 15 minutes, stirring the vegetables halfway through baking.

Pour the balsamic vinegar over the sprouts, and stir the sprouts to distribute the flavors. Roast for another 10 to 12 minutes, until the sprouts are browned and just tender when tested in the center with a small, sharp knife, and the pancetta is cooked.

favoritevariations

- Add ½ cup freshly grated Parmesan cheese to the sprouts as soon as they come out of the oven.
- Add 2 to 3 shallots, quartered, or 1 red onion, thinly sliced.
- Substitute cauliflower or broccoli florets for the Brussels sprouts.

roasted vegetable platter with green sauce

SERVES 4 TO 6 AS A MAIN COURSE OR 6 TO 8 AS A SIDE DISH

A delicious assortment of vegetables—carrots, leeks, potatoes, parsnips, fennel, red pepper, onions, and more—are lightly tossed with olive oil and fresh thyme, and roasted at a high temperature until golden brown on the outside and buttery, tender, and soft inside. The combination of vegetables here is merely a suggestion; see Favorite Variations for other ideas.

The vegetables can be served hot from the oven or at room temperature and are surprisingly good the next day. Serve as a side dish (potatoes and vegetables all in one for a crowd), or accompanied by a loaf of crusty bread, and a selection of cheeses (see page 150) as a main course.

1½ pounds baby potatoes, scrubbed

2 small heads fennel, trimmed, bulb cut into quarters

1 pound medium carrots, peeled, and cut into 1½-inch pieces (if the carrots are very thick cut them in half lengthwise before cutting into 1½-inch pieces)

1 pound parsnips (about 5 medium), peeled and cut into 1½-inch pieces (if the parsnips are very thick, cut in half lengthwise and then into 1½-inch pieces)

3 to 4 small leeks, cut in half lengthwise and then into 1½-inch pieces

1 large red bell pepper, cored and cut into ½-inch thick strips

8 ounces Brussels sprouts (if they are very large, cut in half)

¼ cup plus 2 tablespoons olive oil

2 tablespoons chopped fresh thyme leaves, or 2 teaspoons dried

Salt and freshly ground black pepper

Green Sauce (page 231)

Place a rack in the middle of the oven and preheat the oven to 425°F.

Place the potatoes at one end of a large rimmed baking sheet or roasting pan. Arrange the fennel next, cut side up, followed by the carrots, parsnips, leeks, red pepper, and Brussels sprouts, creating rows of vegetables. Sprinkle with the oil and thyme, and season with the salt and pepper. You can prepare all the vegetables several hours ahead of time; cover and refrigerate until ready to roast. Roast for 30 minutes.

Reduce the temperature to 350°F and carefully flip the vegetables over. Roast for another 30 minutes, or until everything is tender when tested with a small, sharp knife and golden brown. Serve hot or at room temperature with the Green Sauce.

favoritevariations

- Add 12 to 14 cippoline onions.
- Add 1 pound medium asparagus, ends trimmed.
- Add 4 red onions, quartered.
- Add rutabagas, celery root, and turnips, peeled and cut into 1½-inch chunks.
- Add 2 tablespoons chopped fresh rosemary and/or basil leaves.

slow-roasted tomatoes with a basil swirl

SERVES 4 TO 8

August is the best time to make this luscious dish, when tomatoes are fat and ripe and literally dripping from the vine. But this is such a delicious, easy, and adaptable dish that we seek out decent tomatoes year-round, so we don't have to limit ourselves to a short, seasonal tomato season.

A good loaf of crusty bread (such as olive bread warmed in the oven) is an essential accompaniment to these tomatoes; the juices that form in the bottom of the pan (olive oil, garlic, tomato essence, and herbs) make one of the great dipping sauces of all time.

Serve hot from the oven or at room temperature.

4 medium ripe tomatoes, cut in half crosswise
¼ cup olive oil
Salt and freshly ground black pepper

3 garlic cloves, thinly sliced
½ cup Basil Swirl (page 233)
1 small red onion, thinly sliced

Place a rack in the middle of the oven and preheat the oven to 375°F.

Place the tomatoes cut side up in a large broiler pan, baking dish, or ovenproof skillet. Drizzle half of the olive oil over and in between the tomatoes. Sprinkle with salt and pepper. Scatter the garlic over the tomatoes and place about a tablespoon of Basil Swirl on top of each tomato half, reserving the remaining basil for later. Scatter the onions on top and in between the tomatoes. Drizzle the remaining olive oil on top of the tomatoes and onions, and lightly season again with salt and pepper.

Bake for about 45 minutes (if the tomatoes are not particularly ripe it may take closer to an hour), basting the tomatoes once or twice with the oil from the bottom of the pan. The tomatoes are done when they are soft but not falling apart. Remove from the oven and let sit for 5 minutes before topping each tomato with a spoonful of the remaining Basil Swirl. Serve hot, at room temperature, or cold.

favoritevariations

■ Substitute 1 tablespoon pesto for the Basil Swirl.

■ Top each tomato half with a tablespoon of your favorite grated cheese.

■ Crisscross two anchovies on top of each tomato half before baking.

■ Add 1 teaspoon pine nuts, or coarsely chopped walnuts, almonds, cashews, or pistachios to each tomato before baking.

■ Add a tablespoon of chopped pitted black or green olives on top of each tomato for the last 10 minutes of baking time.

fennel gratin "lite"

SERVES 4 TO 6

We are huge fans of creamy gratins—baked dishes of vegetables layered with a touch of stock, heavy cream, and a thin dusting of cheese—but find they can be very heavy and overwhelm the unique taste of each vegetable. We decided to make a lighter version using fennel and no cream. This successful dish is all about the fresh anise flavor of the fennel.

¼ cup extra-virgin olive oil
3 large bulbs fennel, green fronds removed, bulb halved, cored, and cut into thin half-moon slices
1 medium onion, thinly sliced

1 to 1½ cups low-sodium canned vegetable or chicken broth, or homemade chicken broth (page 63)
Salt and freshly ground black pepper
1 cup packed freshly grated Parmesan cheese

Place a rack in the middle of the oven and preheat the oven to 350°F.

Grease the bottom of a large baking dish, ovenproof skillet, or broiler pan with 2 tablespoons of the oil. Arrange the fennel slices in overlapping rows in the dish, sticking some onion in between every 2 to 3 pieces of fennel. Pour 1 cup of the broth and the remaining 2 tablespoons olive oil on top and season with salt and pepper. Bake for 50 minutes.

Raise the oven temperature to 450°F. Sprinkle the fennel evenly with the cheese and spoon some of the stock from the bottom of the pan over the vegetables. If the pan seems dry, add an additional ¼ to ½ cup broth or water. Bake for 15 to 20 minutes, or until the fennel is soft but not limp and the cheese is melted and bubbling.

favoritevariations

- You can make this a more traditional gratin by using ½ cup broth and ½ cup heavy cream instead of broth only.
- Substitute 3 small leeks (white and light green parts only) for the onion.
- Add 3 to 4 peeled garlic cloves, left whole, or 1 tablespoon minced garlic to the gratin.
- Add 2 to 3 tablespoons chopped fresh thyme or basil leaves.

grilled corn on the cob with flavored butters

SERVES 6

We're always happy when the summer's end brings fields lined with sweet, juicy August corn. We peel back the husks, tear out the silk, and rub the corn with a little flavored butter. Then we put the husks back on and throw the corn on a hot grill for just a few minutes to bring out all of the corn's natural sugars.

If you want, you can spear the cobs on wooden or metal skewers before you cook the corn for easy eating. If you use wooden skewers, be sure to soak the skewers in water for about 30 minutes before grilling. The corn makes a great accompaniment to Dry-Rubbed Paper Bag Ribs (page 202).

Some of our favorite flavored butters to use with Grilled Corn on the Cob, all found on pages 244–245, include Herb-Lemon Butter, Lavender Butter, White Truffle Butter, Bacon-Chive Butter, Wild Mushroom Butter, Spicy Lime-Scallion Butter, or Chipotle Pepper Butter.

6 ears corn

3 tablespoons flavored butter of your choice (see pages 244–245), at room temperature

Preheat a charcoal, wood, or gas grill to medium-high (about 350°F).

Carefully peel back the husk from one ear of corn, starting at the top and leaving the bottom part intact. Use your hands, tear out the corn silk. Using your hands or a paper towel, rub ¹/₂ tablespoon of the butter directly over the kernels. Fold the husk back up and over the corn. Repeat with the remaining corn.

Place the corn (in its husk) directly on the grill and cook for 3 minutes. Turn the corn over, and cook for another 2 to 3 minutes, or until the kernels are bright and beginning to char. Serve hot.

favoritevariations

- Sprinkle the corn with fine sea salt, freshly ground black pepper, and chile powder, or cayenne pepper when you add the butter.
- Dip the corn in coconut milk before closing the husks back up to tenderize the corn and add a subtle coconut flavor. You may or may not wish to add the butter.

mashed **parsnips**

SERVES 4 TO 6

When we're craving mashed potatoes but don't want all those carbs (or calories) we like to mash parsnips—an all too little known beige root vegetable with a slightly nutty flavor and creamy, potato-like texture. Parsnips are quite popular in New England where they are planted in the fall and allowed to spend the winter in the ground—the thinking being that the frost creates a sweet vegetable in the spring. We also love roasting them with chicken (page 173), making them into chips (page 210), or adding them to stews with carrots, potatoes, and other root vegetables.

Look for parsnips that are thin and young; the very thick, fat ones tend to be woody and fibrous.

2 pounds parsnips (8 to 10 small to medium), peeled and cut into 1-inch chunks

½ cup sour cream or crème fraîche

Bring a large pot of lightly salted water to boil over high heat. Add the parsnips and cook for 10 to 12 minutes, or until tender when pierced with a small knife. Drain.

Off the heat, place the parsnips back into the pot and mash using a potato masher. Add the sour cream and a generous amount of salt and pepper and mash again. Warm over low heat and serve hot.

favoritevariations

- Make the dish using half parsnip and half celery root, or rutabagas or potato.
- Substitute 3 tablespoons extra-virgin olive oil for the sour cream or crème fraîche for a healthier version of this dish.
- Add ⅓ cup freshly grated Parmesan cheese or any other hard cheese.
- Add ⅓ cup crumbled goat cheese, cream cheese, or mascarpone instead of the sour cream.
- Add 1 tablespoon butter for an extra-rich flavor.
- Add 2 tablespoons chopped fresh chives.
- Add 1 tablespoon chopped fresh thyme or rosemary.
- Use the mashed parsnips as a top "crust" for a stew, casserole, or pot pie (instead of pastry or mashed potatoes) and bake until hot.

grown-up **vegetable medley**

SERVES 6

We won't mention brand names, but we all grew up with little frozen boxes of something called "Vegetable Medley." This was a combination of perfectly diced little carrots mixed with peas and sometimes baby onions. We decided it was time to bring this classic back but with a fresh, new version.

Here we lightly boil fresh carrots and onions, and then sauté them with peas and corn and a vibrant, bright green mint butter. The colors, textures, and flavors of this dish are a far cry from those 1950s creations.

You can steam the carrots and onions and prepare the mint butter several hours ahead of time and put the dish together at the last minute. See photograph on page 190.

8 ounces boiling onions, quartered
1 pound carrots, peeled and cut into ¼-inch
    dice
1½ tablespoons olive oil

1 cup fresh or frozen peas
1 cup fresh or frozen corn kernels
Salt and freshly ground black pepper
About 2 tablespoons Mint Butter (page 244)

Bring a large pot of water to a boil. Add the onions to the water and cook for 4 minutes. Add the carrots and cook for 2 minutes. Drain and place under cold running water to stop the cooking. Drain again and set aside.

In a large skillet, heat the oil over medium-low heat. Add the carrots, onions, peas, and corn, season with salt and pepper, and cook, stirring, for 2 minutes. Add the mint butter and cook for another 4 minutes. Taste for seasoning and add more mint butter if you want a creamier dish.

favoritevariations

■ Use lima beans, fava beans, or edamame beans instead of peas.
■ Use leftover Vegetable Medley as a filling for an omelet or a pot pie.

9

sauces and salsas

winter **parsley pesto**

MAKES ABOUT ¾ CUP

A vibrant green pesto, made with parsley instead of basil, and ideal for winter when fresh herbs are scarce. This pesto may be made several hours ahead of time. Serve with Roasted Winter Vegetable Soup (page 59), with stews, or smothered on a cheese sandwich. Try tossing it with pasta, grilled shrimp, or using it to coat a chicken breast or fish fillet. The pesto will keep, covered and refrigerated, for 2 to 3 days. It can also be frozen (before the cheese is added) for several months.

1 cup packed chopped fresh parsley leaves
1 garlic clove, peeled and left whole
Salt and freshly ground black pepper

½ cup olive oil
¼ cup freshly grated Parmesan cheese

In a food processor or blender, whirl the parsley and garlic with some salt and pepper until finely chopped. With the motor running, slowly add the oil, making sure not to overprocess the pesto; it should still be a little chunky. Remove to a bowl and stir in the cheese. Season to taste.

favoritevariations

- Add ½ cup toasted walnuts, almonds, pistachios, or pine nuts (see page 260) with the parsley.
- Add ¼ cup fresh cilantro leaves.
- Add 1 teaspoon of any of the following ground dried spices: cumin, curry, or cardamom.
- Try freshly grated Romano, Manchego, or any other hard cheese instead of the Parmesan.

the power of parsley

For years it was relegated to a mere garnish, a neglected cluster of curly greens that no one paid much attention to. The truth: Parsley has an amazing amount of flavor and texture. It is slightly peppery, with a genuine crunch and a fresh herb flavor that screams *green*. It is available year-round and will keep in the refrigerator for up to 2 weeks. All this and it's full of vitamins A and C. Curly leaf, the most common type of parsley, is a bit milder than its flat-leaf cousin (which is also called Italian parsley). We like this herb so much we've been known to toss entire salads made of nothing but fresh, coarsely chopped parsley, oil, and vinegar. Use it in soups and stews and in pesto (above), to add color to monochromatic food and freshness to nearly everything.

basil swirl

MAKES ABOUT ½ CUP

Not quite a pesto, this thick mixture of fresh basil, olive oil, sea salt, and freshly ground black pepper adds a vibrant herb flavor and fabulous bright green color to a wide range of dishes. We call it a "swirl," because it's so delicious swirled into soups, stews, sauces, or pasta dishes, on top of roasted vegetables, or in salad dressings.

1½ cups packed fresh basil leaves
½ cup olive oil

Fine sea salt and freshly ground black
    pepper

In a food processor or blender, blend the basil until coarsely chopped. Slowly add the oil and process until the mixture is thick and chunky; it shouldn't be completely smooth. Transfer the basil mixture to a small bowl and season with salt and pepper to taste.

The Basil Swirl will keep, covered, in the refrigerator for about 3 days.

favoritevariation
■ **Use any fresh herb instead of the basil.**

roasted **garlic and horseradish sauce**

MAKES ABOUT 1 CUP

This is an ideal sauce to accompany Beef Tenderloin with Horseradish Crust (page 195), or spread on a roast beef or pork sandwich, or a sandwich made with leftovers from the Roasted Vegetable Platter (page 222). The sauce is fast and simple and can be made several hours ahead of time; cover and refrigerate until ready to serve.

1 large head garlic, roasted (see page 161)
1 cup sour cream

3 to 4 tablespoons drained prepared
    horseradish
Salt and coarsely ground black pepper

Using your hands, squeeze the individual garlic cloves from the skin and set the peeled cloves on a work surface. Coarsely chop the garlic.

In a small bowl, mix the sour cream, chopped garlic, any oil from the garlic pan, and 3 tablespoons horseradish, and season with salt and pepper. Taste for seasoning and add the additional tablespoon of horseradish if you want a sauce with more punch.

chunky **guacamole**

MAKES 3½ CUPS

Good guacamole is all about paying attention to flavors, color, and that most neglected aspect of food—texture. In our guacamole, we cube ripe avocados without ever mushing or mashing them, and gently toss them with a variety of fresh, authentic ingredients. The texture is more like a chopped salad than the usual guacamole dip.

Serve with taco chips, blue corn chips, cooked shrimp, raw vegetables, or as an accompaniment to grilled or sautéed poultry or seafood, or with tacos, burritos (page 187), and tortillas.

The recipe can easily be doubled to serve a crowd.

2 avocados, slightly ripe but not mushy, cut into ½-inch dice

1 large or 2 medium ripe tomatoes, chopped (about 1 cup)

1 small red onion, chopped (about ½ cup)

¼ cup minced fresh cilantro leaves plus extra whole leaves for garnish

½ to ¾ fresh jalapeño pepper, finely chopped, or several dashes of hot pepper sauce

Juice of 1 large lime

Salt and freshly ground black pepper

Place the avocados in a medium bowl and very gently toss with the tomatoes, onion, chopped cilantro, jalapeño, and lime juice and season with salt and pepper. Taste for seasoning and mix in additional hot pepper, salt, or pepper as needed. Garnish with the whole cilantro leaves.

favoritevariations

- Add 1 tablespoon olive oil for a moister guacamole.
- Substitute a chopped chipotle pepper for the jalapeño; it will give the guacamole a smoky flavor.

mango salsa

The vibrant hues of orange, red, purple, and green not only make this salsa gorgeous to look at, but the lush flavors of mango, pepper, fresh cilantro, and lime make this salsa a new favorite. Serve it as a dip with Pita Crackers (page 167), as an accompaniment to Huevos Rancheros (page 36), or with tacos, burritos (page 187), or enchiladas. This is an ideal salsa to make in the winter when mangos are ripe and plentiful and tomatoes are not in season. The salsa can be made several hours ahead of time but doesn't hold up overnight.

2 large ripe mangos, cut into 1/2-inch pieces (about 2 1/2 cups fruit)
1 red bell pepper, cut into 1/4-inch pieces
1/4 cup finely chopped red onion
1/4 cup finely chopped fresh cilantro leaves
2 tablespoons fresh lime juice
Salt and freshly ground black pepper

Mix the mangos, red pepper, onion, cilantro, and lime juice in a large bowl. Season to taste with salt and pepper.

favoritevariations

- Add 1 or 2 finely chopped jalapeño, serrano, or (if you're serious about your spice) habañero peppers.
- Substitute fresh chopped pineapple for all or half of the mango.
- Add 1/4 cup very thinly sliced fresh mint leaves.

classic cocktail sauce

Cocktail sauce is a classic, and if it ain't broke. . . . Here we combine ketchup, horseradish, and hot pepper sauce to produce a sauce that has a slight bite and is ideal with Shrimp Cocktail (page 133). You can also use it as a dip for raw vegetables or the Baked Buffalo Chicken Wings (page 170), or with fried seafood.

1/2 cup ketchup
2 tablespoons drained prepared horseradish
1 tablespoon freshly squeezed lemon juice
2 to 3 dashes hot pepper sauce
Salt and freshly ground black pepper

Mix the ketchup, horseradish, and lemon juice together in a small bowl. Season with hot pepper sauce and salt and pepper to taste. Chill until ready to serve.

fresh tomato salsa

MAKES ABOUT 3½ CUPS

A fresh combination of tomatoes, cilantro, pepper, lime juice, and scallions, this salsa can be served with tacos, tortillas, burritos, or as a dip for chips, shrimp, or raw vegetables. We particularly like it with the Huevos Rancheros (page 36), and the Burrito Party (page 187). See photograph on page 230.

1 pound ripe tomatoes (2 large or 3 medium), cubed
1 green bell pepper, chopped
½ cup chopped scallions (white and green parts)

1 jalapeño pepper, finely chopped, with or without seeds
⅓ cup fresh chopped cilantro leaves
1 tablespoon fresh lime juice
3 tablespoons olive oil
Salt and freshly ground black pepper

In a medium bowl, gently mix all of the ingredients. Taste for seasoning and add salt and pepper as needed. The salsa can be made about an hour or two before serving; cover and refrigerate until ready to serve.

blue cheese dipping sauce

MAKES ABOUT 1¼ CUPS

Serve this dipping sauce with Baked Buffalo Chicken Wings (page 170), or as a thick, delicious dressing for Cobb and Blossom Salad (page 87). It makes a great dip for raw vegetables or cooked shrimp or skewers of grilled beef or chicken.

5 ounces blue cheese, softened and crumbled (about 1¼ cups)
2 chopped scallions (white and green parts)

½ cup sour cream
3 tablespoons milk

Using the back of a spoon, mash the blue cheese in a small bowl until almost smooth—a few chunks are desirable. Mix in the scallions, sour cream, and milk until well blended. Season to taste with salt and pepper.

favoritevariations

■ For a tangy dressing, replace the milk with buttermilk.
■ Use goat cheese instead of blue cheese.
■ Add 2 tablespoons chopped fresh chives.

orange-miso dipping sauce

We warn you: This refreshing, citrusy dip is outrageously good. Try spreading the sauce on grilled chicken or fish, or use it as a simple dip for fresh vegetables, crackers, or shrimp. It's even delicious drizzled over a salad. Our favorite way to serve this sauce is paired with Classic Cocktail Sauce (page 236) for a great Shrimp Cocktail (page 133) and Salmon and Ginger Cakes (page 116).

Miso is a fermented soy bean paste with the consistency of creamy peanut butter. Look for white miso paste in the refrigerated shelves of your grocer's produce section or in Asian grocery shops. The sauce will keep for about 5 days.

1 tablespoon white miso paste
⅔ cup sour cream
½ cup mayonnaise
1 tablespoon grated lemon zest

2 tablespoons freshly squeezed lemon juice
1 tablespoon orange zest
1 tablespoon orange juice
Salt and freshly ground black pepper

Mix all the ingredients together in a bowl until smooth. Season with salt and pepper to taste, and chill until ready to serve.

asian dipping sauce

A delicious dipping sauce for dumplings, stir-fried chicken or fish, or Scallop "Chips" (page 119). The sauce can be made several hours ahead of time; cover and refrigerate until ready to serve.

1 cup soy sauce or tamari
¼ cup finely chopped fresh cilantro leaves
1 scallion (white and green parts), thinly sliced

1 tablespoon finely chopped, peeled fresh ginger
1 teaspoon Asian sesame oil
½ teaspoon Chinese chile paste (optional)

In a small bowl mix all of the ingredients.

pickled **red onions**

MAKES ABOUT 2 CUPS

This recipe is almost too good to be true. Thinly sliced red onions are tossed with cider vinegar for about an hour and, well, that's it. These crisp, vinegary quick pickles are terrific on sandwiches (see Grilled Chicken "Hero" with Garlic Aïoli on page 103), or tossed into salads. They add a tart, fresh taste to rich soups or stews, or served as part of an antipasti platter (see page 217). These pickles will keep refrigerated for over a week.

1 large red onion, thinly sliced
1 cup cider vinegar
1 tablespoon sugar

1 teaspoon salt
Generous grinding of black pepper

Place the onions in a medium nonreactive bowl and pour the vinegar on top. Add the sugar, salt, and pepper and toss well. Cover and refrigerate for 1 hour, stirring once or twice. The onions can stay in the vinegar for about 2 hours but should be drained after that time. Cover and refrigerate. The onions will keep for well over a week.

favoritevariations

- Add 1 tablespoon lightly crushed fennel and coriander seeds for a Middle Eastern–tasting pickle.
- Add a dash of red chile flakes for a slightly spicy pickle.
- Substitute red or white wine vinegar or sherry vinegar for the cider vinegar.
- Try making the pickles using sweet vidalia onions.

green sauce

MAKES ABOUT 1½ CUPS

Imagine an emerald green sauce, chock full of fresh parsley, chives, crunchy sour capers, pungent scallions, and a green, fruity olive oil and you'll get an idea of how enticing this sauce can be. We like to spread it on a roast beef or turkey sandwich, serve it with roasted or grilled fish or poultry, even use it as a dip for Pita Crackers (page 167), assorted raw vegetables, and cooked shrimp. But mostly we love it with vegetables—steamed artichokes or asparagus are terrific pairings. The Roasted Vegetable Platter (page 222) makes this sauce truly shine.

The sauce will keep for about 8 hours without losing its fresh vitality.

2 cups packed fresh parsley leaves
3 scallions (white and green parts), chopped
¼ cup chopped chives

One 3½-ounce jar nonpareil capers, drained
Salt and freshly ground black pepper
¾ cup olive oil

In a food processor or blender, pulse the parsley and scallions until coarsely chopped. Add the chives and pulse four to five times until chopped. Add the capers and pulse again until the sauce is quite thick but not fully blended. Add a very light touch of salt (the capers will add almost enough) and a generous grinding of pepper and pulse again. Add the oil and pulse four to five times. The final sauce should be thick and chunky—a coarsely chopped, very green sauce.

chipotle cream

MAKES ABOUT 1½ CUPS

Two ingredients are whirled together in a food processor or blender to create this quick, extraordinarily flavorful sauce. Serve with burritos (see page 187), tacos, and tortillas, as a dip for cooked shrimp, raw vegetables, and blue corn chips, or as a side sauce for roasted or grilled poultry, pork, beef, or vegetables.

¾ cup chipotle peppers in adobo sauce
  (see Note)

1 cup sour cream

In the bowl of a food processor or blender, process the peppers and the sauce they come in for about 5 seconds. Add the sour cream and puree until smooth. Place in a serving bowl, cover, and chill until ready to serve. The sauce can be made up to 8 hours ahead of time.

NOTE: Chipotles are dried smoked jalapeño peppers. Sold in small jars and cans, they have a wonderfully smoky, spicy flavor.

sweet and spicy **bbq sauce**

MAKES ABOUT 1½ CUPS SAUCE

This sauce is loosely adapted from the one in our earlier book, *Stonewall Kitchen Harvest.* Over the years, it has become a real favorite on Dry-Rubbed Paper Bag Ribs (page 202), grilled chicken, burgers (page 193), barbecued brisket, or steaks. It will keep, covered and refrigerated, for about a week.

1 tablespoon vegetable oil
1½ tablespoons finely chopped, peeled, fresh ginger
1 garlic clove, minced
½ to 1 teaspoon Chinese chile paste or hot pepper sauce to taste

2 tablespoons soy sauce
2 tablespoons balsamic vinegar
1½ cups ketchup
½ cup pure maple syrup
Salt and freshly ground black pepper

In a medium saucepan, heat the oil over medium heat. Add the ginger and garlic and cook for about 3 minutes, or until they just begin to turn golden brown. Stir in the chile paste and cook for 5 seconds. Add the soy sauce and vinegar and then stir in the ketchup and maple syrup until smooth. Add salt and pepper to taste and simmer over very low heat for about 8 minutes, or until thickened. Let cool. (The sauce can be made about a week ahead of time and refrigerated.)

favoritevariations
- Use honey instead of maple syrup.
- Add 1 tablespoon Worcestershire sauce for added spice.
- Add 1 teaspoon grated orange zest and 1 tablespoon fresh orange juice.

garlic **aïoli**

MAKES ABOUT ½ CUP

If you start with good, store-bought mayonnaise, this sauce gives you a lot of punch with very little effort. Sweet, pungent roasted Garlic Aïoli makes almost any sandwich more exciting; see the Grilled Chicken "Hero" (page 103), for example. You can also use it to make a seriously garlicky chicken or egg salad, to wake up a roast beef sandwich, or as a condiment for grilled steaks, fish, or chicken.

1 large head garlic, roasted (see page 161)   Salt and freshly ground black pepper
⅓ cup mayonnaise

Remove the garlic from its skin. Put the garlic in a small bowl and mash the cloves with a fork. Add the mayonnaise and stir well to combine. Season the aïoli with salt and pepper to taste.

favoritevariations

- Add 2 tablespoons chopped fresh chives, basil, or parsley.
- Add 2 tablespoons chopped roasted sweet red pepper to give the aïoli a sweet flavor and a gorgeous rosy color.
- See the Lobster BLT with basil aïoli (page 104) for another aïoli variation.

what flavor is your butter?

Flavored butter highlights the flavor of other dishes and adds a richness and complexity that is generally only achieved with a more complicated sauce. We're talking about combinations like horseradish butter on grilled swordfish, tarragon-chive-lemon butter on a lamb chop, or a raspberry-cinnamon butter tucked inside a warm muffin.

The possibilities, we have found, are endless. Below are a few of our favorite combinations along with some suggestions for using them. Read these ideas and then have fun coming up with your own combinations.

The butters can be made several days ahead of time; cover and refrigerate until ready to use, about 5 days. We also like making flavored butter in small ramekins, covering them with plastic wrap, and freezing them for up to 3 months. Or roll flavored butter up into a log shape (like a fat cigar) and wrap in plastic wrap before freezing.

Place ¼ cup (½ stick) softened butter in a small bowl. Using a fork, mix in any of the following:

- **Horseradish Butter:** 2 tablespoons drained, prepared horseradish or beet horseradish. Serve with grilled fish, roast beef or corned beef, steak, or spread it on matzo.

- **Herb-Lemon Butter:** 2 tablespoons chopped fresh herbs, 1 tablespoon lemon juice, and a generous grinding of black pepper. Spread on any type of grilled food, on a tomato cut in half and then broiled or baked, or on toast; or add to sautés with vegetables, chicken, or fish; pasta or rice dishes; or soups and stews.

- **Mint Butter:** 2 tablespoons chopped fresh mint and a grinding of pepper. Use with the Grown-Up Vegetable Medley (page 229), Green Beans with Tomatoes and Kalamata Olives (page 213), Grilled Corn on the Cob (page 227), lamb chops, couscous, Israeli couscous, roasted fish steaks like halibut, or sautéed or grilled zucchini slices.

- **Smoked Salmon Butter:** 2 to 3 tablespoons finely chopped smoked salmon or any type of smoked fish and a grinding of black pepper and ½ teaspoon grated lemon zest. Use in scrambled eggs, omelets, or to top fresh salmon, or any type of seafood. Add to risotto or pasta.

- **Bacon-Chive Butter:** 2 crumbled slices cooked bacon and 1 tablespoon minced chives. Add to baked potatoes, pasta dishes, risotto, grilled steaks, burgers (see page 193), seafood, chops, toast, or bagels.

- **Wild Mushroom Butter:** 2 tablespoons reconstituted dried wild mushrooms (soak mushrooms in warm water for 5 minutes, drain, pat dry, and then chop) and 1 teaspoon chopped fresh tarragon, if desired. Add to veal, chicken, beef, or game dishes, or risotto, soups, and stews; spread on a grilled cheese sandwich or over sautéed peas or any vegetable.

- **Chipotle Pepper Butter:** 1 to 2 tablespoons finely chopped chipotle peppers. Use with grilled meat, poultry, or fish, or egg dishes, or spread on tortillas before assembling tacos.
- **Lavender Butter:** ½ teaspoon chopped dried organic lavender. Spread on Grilled Corn on the Cob (page 227), steak, grilled chicken, toast, scones, or pound cake.
- **White Truffle Butter:** ½ teaspoon white truffle oil. Use with Grilled Corn on the Cob (page 227); steak; pasta; baked, roasted, or mashed potatoes; roasted mushrooms, peas, green beans, or any steamed green vegetable.
- **Coconut Butter:** 2 tablespoons shredded unsweetened coconut. Add to stir fried or broiled shrimp, fish fillets, pancakes, or waffles; or spread on a wedge of fresh pineapple or a grapefruit half and grill or place under the broiler.
- **Spicy Lime-Scallion Butter:** 2 tablespoons lime juice, 1 tablespoon grated lime zest, 1 finely chopped scallion (white and green parts), and ½ teaspoon Chinese chile paste or hot pepper sauce. Use this tangy, citrus and spice butter with fish, shrimp, stir-fries, chicken and beef dishes, or as a topping for Asian noodles.
- **Caper-Olive Butter:** 3 tablespoons chopped olives, 1 tablespoon coarsely chopped drained capers, and 1 tablespoon olive oil. Spread on fish, shellfish, steak, chicken breasts, slices of French bread, bagels, sautéed vegetables, pasta, or couscous.
- **Pea Butter:** Mash ¼ cup cooked peas, sea salt, and pepper to taste. Spread a tiny bit of the pea butter on top of grilled or baked salmon, lamb chops, or on steamed carrots.
- **Jam Butter:** 1 to 2 tablespoons of your favorite jam. Use on toast, muffins, or biscuits, or inside an omelet.
- **Sweey Cranberry-Ginger Butter:** 2 tablespoons finely chopped fresh or frozen cranberries, 1 teaspoon grated or finely chopped peeled, fresh ginger, and 1 tablespoon sugar. Spread on muffins, pancakes, sweet potatoes, or toast.
- **Maple-Nutmeg-Cinnamon Butter:** 2 tablespoons pure maple syrup and ⅛ teaspoon each grated nutmeg and ground cinnamon. Spread on pancakes, waffles, muffins, toast, scones, squash, cooked carrots or beans, cooked salmon or fish fillets, pork chops, or pork tenderloin.
- **Sweet Chocolate Butter:** 3 tablespoons melted dark, bittersweet, or milk chocolate or chocolate fudge sauce and 1 teaspoon sugar. Spread on toast or muffins, or add to pancakes and waffles. Make a tea time treat by spreading this chocolate butter on thin bread (crusts removed) and topping with fresh raspberries.

dessert

chocolate **mousse**

SERVES 6

Chocolate mousse was overdone in the 1970s, but we never really tired of it. Because you only need a few ingredients to make this French classic, it's important to use the best chocolate and freshest milk and cream you can find.

You can serve the mousse as-is, or layer it into a fancy parfait; see Favorite Variations below.

6 ounces semisweet or bittersweet (about 55%) chocolate, chopped
4 ounces milk chocolate, chopped

½ cup milk
1 cup heavy (whipping) cream
½ teaspoon vanilla

Melt the two types of chocolate in the microwave or a double boiler or in a medium saucepan over very low heat, stirring with a spatula until melted and smooth. The chocolate should be warm to the touch but not hot.

Meanwhile, place the milk in a medium saucepan over medium-low heat until simmering. Using a mixer, whip the cream until it holds soft peaks; whisk in the vanilla.

Whisk the hot milk into the warm chocolate until smooth. Using a spatula, slowly fold the chocolate mixture into the whipped cream until well blended. Pour into a serving bowl, individual ramekins, or small bowls, cover, and chill for at least 2 hours to set before serving.

favoritevariations

- Add 1 teaspoon grated tangerine or orange zest to the mousse.
- Add a drop of orange or almond oil to the mousse.
- Add 1 teaspoon Amaretto, Grand Marnier, or your favorite liqueur to the mousse.
- Dissolve 1 teaspoon ground espresso powder in 1 tablespoon hot water and add to the mousse.
- Add a dash of ground ginger, cinnamon, cardamom, or nutmeg to the mousse or sprinkle as a garnish on top.
- To make a mousse parfait: Whip 1 cup heavy cream with 2 tablespoons sugar and ½ teaspoon vanilla until peaks form. Divide half the mousse into the bottom of six wine goblets (widemouth red wineglasses work best), parfait glasses, or glass bowls. Add a dollop of whipped cream on top and divide the remaining mousse on top. Add the remaining whipped cream. Using a box grater, grate a bit of a milk or dark chocolate bar on top as a garnish.
- Garnish the mousse with fresh raspberries, sliced strawberries, candied ginger, candied citrus peel, or candied rose petals.
- Top the mousse with a dollop of crème fraîche or mascarpone mixed with a touch of confectioners' sugar.
- Use a wide vegetable peeler to make chocolate shavings from a bar or chunk of dark, semi-dark, milk, or white chocolate to garnish the mousse.

mini **raspberry-filled chocolate cakes**

SERVES 6

Molten chocolate cakes were all the rage for a while, with every trendy restaurant serving their own version of this slightly undercooked, oozing chocolate cake. What we always liked about this cake is that it reminds us of a cross between a really extraordinary chocolate pudding and the best chocolate cake, the kind we enjoyed as kids. This is very rich stuff—ideal for a romantic dessert or an elegant dinner.

The cakes can be made hours or days ahead of time and refrigerated or frozen.

Vegetable oil spray for greasing the ramekins
¾ cup (1½ sticks) unsalted butter
8 ounces good-quality semisweet or bittersweet (60%) chocolate, chopped

3 large eggs
3 large egg yolks
⅓ cup sugar
3 tablespoons all-purpose flour
1 cup fresh or frozen raspberries

Place a rack in the middle of the oven and preheat the oven to 450°F.

Grease the bottom and sides of six eight-ounce ramekins with the vegetable spray and set aside.

In a medium saucepan melt the butter over low heat until sizzling but not turning brown. Remove from the heat and add the chocolate; using a soft spatula, stir until the chocolate is melted and the mixture is smooth.

In an electric mixer, whisk the eggs, egg yolks, and sugar for about 5 minutes on medium speed, or until light and fluffy. Add the chocolate mixture and mix until just incorporated. Sprinkle in the flour and mix until just blended. Fill each of the ramekins about one-third of the way. Divide the raspberries on top of the chocolate in the middle of the ramekins and spoon the remaining chocolate mixture on top.

Place the ramekins on a cookie sheet and bake on the middle shelf for 15 minutes. (If the cakes were refrigerated, bake for 16 to 17 minutes; if they were frozen, bake for 18 to 20 minutes.) The cakes are done when they are set on the sides, but still soft in the center. Remove from the oven, run a small knife around the edge of each cake, and carefully invert onto a plate. (Alternatively, serve directly from the ramekin.) When you split open the hot cake the chocolate and raspberries will ooze out of the middle.

favoritevariations

■ Substitute vanilla sugar (bury a split vanilla bean in a few cups of sugar for several days) for the regular sugar.

■ Use blueberries, strawberries, or blackberries instead of raspberries.

■ Add ¼ teaspoon almond or orange extract to the melted chocolate mixture before adding it to the beaten eggs.

ultimate **brownies**

Who are we to say that the world needs yet another brownie recipe? But this one, ultrachocolatey and chewy with a great dense texture, stands out as a winner. The brownie batter uses very little flour; our other trick is that we transfer the hot brownie pan into the refrigerator to create a chewy texture.

Serve the brownies alone, or make a brownie sundae by topping the brownies with a drizzle of Ultimate Chocolate Sauce (page 261) and a scoop of your favorite ice cream.

2 sticks unsalted butter, plus some for greasing the pan

1 cup all-purpose flour plus extra for the pan

12 ounces semisweet or bittersweet (55%) chocolate, chopped

1 teaspoon instant espresso powder

1½ cups sugar

4 large eggs

1½ teaspoons vanilla extract

Place a rack in the middle of the oven and preheat the oven to 325°F. Butter and flour a 13 × 9-inch baking pan.

In a small saucepan set over very low heat, melt the butter. Remove from the heat and add the chocolate. Using a soft spatula, stir to melt the chocolate and create a smooth sauce. Add the espresso powder and stir to combine.

In a mixer, whip the sugar and eggs for about 4 minutes on medium speed, or until light and fluffy. Add the vanilla and the chocolate mixture and blend well. Remove the bowl from the mixer, sift the flour on top, and gently fold it in by hand until blended, being careful not to overmix the batter. Pour into the prepared baking pan and bake for 35 minutes.

Remove from the oven and let cool for 10 minutes. Place in the refrigerator until completely cool. Cut into 20 squares.

favoritevariations

■ Add 1 cup chopped walnuts, pecans, pistachios, or almonds to the batter just before baking.

■ Add ½ teaspoon mint extract to the batter.

■ Add ⅛ teaspoon orange or almond oil to the batter.

■ Add 1 teaspoon grated lemon or orange zest to the batter.

chocolate crepes with tangerines and dark chocolate–orange sauce

For some reason many cooks have the mistaken idea that crepes are difficult or time consuming to make. Nothing could be further from the truth. If you've made crepes before, you know that the first crepe always goes to the cook. In other words, don't be discouraged if the first crepe is less than perfect. Once the pan is hot and greased the crepes will improve. Serve the crepes hot, drizzled with the chocolate sauce, or spread the sauce inside the crepes, fold them into quarters, and serve at room temperature. Either way, the chocolate-tangerine combination is at once a deeply satisfying and refreshing way to end a meal. These crepes would also be an excellent choice for brunch, served with fresh-squeezed orange juice mimosas.

for the crepes
2 ounces semisweet or bittersweet (about 55%) chocolate, chopped
2 tablespoons unsalted butter plus more for the pan
3 large eggs
¼ cup sugar
¼ teaspoon salt
1⅓ cups milk
½ teaspoon vanilla
2 tablespoons cocoa powder
1 cup all-purpose flour

for the dark chocolate sauce
⅓ cup milk
¼ cup heavy cream
6 ounces semisweet chocolate, finely chopped
1 tablespoon orange-flavored liqueur, such as Grand Marnier, or ¼ teaspoon orange or almond extract

for the garnish
3 tangerines, peeled, sectioned, membranes removed and cut into 1-inch pieces
Confectioners' sugar for dusting

To make the crepe batter: Melt the chocolate and butter together in a small saucepan over low heat, stirring constantly. Remove from the heat once the chocolate is almost completely melted, and set aside.

In a large bowl, beat the eggs with a whisk until blended. Add the sugar and salt and whisk to combine. Pour in the milk and vanilla, and whisk until blended. Sift the cocoa powder and flour over the surface of the batter, and whisk them into the batter until no lumps remain. Slowly drizzle in the melted chocolate mixture, whisking constantly. Let the batter sit, covered, for about 30 minutes or refrigerate overnight. Bring to room temperature before using.

To make the sauce: Bring the milk and cream to a simmer in a small saucepan. Remove from the heat, add the chocolate, and stir until smooth. Stir in the liqueur. Set aside until ready to use. (The chocolate sauce may be made a day ahead of time, covered and refrigerated, and reheated in a saucepan over low heat until warm.)

RECIPE CONTINUES ▶

To cook the crepes: Heat a 6- to 8-inch nonstick skillet or crepe pan over medium heat. When the pan is hot, add about $1/2$ teaspoon butter and let it melt, swirling it around the entire surface of the skillet. Add $1/3$ cup of the crepe batter. Swirl the pan to encourage the batter to coat the entire surface of the pan. Cook for 30 seconds to one minute, or until the crepe has set and browned slightly on the bottom side. Flip carefully and cook for another 30 seconds or so. Transfer to a plate. Repeat with remaining batter, adding a small amount of butter to grease the pan after every few crepes, and place finished crepes on the plate.

(You can make crepes the day before serving. Cover and refrigerate overnight. Wrap the crepes in foil and reheat in a 250°F oven for about 10 minutes.)

Fold the hot crepes into quarters. Place 1 or 2 crepes on each plate, drizzle each with chocolate sauce, and top with tangerine sections and a dusting of powdered sugar.

favoritevariation

■ Use milk chocolate instead of dark chocolate for a creamier, sweeter crepe and sauce.

chop a choc

Here's a little tip that makes chopping a block of chocolate or a chocolate bar much simpler and easier: Use a long serrated knife and slice the chocolate as if you were cutting a thin slice of bread. The serrated knife will cause the chocolate to crumble and break off. You can then use a regular knife to chop the chocolate more finely if need be.

the mysteries of chocolate

When we're feeling down and blue, or celebratory and elated, it's chocolate we turn to. Instant joy. It still gives us that same feeling it did when we were kids—one bite and we're transformed into happier creatures.

Chocolate may remind us of being kids, but the world of chocolate has grown up. These days choosing a chocolate bar—for eating or baking—is something far more complex than it was back in the days when all we craved was a Hershey's bar. What follows is a basic primer that will help you make sense of some of the new terminology, as well as guide you in cooking with and shopping for chocolate.

THE PERCENTAGE ISSUE One of the most confusing things about chocolate these days is the percentages you often see printed on chocolate bars and in recipes. When you see a recipe that calls for 55 percent or 60 percent semisweet or bittersweet chocolate, or a chocolate bar with this on the label, the percentage refers to how much of the chocolate bar is pure ground up cacao bean (including cocoa butter) as opposed to sugar (unless, of course, we're talking about milk chocolate which, in addition to cacao and sugar, also contains milk). Standard semisweet and bittersweet chocolate contain 50 percent to 60 percent cacao and thus 50 percent to 40 percent sugar. It's increasingly common to see quality chocolates with even higher percentages of cacao and less sugar.

As we discovered with wine and then olive oil, Americans are beginning to appreciate the complexity of flavors found in pure chocolate. But eating and cooking with these higher percentage chocolates does take some getting used to. If you're used to biting into a chocolate bar that is 50 percent sugar you may be surprised (even shocked) at the intensity found in a bar of good bittersweet chocolate. When you eat these higher percentage chocolates chances are good that you'll experience a wider range of flavors—a pleasing bitterness, acidity, astringency, and sweetness.

COOKING WITH CHOCOLATE In several recipes you'll notice that we call for a specific type of chocolate, such as bittersweet, semisweet, or milk chocolate. We recommend sticking with the type of chocolate that is called for. We also sometimes call for a chocolate containing a specific percentage of cacao beans. Most of the recipes in this book, unless otherwise indicated, were made using semisweet or bittersweet chocolate with a 55 percent to 62 percent cacao content. We highly recommend finding chocolate with percentages in this range, or your recipes may not be as successful.

SHOPPING FOR CHOCOLATE There is a whole new world of artisanally made chocolate sold in specialty food shops, chocolate shops, and even plain old grocery stores. Some of the brands we look for include: Scharffen Berger (www.scharffenberger.com), Valrhona (www.valrhona.com), Green & Black's Organic Chocolate (www.greenandblacks.com), Callebaut (www.ecallebaut.com) and El Rey (www.chocosphere.com).

Keep in mind that many popular, widely available types of chocolate don't list percentages on their label. Some of the more commonly available types of chocolate that fit within the 55 percent to 62 percent category include bittersweet and semisweet chocolate made by Ghirardelli, Hershey, and Lindt.

STORING CHOCOLATE Always store chocolate in a cool, dry spot that is no higher than 75°F. Higher temperatures will cause chocolate to develop a whitish layer, a kind of film that is called a "bloom." The chocolate is still perfectly good to eat.

chocolate-dipped **pistachio-orange biscotti**

These twice-baked cookies are laced with toasted pistachio nuts, orange rind, and orange juice and then dipped into semisweet chocolate to create a crunchy, satisfying biscotti. Serve with hot chocolate, tiny cups of strong espresso, café au lait, or a pot of tea.

2 cups raw shelled pistachios, toasted (page 260)
2 cups plus 2 tablespoons all-purpose flour plus more for dusting
1 cup sugar
1½ teaspoons baking powder
½ teaspoon salt
¼ cup (½ stick) unsalted butter, cold, cut into 4 pieces

2 large eggs
1 teaspoon vanilla
1 packed teaspoon grated orange zest
¼ cup orange juice, preferably fresh
6 ounces semisweet or bittersweet (about 55%) chocolate, or 1 cup semisweet chocolate chips

Place a rack in the center of the oven and preheat the oven to 350°F. Line a cookie sheet with parchment paper.

Finely chop half the pistachios and combine in a small bowl with the remaining whole nuts; set aside.

In a large bowl, stir together the flour, sugar, baking powder, and salt until blended. Add the butter and blend into dry ingredients using your fingertips or a pastry cutter, until the mixture resembles coarse sand. Mix the eggs, vanilla, zest, and juice in a separate bowl until well blended. Add the wet ingredients to dry ingredients and stir with a wooden spoon until just blended. Fold in the chopped and whole pistachios.

Generously flour a clean working area. Using floured hands, divide the dough into two equal portions. Form each piece into a flat log roughly 12 × 8 and 1 inch high, adding additional flour as needed to prevent the dough from sticking to the counter. Carefully place the logs 2 to 3 inches apart on the parchment-covered baking sheet.

Bake the logs for 25 minutes, or until firm to the touch and just beginning to brown. Remove from the oven, reduce the oven temperature to 300°F, and let the biscotti cool for about 10 minutes.

Transfer the logs to a cutting board. Using a sharp, serrated knife and a gentle sawing motion, cut logs on a slight diagonal into ½-inch-wide pieces. Place the biscotti cut side up on one or two cookie sheets. Bake for 30 minutes, turning the biscotti once halfway through baking. The biscotti should be firm to the touch and golden brown on both sides. Remove from the baking sheet and cool completely on wire racks.

RECIPE CONTINUES ▶

While the biscotti are cooling, melt the chocolate in the microwave, in a double boiler, or over very low heat. When almost all of the chocolate has melted, remove from the heat and let rest for 5 minutes. Dip one end of the cookie or one flat side of each biscotti into the chocolate and hold vertically to let excess chocolate drip off. Place the biscotti chocolate-side up on wax paper to cool until the chocolate hardens, 3 to 4 hours. The biscotti will keep, in a cool, dark, well-sealed tin or plastic bag, for several days.

favoritevariations

- Substitute almonds, pine nuts, or hazelnuts for the pistachios.
- Dip the biscotti into white or milk chocolate instead of dark chocolate.
- For double-chocolate pistachio biscotti, sift $\frac{1}{4}$ cup high-quality cocoa powder into the dry ingredients.
- Substitute fresh tangerine or clementine juice for the orange juice.
- Add 2 tablespoons chopped dried cherries or cranberries.

would you care for those nuts toasted?

Many recipes in this book call for nuts to be lightly toasted before using them in cookies, cakes, sauces, or on top of salads. Is toasting nuts just a fussy, unnecessary step, or is it actually worth the bother?

When you toast nuts in a hot oven it releases the nuts' natural oils and causes them to become particularly fragrant and flavorful. So, in most cases, it's well worth taking the extra 10 minutes to toast the nuts lightly and release all their nuttiness.

To toast nuts, place them on a cookie sheet in a preheated 350°F oven for 5 to 10 minutes. They are ready when you can smell them and they are beginning to turn very pale golden brown. Let cool before chopping or adding to recipes.

ultimate **chocolate sauce**

We strongly urge you to pour this simple sauce hot from the pan over a scoop of vanilla or ginger ice cream. Even better, drizzle a bit over Ultimate Brownies (page 252), top it off with a scoop of ice cream, and drizzle with more chocolate sauce! It's the basis of our excellent Quick Ice Cream Pie (page 262).

The sauce will keep, tightly sealed in a jar, for about a week in the refrigerator. To reheat, place the opened jar in a pot filled almost halfway with simmering water, and heat until warm and pourable.

½ cup (1 stick) unsalted butter
1 cup semisweet or bittersweet chocolate chips (about 55%), or 6 ounces chopped chocolate

½ cup light corn syrup
⅛ teaspoon salt

In a medium saucepan, melt the butter, chocolate, corn syrup, and salt over medium-low heat until just simmering, stirring frequently to create a smooth, thick sauce. Serve hot or at room temperature.

favoritevariations

■ Add 1 to 2 teaspoons orange liqueur, such as Grand Marnier, or almond-flavored liqueur, such as Amaretto.
■ Add a tablespoon or two of toasted unsweetened coconut flakes.
■ Add 1 teaspoon grated orange or lemon zest.
■ Add 1 to 2 tablespoons slivered crystallized ginger.

quick **ice cream pie**

SERVES 6 TO 8

There are few desserts as refreshing, nostalgic, and simple as a well-made ice cream pie. This frozen dessert uses a premade graham cracker crust, your favorite ice cream, and Ultimate Chocolate Sauce (page 261). Don't be misled; this pie is sophisticated and interesting enough to be served at a dinner party. It's also a great dessert for a special family meal. The pie takes virtually no time to make, but you will need to leave about 1 hour and 15 minutes to let it freeze properly.

The pie can be made ahead of time; cover and place in the freezer for up to 24 hours before serving.

About ¾ cup Ultimate Chocolate Sauce (page 261)
1 premade 8-inch graham cracker crust
2 pints good-quality ice cream, almost at room temperature (soft enough to spread; see Note)

1 cup heavy (whipping) cream
2 tablespoons sugar

Use a spoon to drizzle about ¼ cup of the chocolate sauce on the bottom of the crust and spread with a soft spatula. Very gently spoon 1 pint of the ice cream into the crust and spread it evenly to create an ice cream layer. Drizzle another ¼ cup of the chocolate sauce over the ice cream, using a soft spatula to almost cover the first layer. Freeze the pie until the chocolate hardens, about 15 minutes. Spread the other pint of ice cream into the pie, doming it slightly it the center. Freeze until the pie is firm, about 1 hour.

Meanwhile, using an electric mixer, whip the cream until soft peaks begin to form, 2 to 3 minutes on high speed. Add the sugar, and continue beating until the cream is stiff. Using a spoon or a pastry bag fitted with a star tip, decorate the pie with the whipped cream, and then drizzle with the remaining chocolate sauce.

NOTE: Some of our favorite ice cream combinations include coffee and vanilla; caramel and chocolate; all dulce de leche; mint chocolate chip and chocolate; ginger and vanilla; raspberry sorbet and vanilla ice cream; strawberry ice cream and raspberry sorbet; and lemon sorbet with vanilla.

favoritevariations
- Substitute a cookie crust for the graham cracker crust.
- Top the pie with crushed peanuts, walnuts, pistachios, or almonds.
- Top the pie with assorted fresh berries.

a quick pastry bag

If you don't have a pastry bag, or find them overly fussy to use, you can make a simple, makeshift pastry bag using a regular plastic bag. Take a large plastic bag (if it's the kind with a "zipper" closure on top, simply cut it off with a scissor) and fill the bag less than halfway with your whipped cream, pastry cream, or filling. Use your hands to close the bag at the top, squeezing any air out of the bag before twisting the top into a swirl that will close the bag. Take scissors and snip off a tiny portion at the tip of the bag and use your plastic bag as you would a pastry bag.

oatmeal, fig, and ginger cookies

MAKES ABOUT 30 COOKIES

Oatmeal Raisin Cookies are a real favorite with their chewy texture and subtly sweet flavor. This version takes the classic cookie and gives it a new twist, by adding fruity figs and fragrant crystallized ginger.

This dough freezes well: Freeze the dough balls on a wax paper–lined cookie sheet until solid, and then transfer to a resealable plastic bag. Squeeze out all of the air from the bag before sealing. Freeze for up to 3 weeks. The dough can be baked straight from the freezer for about 18 to 22 minutes.

1 cup (2 sticks) unsalted butter, at room
    temperature
1 cup packed light brown sugar
1¼ cups sugar
2 teaspoons vanilla
2 large eggs

1½ cups all-purpose flour
1 teaspoon baking powder
½ teaspoon salt
3 cups old-fashioned oats
1¼ cups chopped dried figs
½ cup chopped crystallized ginger

Place a rack in the middle of the oven and preheat the oven to 350°F. Line two cookie sheets with parchment paper (or grease the sheets) and set aside.

In an electric mixer fitted with the paddle attachment, beat the butter and two sugars together on medium speed until light and fluffy, about 3 minutes. Add the vanilla and mix on low speed until just combined; then add the eggs one at a time, scraping down the sides of the bowl as necessary between additions.

In a separate bowl, blend the flour, baking powder, and salt together with a whisk. With the mixer on low, slowly add the flour mixture and mix until just combined. Using a spoon or spatula, stir in the oats, figs, and ginger, separating the dried fruit with your hands as you drop it in to make sure it gets evenly distributed.

Form the dough into 2-inch balls, using roughly 2 tablespoons dough for each, and place 2 inches apart on the prepared cookie sheets. Bake for 15 to 18 minutes, rotating the sheets front to back and top to bottom in the oven about halfway through cooking. The cookies should be golden brown at the edges. Let cool for 5 minutes on the cookie sheets, then transfer to a wire rack to cool completely. Store cooled cookies in an airtight container for up to 3 days.

favoritevariations

Try substituting the following for the figs and ginger:

- Traditional Oatmeal Raisin Cookies: 1½ cups raisins.
- Apricot-Almond Oatmeal Cookies: 1 cup toasted slivered almonds, 1 cup chopped dried apricots, and 1 teaspoon cardamom.
- Cranberry-Orange Oatmeal Cookies: 1½ cups dried cranberries, 2 tablespoons grated orange zest.
- Chocolate-Dipped Oatmeal Chocolate Chip Cookies: Substitute 1 cup chocolate chips for the dried fruit. Melt an additional 2 cups chocolate chips and dip cooled cookies into chocolate to cover half of the cookie. Let harden overnight on wax paper.

lemon-ginger **cheesecake**

SERVES 8 TO 10

We think this recipe is everything a cheesecake should be—light, fluffy, and creamy. Best of all, the cake can be made 2 full days ahead of time; cover and refrigerate until ready to serve.

for the crust
½ cup (1 stick) unsalted butter, melted, plus
    extra for greasing the pan
1½ cups graham cracker crumbs (see Note)
½ cup sifted confectioners' sugar
½ teaspoon ground cinnamon
½ teaspoon ground ginger

for the cheesecake
2 pounds cream cheese, at room
    temperature

1¼ cups sugar
4 large eggs, at room temperature
Grated zest from 1 large lemon (about
    1 tablespoon)
Juice from 1 large lemon (2½ to
    3 tablespoons)
½ teaspoon vanilla extract
1 teaspoon ground ginger
6 strips crystallized ginger, cut into thin
    strips for garnish
Confectioners' sugar for decorating

Grease the bottom and sides of a 10-inch springform pan with butter.

In a small bowl, mix the graham cracker crumbs, confectioners' sugar, melted butter, cinnamon, and ginger, stirring until the mixture comes together. Press the crust evenly onto the bottom of the prepared pan and chill while you make the filling, or cover and refrigerate overnight.

Place a rack in the middle of the oven and preheat the oven to 350°F. In an electric mixer fitted with the paddle attachment, whip the cream cheese until smooth, using a spatula to scrape off any that gets stuck inside the paddle. Turn the machine on low and gradually add the sugar in a slow, steady stream. Then add the eggs, one at a time, scraping down the sides of the bowl between additions if needed. Increase the speed to medium high and beat for 3 minutes, until the filling is light and fluffy. Add the lemon zest and juice, vanilla, and ground ginger and mix for another 2 minutes, scraping the bowl and paddle as needed until the ingredients are fully incorporated.

Pour the filling into the chilled crust and bake for 1 hour. The cake is done when it is still soft in the center; the whole cake should jiggle a bit when nudged. Remove from the oven and let cool.

Remove the cake from the pan and place on a serving plate. Arrange the crystallized ginger slices on top. Just before serving, sprinkle lightly with sifted confectioners' sugar.

NOTE: To make graham cracker crumbs, place graham crackers in a closed plastic bag and crush them with a rolling pin until fairly finely ground, or grind them in a food processor.

favoritevariation

■ To make an amazing goat cheese–flavored cheesecake, use 1 pound cream cheese and 1 pound soft goat cheese and increase the sugar to 1½ cups.

lemon cake with lemon-vanilla glaze

We appreciate a fancy, multilayered, show-off cake as much as the next person, but sometimes there's nothing better than a simple, light, low-fat lemon cake. This is the recipe to try if you're one of those cooks who says they "just can't bake." A no-fail simple cake batter made from lemon juice, lemon zest, buttermilk, milk, and eggs is baked for under an hour, and topped with the simplest glaze imaginable. Serve it with a pot of tea or a pitcher of iced tea.

This cake will stay moist and fresh for several days; cover in plastic wrap and refrigerate.

for the cake
Butter for greasing the pan
1½ cups all-purpose flour, plus extra for
    the pan
2 teaspoons baking powder
Pinch of salt
¾ cup sugar
1 cup buttermilk
2 large eggs
¼ teaspoon vanilla extract
Grated zest from 1 large lemon (about
    1 tablespoon), or 1 Meyer lemon
½ cup vegetable oil, such as safflower oil

for the glaze
Grated zest from 2 large lemons (about
    2 tablespoons)
Juice from 2 large lemons (about
    6 tablespoons), or 4 Meyer lemons
¾ cup sugar
⅛ teaspoon vanilla extract

Place a rack in the middle of the oven and preheat the oven to 350°F. Grease and lightly flour the bottom and sides of an 8-inch cake pan and set aside.

To make the cake: Sift the flour, baking powder, and salt together in a medium bowl, and set aside.

In a large bowl, mix the sugar and buttermilk using an electric mixer or whisk. Add the eggs and mix well. Add the vanilla and lemon zest and mix well. Gradually mix in the flour mixture until smooth. Add the oil and mix briefly. Pour the batter into the prepared pan and bake for 30 to 45 minutes, or until a toothpick inserted in the center comes out clean.

To make the glaze: Mix the lemon zest, lemon juice, sugar, and vanilla in a small saucepan, and bring to simmer over medium heat, stirring gently. Reduce the heat to low and let simmer about 4 minutes until smooth and slightly thickened. Set aside.

Remove the cake from the oven and, using a kitchen knife, loosen the sides all around the pan. Top the pan with a large plate and flip the whole thing over to remove the cake from the pan. Invert onto another plate so that the cake is right side up. Brush the top of the hot cake lightly with the glaze. Let cool for 5 minutes. Brush with the glaze again. Let cool for 5 more minutes and then pour the remaining glaze on top of the cake. Cut into thin slices and serve slightly warm or at room temperature.

pineapple **upside-down spice cake**

SERVES 6 TO 8

Imagine a whole gorgeous show-off cake made in a cast-iron skillet!

for the pineapple topping
1 small fresh pineapple (2½ to 3 pounds)
¼ cup (½ stick) unsalted butter
¾ cup packed light brown sugar

for the cake
1½ cups all-purpose flour
2 teaspoons baking powder
1 teaspoon ground cardamom

1 teaspoon ground ginger
⅛ teaspoon ground allspice
Pinch of salt
½ cup (1 stick) unsalted butter, at room temperature
1 cup sugar
2 large eggs
½ teaspoon vanilla extract
½ cup fresh orange juice

Place a rack in the middle of the oven and preheat the oven to 375°F.

To make the topping: Cut the tough outer skin and any eyes off the outside of the pineapple. Cut in half lengthwise, and cut out the core with a small, sharp knife. Cut the pineapple into ¼-inch-thick half-moons. You should have about 2½ cups pineapple.

In a 10-inch cast-iron or heavy skillet, heat the butter over low heat. Increase the heat to medium, add the brown sugar, stir and let cook for 3 to 5 minutes, or until the mixture is bubbling. Remove from the heat.

Carefully lay the pineapple slices on top of the brown sugar mixture, fitting the pieces together like a puzzle, and pressing them down to create a flat layer. You will have more than one layer—fit the pineapple into the pan as tightly as possible.

To make the cake: In a bowl, whisk or sift together the flour, baking powder, cardamom, ginger, allspice, and salt and set aside.

Working with an electric mixer fitted with a paddle attachment, beat the butter until soft and light on medium speed, 2 to 3 minutes. Add the sugar and beat until light and fluffy, about 4 minutes. Add the eggs, one at a time, beating well between additions and scraping the sides of the bowl if necessary. Add the vanilla and mix well. Add half of the flour mixture and beat on low speed until blended. Add the orange juice and then the remaining flour mixture, mixing just until blended. Pour the (thick) cake batter on top of the pineapple slices and, using a soft spatula, spread it out evenly. Bake for 30 to 40 minutes, or until a toothpick inserted in the center comes out clean. Remove from the oven and let the cake cool for about 5 minutes, but not longer or it may stick to the pan. Place a large serving plate on top of the skillet and, very carefully, flip the cake over onto the plate. Let cool slightly and serve warm or at room temperature.

favoritevariations

■ Squeeze the juice from fresh blood oranges or a grapefruit and use instead of regular orange juice.

■ Add 1 tablespoon light rum to the cake batter with the orange juice.

raspberry squares with brown sugar crumb topping

MAKES 12 TO 16 SQUARES

Three layers combine to make these simple squares, each one contributing a great flavor, texture, and color: a quick shortbread, raspberries and raspberry jam, and a crunchy, buttery brown sugar combination to top it all off. These fruit-filled squares are equally at home at an elegant dinner or packed up for a picnic or barbecue.

Surprisingly, these squares work equally well with fresh or frozen berries.

for the crust
1½ cups all-purpose flour
½ cup confectioners' sugar, sifted
¼ teaspoon salt
¾ cup (1½ sticks) unsalted butter, cold, cut into 8 pieces

for the filling
½ cup raspberry jam, with or without seeds
4 cups fresh or frozen raspberries
2 to 4 tablespoons all-purpose flour

for the topping
½ cup (1 stick) unsalted butter, cold, cut into ½-inch cubes
1 cup all-purpose flour
1 cup packed light brown sugar

Place a rack in the middle of the oven and preheat the oven to 375°F.

To make the crust: Combine the flour, confectioners' sugar, salt, and butter in a food processor or medium bowl. Pulse about 30 times, or work the butter in with a pastry blender or your fingers, until the butter is the size of small peas. Sprinkle the mixture evenly into an ungreased 9 × 13-inch baking pan. Using your hands, press the mixture into the bottom of the pan about ½ inch up the sides of the pan. Bake the crust for 10 to 12 minutes, or until firm and barely beginning to brown.

Meanwhile, make the filling: Melt the jam in a small saucepan over medium heat, just until thinned out and liquefied.

In a medium bowl, gently mix the raspberries with enough flour until fully coated, and set aside.

Make the topping: Combine the butter, flour, and brown sugar in a food processor or medium bowl and pulse or work the butter in with a pastry blender or your fingers until the mixture begins to come together and starts to move away from the sides of the bowl; set aside.

When the crust is done, remove it from the oven. Use the back of a kitchen spoon or a pastry brush to spread the jam evenly over the hot crust. Sprinkle the berries and any flour remaining in the bowl evenly over the jam. Using your hands, sprinkle the topping evenly over the berries, breaking up any clumps larger than a nickel. Bake for 25 to 30 minutes, or until the berries are bubbling and the topping is brown. Remove from the oven and cool completely before cutting into squares.

favoritevariations

- Substitute other berries, such as blueberries, strawberries, or blackberries, and jams for the raspberries and raspberry jam.
- Try substituting lemon marmalade, fig jam, or strawberry preserves for the raspberry jam.
- Add 1 teaspoon ground ginger to the crust ingredients, 2 teaspoons grated fresh ginger to the jam, and 2 teaspoons ground ginger to the topping.

strawberry and rhubarb **crostata**

A crostata is a freeform rustic tart, ideal for those who feel that baking a pie is too much of a commitment. In this crostata, a flaky, buttery circle of dough is filled with fresh spring berries, rhubarb, a touch of fresh-squeezed orange juice, and light brown sugar. We like to serve this with vanilla-scented whipped cream. You can make the dough a day ahead of time or freeze it (wrapped in plastic wrap and then in foil) for up to 2 months before using.

for the dough
2 cups all-purpose flour plus extra for rolling
    out the dough
3 tablespoons sugar
Pinch of salt
¾ cup (1½ sticks) unsalted butter, cold,
    cut into cubes
About ½ cup ice cold water

for the strawberry filling
3½ cups fresh strawberries (about 1 pound),
    cut into thick slices

1 cup chopped rhubarb
About ¼ cup packed light brown sugar
    (see Note)
1½ tablespoons all-purpose flour
2 tablespoons fresh orange juice

for the vanilla whipped cream
1 cup heavy (whipping) cream
1 teaspoon vanilla extract
2 tablespoons sugar

To prepare the dough: In the bowl of a food processor, whirl the flour, sugar, and salt until combined. Add the butter and pulse the mixture about 15 times, until the butter resembles small peas. With the motor on, add enough ice water until the dough just begins to pull away from the sides of the bowl and comes together. Don't worry if it still looks crumbly. You can also make the dough by hand: Mix the flour, sugar, and salt in a bowl. Using a pastry blender, add the butter and work it into the flour until it resembles coarse cornmeal. Pour in enough water until the dough begins to come together. Pour the dough onto a large sheet of aluminum foil and close the foil up to create a ball with the dough. Refrigerate for at least 1 hour and up to 24 hours.

To prepare the filling: In a large bowl, mix the berries, rhubarb, brown sugar, flour, and orange juice and stir well to make sure the fruit is thoroughly coated. Let marinate, stirring once or twice, while you roll out the dough.

Place a rack in the middle of the oven and preheat the oven to 450°F.

Unwrap the dough. Working on a lightly floured surface, roll the dough out to a circle about 12 to 14 inches in diameter. Place the circle on a large, ungreased cookie sheet. Using a slotted spoon, place the fruit into the center of the dough, leaving a border of about 2 inches. Pour any accumulated fruit juices from the bottom of the bowl over the fruit. Drape the edges of the dough over the filling and press down lightly to crimp them. The dough won't cover the filling

RECIPE CONTINUES ▶

completely; you should have a fair amount of exposed fruit in the center. (The crostata can be made several hours ahead of time; cover and refrigerate until ready to bake.) Bake for 20 to 25 minutes (or about 28 minutes if the crostata was refrigerated), or until the dough is a light golden brown, the fruit in the center looks soft, and the juices are bubbling. Remove from the oven and let cool for about 5 minutes.

In an electric mixer, whip the cream on medium speed until soft peaks form, about 5 minutes. Add the sugar and vanilla and whip until the cream holds its shape.

Transfer the crostata to a large serving plate and serve warm or at room temperature, with the whipped cream on the side.

NOTE: The amount of sugar you use really depends on the sweetness of the berries; taste and add more if needed.

favoritevariations

- Substitute blueberries, raspberries, or blackberries alone or in combination for the strawberries and/or rhubarb.
- Make an apple or pear crostata by substituting 4 peeled and thinly sliced tart apples or pears (or a combination) for the berries and rhubarb. Substitute apple cider for the orange juice and brush the pastry with apple cider once or twice during the last 10 minutes of baking.
- Add 1 teaspoon ground ginger or ground cinnamon or nutmeg to the fruit mixture.

one fifty ate's maple on snow

Kathy first tasted this wonderful winter treat at the restaurant/bakery One Fifty Ate in South Portland, Maine. It was a bitterly cold December evening and dinner was hearty, comforting, and delicious. For dessert, there was an item on the menu that sounded too wonderful to pass up: "Maple on Snow." The waitress brought a white bowl of fresh snow (we had just had close to a foot of powder) to the table. One bite of icy cold freshness, with a hint of something creamy and the undeniable flavor of maple syrup was the perfect ending to the meal. During the next snowfall, try this simple dessert:

Scoop up 1 cup *fresh, clean* snow and put it into a bowl. Drizzle 1 tablespoon heavy cream and 2 tablespoons maple syrup on top and serve, accompanied by a cookie. If you can't avoid winter, eat it!

trio of **milkshakes**

■ **ginger-coconut** milkshake

SERVES 2 TO 4

We combined ginger ice cream and coconut milk to create this exotic-flavored drink. How can only two ingredients whirled together fill the mouth with *so* many flavors? Serve it as dessert or a drink; the recipe can easily be doubled or tripled.

1 pint ginger ice cream   ¼ cup unsweetened coconut milk

Add both ingredients to the jar of a blender and blend until completely smooth. Serve immediately.

favoritevariations

■ Add ¼ cup rum.
■ Add ¼ cup lemon-flavored vodka.
■ Add 1 tablespoon finely chopped lemongrass or grated lemon rind.

■ **chocolate-maple** milkshake

SERVES 2 TO 4

When the maple syrup flows each spring in New England we do our best to get our hands on the best-quality grade A medium amber maple syrup and highlight its flavor in the simplest of preparations. The syrup transforms an ordinary chocolate milkshake into something out of the ordinary. The recipe can easily be doubled or tripled.

1 pint good-quality chocolate ice cream   ½ cup pure maple syrup
¼ cup milk

Combine all of the ingredients in a blender and blend until completely smooth. Serve immediately.

favoritevariations

■ Substitute vanilla ice cream for the chocolate.
■ Add ¼ cup rum.

■ **mango-lemon-coconut** milkshake

SERVES 2 TO 4

The "milk" in this recipe is coconut milk, which combines beautifully with puckery lemon sorbet and ripe sweet mango for a completely refreshing dessert. Topped with a fresh mint leaf, this thick slush redefines "summer cooler." The recipe can easily be doubled or tripled.

1 pint high-quality lemon sorbet
¾ cup canned unsweetened coconut milk
1 cup ice

1 mango, peeled, pitted, and chopped
Fresh mint leaves for garnish (optional)

Combine the sorbet, coconut milk, ice, and mango in a blender and blend until completely smooth. Serve immediately, garnished with mint leaves.

favoritevariations
- Substitute 1½ cups chopped pineapple or berries for the mango.
- Add 2 teaspoons finely grated lime zest and 1 tablespoon fresh lime juice.
- Add 1 tablespoon chopped mint to the blender.
- Add ¼ cup rum.

stonewall kitchen **favorite menus**

summer cookout

Trio of Deviled Eggs, **page 84**

Dry-Rubbed Paper Bag Pork Ribs, **page 202**

Sweet and Spicy Barbecue Sauce, **page 242**

Tangy Coleslaw, **page 73**

Bacon and Chive Biscuits, **page 27**

Quick Ice Cream Pie, **page 262**

mediterranean barbecue for a crowd

Chopped Greek Salad, **page 88**

Olive and Anchovy Toasts, **page 166**

Grilled Herbed Butterflied Leg of Lamb with Mint–Red Wine Sauce, **page 198**

Mediterranean Orzo Salad, **page 143**

Lemon Cake with Lemon-Vanilla Glaze, **page 269** with Lemon Sorbet

spring sunday brunch

Trio of Fruit Salads with Flavored Sugar Syrups, **page 18–20**

New Eggs Benedict, **page 40**, Spinach, Proscuitto, Sun-Dried Tomato, and Cheese Frittata, **page 33**, or Walnut Pancakes with Carmelized Bananas, **page 28**

Raspberry Muffins with Crumb Topping, **page 21**, or Blueberry-Buttermilk Muffins, **page 22**

Espresso with Coffee Ice Cubes, **page 113**

Iced Tea with Mint Syrup, **page 20**, and Iced Tea Cubes, **page 113**

winter dinner party

New England Five-Onion Soup with Cheddar Croûtes, **page 64**

Roast Pork Loin with Honey and Thyme, **page 204**

Roasted Vegetable Platter with Green Sauce, **page 222**

Twice-Baked Potatoes with Chive-Scallion-Pancetta Stuffing, **page 156**, or Ultimate Mashed Potatoes, **page 160**

Mini Raspberry-Filled Chocolate Cakes, **page 251**

family snow ball/ice skating party

Coq au Vin with Cippoline Onions (for the adults), **page 181**, and Mashed Parsnips, **page 228**, or Ultimate Mashed Potatoes, **page 160**

Four-Cheese Macaroni with Thyme-Parmesan Crust, **page 148**, or Spaghetti and Three-Meat Meatballs, **page 145** (for the kids)

Green Salad

Crusty Bread

Lemon-Ginger Cheesecake, **page 266**

thanksgiving dinner for family and friends

Corn and Sweet Potato Chowder with Saffron Cream, **page 56**

Roast Stuffed Turkey with Vegetables, **page 183**

Herbed Bread and Celery Stuffing, **page 162**

Cardamom Creamed Spinach, **page 218**

Ultimate Mashed Potatoes, **page 160**

Roasted Brussels Sprouts with Pancetta and Balsamic Glaze, **page 221**

Apple Crostata (variation on Strawberry and Rhubarb Crostata), **page 275**

acknowledgments

Many thanks to our agent, Deborah Krasner, for all her hard work in making this book come together.

Thank you to Rica Allannic, our editor, for all her careful edits and diligent work. You have shaped this into a book we are all proud of. And many thanks to Jane Treuhaft for designing yet another spectacular book.

Our photo shoot, which took place in a wonderful house on the York River in Maine, was two weeks of hard work, much laughing, and great fun. We were lucky enough to work with some major talent. Our "master" food stylist, William Smith, made all our favorites look like works of art. Many thanks to our assistant, Mary Bengtson, and for special help from Andrea Kuhno. Cynthia Marnahas has helped in innumerable ways—many thanks, Cindy.

Special thanks from Kathy:

Thank you Jim and Jonathan for allowing me the honor to work on another book. You are both a joy to work with. And to Jim for his incredible eye with the photography in this book, and his uncanny ability to capture these dishes in such an artistic way.

Jess Thomson walked into my life several winters ago, a student at the Cambridge School of Culinary Arts looking for an internship. She has worked with me on two books. For this book she was so much more than an assistant. Jess literally bursts into my kitchen with ideas, new techniques, and her amazing touch with food. Jess, you are a major talent and a real inspiration. Thank you for all your hard work and enthusiasm. I feel very lucky to have you as a friend.

Thanks to Deborah Krasner for all she does—friend, agent, and all-round great listener.

Thanks to Alice Medrich, author of *Bittersweet,* for her help with the chocolate information.

Thanks to all the friends and neighbors who *so* willingly stopped by my kitchen to taste and share their ideas on these favorites.

Thanks to my mother-in-law, Nancy, for simply being who she is. And to my family: John, my constant, my editor, thank you for the endless love; to Maya and Emma, thank you for your love, your beauty, and all the honest feedback about your mother's cooking and experimentation.

Special thanks from Jim and Jonathan:

Without Kathy Gunst's incredible talents, this book would still be a seed in our minds waiting to be brought to reality. Her intuitive grasp of what we wanted to impart in *Favorites* was the guiding force behind this book. As a co-author, she was more than flexible, putting up with our crazy schedules and the time restrictions we always work under. We appreciate her good humor, patience, and above all, her skills in the kitchen and her way with words. Thank you, Kathy, from all of us.

We also want to thank both of our families and our close friends who, in a way, inspired this cookbook. We enjoy cooking for them using simple, fresh foods and trying classic recipes, usually with a twist of our own. When our guests enjoy the dishes, we know we have another *favorite* to add to our list.

We especially want to pass along appreciation for our wonderful, loyal customers. You are the foundation and the motivation for all we do. Our hope is that you enjoy each new endeavor along with us as we continue with this adventure.

To Ina and Frank, thanks for the inspiration, support, and friendship. We are delighted to work with you and proud to be involved with both of you.

To the staff at Stonewall Kitchen, we continue to be sincerely grateful for all that you do to continue the growth of our company. This book is a reflection of what all of you do every day for us. Thank you for your hard work, loyalty, and friendships over the years.

index

Note: *Italicized* page numbers refer to photographs.

obstersalad**spaghetticarbonara**chickenstev